Speculative Realism and Science Fiction

Speculative Realism

Series Editor: Graham Harman

Editorial Advisory Board
Jane Bennett, Levi Bryant, Patricia Clough, Iain Hamilton Grant, Myra Hird, Adrian Johnston, Eileen A. Joy.

Books available
Onto-Cartography: An Ontology of Machines and Media, Levi R. Bryant
Form and Object: A Treatise on Things, Tristan Garcia, translated by Mark Allan Ohm and Jon Cogburn
Adventures in Transcendental Materialism: Dialogues with Contemporary Thinkers, Adrian Johnston
The End of Phenomenology: Metaphysics and the New Realism, Tom Sparrow
Fields of Sense: A New Realist Ontology, Markus Gabriel
Quentin Meillassoux: Philosophy in the Making Second Edition, Graham Harman
Assemblage Theory, Manuel DeLanda
Romantic Realities: Speculative Realism and British Romanticism, Evan Gottlieb
Garcian Meditations: The Dialectics of Persistence in Form and Object, Jon Cogburn
Speculative Realism and Science Fiction, Brian Willems
Speculative Empiricism: Revisiting Whitehead, Didier Debaise, translated by Tomas Weber

Forthcoming books
After Quietism: Analytic Philosophies of Immanence and the New Metaphysics, Jon Cogburn
Infrastructure, Graham Harman

Visit the Speculative Realism website at: edinburghuniversitypress.com/series/specr

Speculative Realism and Science Fiction

Brian Willems

EDINBURGH
University Press

To Jasna

Edinburgh University Press is one of the leading university presses in the UK. We publish academic books and journals in our selected subject areas across the humanities and social sciences, combining cutting-edge scholarship with high editorial and production values to produce academic works of lasting importance. For more information visit our website: edinburghuniversitypress.com

© Brian Willems, 2017

Edinburgh University Press Ltd
The Tun – Holyrood Road, 12(2f) Jackson's Entry, Edinburgh EH8 8PJ

Typeset in 11/13 Adobe Sabon by
Servis Filmsetting Ltd, Stockport, Cheshire

A CIP record for this book is available from the British Library

ISBN 978 1 4744 2269 7 (hardback)
ISBN 978 1 4744 2271 0 (webready PDF)
ISBN 978 1 4744 2270 3 (paperback)
ISBN 978 1 4744 2272 7 (epub)

The right of Brian Willems to be identified as the author of this work has been asserted in accordance with the Copyright, Designs and Patents Act 1988, and the Copyright and Related Rights Regulations 2003 (SI No. 2498).

Contents

Acknowledgements	vi
Series Editor's Preface	vii
Introduction	1
1. The Zug Effect	6
2. Divine Paraphrase: Cormac McCarthy	40
3. Double-Vision: Neil Gaiman	60
4. Subtraction and Contradiction: China Miéville	86
5. Tension and Phase: Doris Lessing	112
6. Animal Death: Paolo Bacigalupi	133
7. Transcription: Kim Stanley Robinson	181
Conclusion	197
Bibliography	205
Index	220

Acknowledgements

First and foremost, thank you to Graham Harman, Carol Macdonald and all those at Edinburgh University Press for supporting this project. Thank you also to Boris Škvorc and everyone at the Faculty of Humanities and Social Sciences at the University of Split who helped make this book possible, including a grant to do research at the British Library in April 2016. Appreciation is also due to Diana Thater for the use of the image from *Science, Fiction* (2014) for the book cover, and to Larry Rickels for all his help. A section of the Introduction on outer space sounds originally appeared as part of 'The Sounds of Space', in *Reality Unbound: New Departures in Science Fiction Cinema*, ed. Aidan Power et al., Berlin: Bertz + Fischer, 2016. Selections from the third and fourth chapters appeared in 'Emerging Sight, Emerging Blindness', in *On Blinking*, ed. Jeremy Fernando and Sarah Brigid Hannis, Tirana: Uitgeverij Press, 2012.

Series Editor's Preface

True to its title, Brian Willems's *Speculative Realism and Science Fiction* is a thorough and focused treatment of the relationship between the two movements it names: a recent school of philosophy and a much older genre of literature. From the moment that Speculative Realism was born in 2007, its connections with science fiction were both obvious and openly declared.[1] Both currents hope to draw us away from academic fixation on the infinite subtleties of human cognition, and into a larger speculative cosmos. Admittedly, there seem to be two distinct missions at work here: science fiction often portrays a universe that is an imaginative fabrication of the author; Speculative Realism, as a type of philosophy, is duty-bound to speak about the world as it is. Yet the two traditions soon draw closer again when we realise that Speculative Realism, in all its variations, tends to uphold a reality that is significantly more bizarre than that accepted by everyday common sense. For examples, we need only consider Quentin Meillassoux's view that God does not exist but might exist in the future, or the object-oriented doctrine that causal relations between real things occur only through the medium of aesthetic images, neither of them making a good fit with even the most outlandish speculations of contemporary physics.

There is also the well-known fact that the four participants of the original Speculative Realism workshop (Brassier, Grant, Harman, Meillassoux) soon discovered that the only author admired by all four was not one of the great canonical philosophers, but the American science fiction and horror writer H. P. Lovecraft. My own publications on Lovecraft offered one possible

[1] Ray Brassier, Iain Hamilton Grant, Graham Harman and Quentin Meillassoux, 'Speculative Realism', *Collapse* III (2007), 306–449.

approach to linking Speculative Realism with science fiction, while Meillassoux's widely read pamphlet on 'extro-science fiction' provided another.[2] Moreover, such prominent science fiction authors as China Miéville, Kim Stanley Robinson and Bruce Sterling have shown some degree of interest in the activities of Speculative Realist philosophers.[3]

Nonetheless, the science fiction authors covered by the original figures of Speculative Realism have been limited mainly to Lovecraft and a handful of others. Yes, there were certain philosophers who later appeared in the vicinity of Speculative Realism – Steven Shaviro and Tristan Garcia come to mind – with a broader command of science fiction literature than the original four participants. Yet none has attempted a wide survey of the topic. Into this vacuum steps Willems, who seems to have known his science fiction before Speculative Realism even existed as a collective enterprise. He even broadens the definition of science fiction to encompass two novelists, Cormac McCarthy and the Nobel Prize winner Doris Lessing, who are not really science fiction authors in the strict sense, even if – much like Franz Kafka – they might be seen as sf's fellow travellers. Since Willems's Introduction already gives us a chapter-by-chapter survey of his subjects of interest, we can limit ourselves to a few remarks on what he calls 'the Zug effect', the central theme of his book.

One of the key principles of the object-oriented strand of Speculative Realism is that the object lies somewhere beyond all of our attempts to interact with or speak about it. Though this was already to some extent true of the tool-analysis in Martin Heidegger's 1927 masterwork *Being and Time*, the object-oriented thinkers hold that objects are strange to each other, not just to the human mind as in Heidegger. Now it is true that most writers of fiction, and even of science fiction, are unlikely to portray object-object interactions in the absence of any sentient observer. Yet there are moments when this happens, and a much greater number of moments in which science fiction depicts reality in a distant

---

[2] Graham Harman, 'On the Horror of Phenomenology: Lovecraft and Husserl', *Collapse* IV (2008), 333–64; Graham Harman, *Weird Realism: Lovecraft and Philosophy* (Winchester: Zero Books, 2012); Quentin Meillassoux, *Science Fiction and Extro-Science Fiction*, trans. Alyosha Edlebi (Minneapolis: Univocal, 2015).

[3] See, for instance, Sterling's post on the *Wired* blog, 'Speculative Realism as "Philosophy Fiction"', 19 February 2011, https://www.wired.com/2011/02/speculative-realism-as-philosophy-fiction/

strangeness foreign to the tradition of realistic fiction. As Willems puts it:

> Dark objects are, paradoxically, represented in a number of different ways: through symbiosis, disruptions of vision and the loss of language. The Zug effect is the name given to this paradox, which can also be thought of as the appearance of speculative realism within science fiction.

Each of Willems's chapters gives examples of the Zug effect and its disruptions, making use each time of different writers and different philosophical partners from the Speculative Realism movement. For instance, Willems speaks of the 'crisis energy' central to *Perdido Street Station*, China Miéville's most famous novel. Though the active communist Miéville most probably had dialectical philosophy in mind when he conceived of this contradictory energy, Willems does a fine job of steering the discussion on to a different road. He does this by means of a surprising comparison between Miéville and Manuel DeLanda, who is both the greatest renegade Deleuzean philosopher of the past twenty years and a wonderful interpreter of the natural sciences.

The human-centred bias of modern philosophy is proverbial. One of the pillars of this bias, beginning with the philosophy of René Descartes, is the assumption of a vast ontological rift between 'rational' human beings and 'irrational' animals. This bland commonsensical distinction is repeated today in Robert Brandom's trumped-up duel between 'sapience' and 'sentience', in which a fog-generating cliché is ennobled with the ring of new terminology. Willems's interesting way of disarming this cliché is to give us a tour of Paolo Bacigalupi's 2009 novel *The Windup Girl*, 'an antagonistic space in which both animal and human find themselves mutually disturbed'. While it may come as no surprise that my own work and Levi Bryant's are used to affirm this novel's assault on anthropocentrism, Willems makes a bolder move in bringing into play Theodor Adorno: an older name from an earlier age, one less concerned to reject the modernist boxing match of human vs. world. Willems proceeds to still bolder cosmological speculations in his treatment of Kim Stanley Robinson's relation to the eco-philosophy of Timothy Morton, one of the foremost public intellectuals of what is now called the Anthropocene. He closes with the argument that 'the unrepresentable is not, contrary to Meillassoux, foreign to science fiction, but rather at the heart of it', placing Willems closer to object-oriented currents than to Meillassoux's heavily mathematised 'speculative materialism'.

So numerous are the points of connection between Speculative Realism and science fiction that others are likely to follow the path laid out in Willems's pioneering book. But several features of the present work will be difficult to match: Willems's clarity of exposition, his broad selection of examples, and his thorough familiarity with both recent science fiction and the authors of Speculative Realism, some of them not especially easy to read. Willems's focus on the Zug effect as central to both currents is itself an inspired viewpoint, and something like this idea will have to be among the building blocks of any future comparison between these trends. But above all, in its lucidity and its sense of wonder, this book makes for pleasurable reading. I invite you to partake of its pleasures.

Graham Harman
Dubuque, Iowa
December 2016

Introduction

The real monsters are not aliens from outer space but humans on Earth. Nuclear radiation poisoning, environmental catastrophes and genetic manipulation gone wrong are only some of the ways that science fiction horrors are being realised. Yet if humans have become the new monsters, what happens when their dominance is removed? Are there other organisations of knowledge, time and space which could lead to a better future than the one now being created? The philosophical field of speculative realism takes this issue to heart by questioning the anthropocentrism of the present. Science fiction literature often complements this trend by imagining alternative worlds in which humans are no longer the only organisers of knowledge. The combination of both of these perspectives can lead to strategies for imagining a world different from the tragedy we are now making.

A human-centred approach to the environment is leading to ecological collapse. When non-human things are taken to be equally as valid objects of investigation as humans, a more responsible and truthful view of the world can take place. A number of works of science fiction that question anthropomorphism are used in this book to develop some of the ideas of speculative realism. Each chapter takes one aspect of the connection between the two into consideration.

The first chapter defines the kind of science fiction that is engaged with throughout the book and offers an overview of the main speculative realist positions. Both science and science fiction are seen as non-axiomatic, meaning that they incorporate ambiguity into their procedures and strategies. This relates to speculative realism via Quentin Meillassoux's definition of 'Type-2' science fictional worlds. These are worlds, much like our own, in which events take place that will never fit into a standard scientific framework, although science itself is actually much more complex than Meillassoux allows. The reason that Type-2 worlds appear is due to what is called the Zug effect. In order to develop this idea, the location of nonsense within sense is developed in a number of novels. In Damon Knight's *Beyond the Barrier* (1964), the Zug effect is explained when a number of 'dark objects' appear which have no cognitive connection to any other objects; in addition, the descriptions of outer space make little pretence at being understandable within the context of realism. Joanna Russ's *And Chaos Died* (1970) takes the concept of dark objects one step further by making a lack of understanding a requirement of utopia. Kim Stanley Robinson's *2312* (2012) features an interplanetary 'darkliner' spaceship aboard which the passengers spend the whole journey without sight. All the examples in the first chapter thus engage with the concept of dark or dormant objects, which Graham Harman and Levi Bryant have both developed in their own ways. These novels show the difference between unknown objects that are subject to eventual understanding (Darko Suvin's novum) and objects that remain forever unknown (Samuel Delany's inmixing). In other words, the dark objects examined in these examples have qualities that are withdrawn from a possible framework of understanding. Such objects are seen as being both part of the current state of ecological collapse called the Anthropocene, and as offering a possible way to think outside its constraints.

Meillassoux's thought is then developed in a reading of Cormac McCarthy's novel *The Road* (2006) and its film adaptation. Type-2 worlds contain elements not expected to fall under traditional scientific explanation. In this chapter, such objects are defined as being 'divine' in the sense that they are removed from the world of explanation. In the novel, a boy and his father struggle to survive in post-apocalyptic America. The boy's impoverished language is read as merely paraphrasing his desolate surroundings. This lack of language is seen as divine because the novel shows it to be not-of-this-world, and thus more closely related to things in the world rather than the context that makes sense of those things.

The third chapter addresses the following question: if the Zug effect is that which exists outside of traditional science, how then can it be known or experienced? The answer is posited through a reading of Harman's indirectness, which is developed through the idea of the 'double-vision' of the coupling of sight/non-sight in selected fiction by Neil Gaiman. In *American Gods* (2001), *Anansi*

Boys (2005) and 'How to Talk to Girls at Parties' (2007), double-vision functions as a synchronic representation of diachronic events. Martin Heidegger, Mikhail Bakhtin and Franco Moretti are used to show how this representation makes fleeting change visible. These moments consist of the co-presencing of the changed and the unchanged within a single being at one moment in time. While change is everywhere around us, in germination, growth and decay, the term double-vision indicates the potential of seeing more than one side of a transformation simultaneously, thereby presenting a moment of stasis within change.

Up to this point in the book, the Zug effect can be seen only indirectly. However, in order for this vision to take place, a certain sense of stasis is required. Chapter 4 uses China Miéville's second novel, *Perdido Street Station* (2000), to provide two alternative modes of vision: subtraction and contradiction. *Perdido Street Station* initially posits that an experience of double-vision is essentially immobile. For, while a multitude is represented simultaneously, this multitude, in such an experience, is stationary. Manuel DeLanda's readings of subtraction and exteriority are used to develop how Miéville's novel posits two possible ways to 'rectify' this stillness: first through the addition of movement within double-vision, and second through a lack of codifying constraints. Both are also read as strategies for combating the helplessness often felt within the Anthropocene. Graham Harman's discussion of the 'mere' [*bloß*] in Heidegger is taken in conjunction with the 'flow' of Latour's figuration in order to develop this concept of movement in non-human identities in the novel. Regarding the law of non-contradiction, the crisis energy of *Perdido Street Station* is read as only being able to function within a contradictory state.

Chapter 5 develops the notion of contradiction introduced in the previous chapter through a reading of Doris Lessing's novel *The Cleft* (2007). The novel foregrounds two issues that have been raised in this book earlier: the aporia of language and the problem of restlessness (movement). It shows how both of these issues lie in contradiction to each other on the 'surface' rather than at any kind of mythological depth. The novel is also read as a metaphor for a more complicated and realistic reading of science than Meillassoux allows. The novel is a fable-like story that presumes that 'in the beginning' of humankind there were only females, who would become impregnated by the moon. The novel tells how the first males, called either 'Monsters' or 'Squirts', came about and the changes they wrought on the society of the Clefts. The arrival of the males in the all-female society of the Clefts causes both the eruption of language and the beginnings of restlessness. While this novel is seen to be problematic in a number of ways, it is also seen as providing a strong argument for what Harman describes as a new 'phase' in the life of an object. The focus of this chapter is to show how challenges to anthropomorphism lie on the surface of objects rather than being hidden.

All the chapters up to this point develop readings of a number of seemingly non-human traits, including randomness, movement and flatness. In Chapter 6 the death of an animal is seen as a key figure in examining the centrality of death in the construction of what it means to be human. In Paolo Bacigalupi's novel *The Windup Girl* (2009), the Zug effect is found within narrative strategies of representing an antagonistic space in which both animal and human find themselves mutually disturbed. This dual configuration, which can be another way to see 'around' the Anthropocene, is not only found in Harman's reading of tool-being and Bryant's concept of machine interaction but also in Adorno's *Aesthetic Theory* (1970). Here, Adorno develops a reading of natural beauty and art in which the antagonism between the two is actually read as the fulfilment of one in the other. This antagonism is used to develop a non-dialectical reading of the novel, which not only finds a representation in the biologically engineered fruit called a *ngaw* but also in a key scene of the novel, the death of an animal called a megodont. It is the death of this animal that provides a short circuit by locating both sides of the antagonistic relationship in a single entity. The figure of the windup girl Emiko then reschedules this antagonism on the human scale.

The last chapter asks what happens when the human is reinserted into a non-anthropocentric view of the world. Part of the answer to this lies in the structure of the main novel under discussion, Kim Stanley Robinson's *The Years of Rice and Salt* (2002). The novel is an alternative history, which imagines an alternative past in which Islam became the dominant world-religion. The form of alternative history is argued to show that it is not the future which offers the chance of possibility but, paradoxically, the past. Robinson's novel is considered in this context through Timothy Morton's readings of the bardo (the place of reincarnation in Buddhist thought). The novel represents ten cycles of reincarnation. In each cycle the two main characters have the same first letters to their names: 'b' and 'k'. In the first chapter they are Bold and Kyu, in the last, Bao and Kung. The key to the novel lies in the presence of the Zug effect between incarnations, in the bardo. Due to the structure of reincarnation's dependence on past behaviour, the bardo represents the possibilities of what came before. The appearance of the bardo in Robinson's other work is used to develop this reading, as are some early novels by J. G. Ballard.

Although a number of different texts are used in a variety of ways, what ties them together is the way in which science fiction and speculative realism mirror each other. The thrust of speculative realism is to foreground how the withdrawn or dark nature of objects has the potential to make new connections with other objects, although they can also remain removed from any connection whatsoever. By both fusing new qualities to objects, and fissioning old qualities from them, the darkness of objects is what makes them speculative, meaning what allows alternatives to human-organised knowledge to take place. Science fiction is essential to this discussion because it offers a playground of Type-2 worlds in which multiple strategies for representing the unrepresentable are developed. The unrepresentable is not, contrary to Meillassoux, foreign to science fiction, but rather at the heart of it.

Dark objects are, paradoxically, represented in a number of different ways: through symbiosis, disruptions of vision and the loss of language. The Zug effect is the name given to this paradox, which can also be thought of as the appearance of speculative realism within science fiction. The aim of this book is to trace the appearance of the Zug effect throughout a number of different examples of the genre. The Zug effect relates to the Anthropocene because it is a strategy for imagining different futures when all seems hopeless. However, the form this imagining takes is often through the most frightening destruction of everything humanity holds dear. As it should.

1

The Zug Effect

> *He* was the one surviving Zug: he himself was the monster he had been sent to kill.
>
> Damon Knight, *Beyond the Barrier* (1964)

Ambiguities of Science, Ambiguities of Science Fiction

The Zug effect is part of only certain moments in science fiction (often abbreviated 'sf') which are open to representing ambiguity. The definition of what sf is has a varied history, which is of great importance when locating moments of speculative realist sf within the genre and along its edges. Traditionally, J. O. Bailey's typological study *Pilgrims through Space and Time*, from 1947, is placed at the origin of critical thought on sf. This was followed by Kingsley Amis's more evaluative effort in *New Maps of Hell* (1960). Bailey centralised the concept of *extrapolation* for the definition of sf (Bailey 1972: 11). Amis ended his study with a valorisation of the satiric qualities of Frederik Pohl's and C. M. Kornbluth's co-written *The Space Merchants* (1952) (Amis 1960: 113–15). Amis uses their novel to call for a more political engagement for the genre. Gary Westfahl challenges this chronology by locating the 'naïve and simplistic' (Westfahl 1998: 2) critical attempts of legendary sf editor Hugo Gernsback at defining the genre at the heart of sf theory. Westfahl's descriptive rather than prescriptive approach (the latter exemplified by the work of Brian Aldiss) leads him to develop what sf is rather than what it should be: 'science fiction has three elements – fiction, science and prophecy [...]; it has three corresponding natural sets of readers and writers – the general public, young people and scientists; and it has three corresponding purposes – to provide entertainment, scientific education, and stimulating ideas for inventions' (1998: 58).

However, Darko Suvin's work, as exemplified in *Metamorphoses of Science Fiction* (1979), is the touchstone for much sf criticism of the last fifty years or so. Suvin concretised two terms that have become key words in sf criticism: cognitive estrangement, seeing the norms of any age as transitory (Suvin 1979: 12), and the novum, *'a totalizing phenomenon or relationship deviating from the author's and implied reader's norm of reality'* (Suvin 2010: 68, italics in original). Using these concepts as a guide, sf criticism split into two camps at this point: a structuralist approach as seen in the work of Tzvetan Todorov, Mark Rose and Carl Malmgren, and a poststructuralist approach as found in the work of Gwyneth Jones, Samuel Delany and Fredric Jameson. It is within the latter camp that more philosophical readings of sf have often been subsumed, including Theodor Adorno's work on *Brave New World* (1932), Jean Baudrillard's thoughts on J. G. Ballard, Maurice Blanchot's essay on the 'proper' use of sf and Slavoj Žižek's reading of the 1999 film *The Matrix* (Adorno 1983; Baudrillard 2006; Blanchot 2006; Žižek 1999). However, what most of these approaches have in common is that they still assume sf to be roughly as defined by Gernsback, meaning that fiction, science and prophecy combine to make extrapolations about future events. One of the key elements of this book is that it offers a different definition of sf because it focuses on the roles of ambiguity and the unknowable in the genre; thus it will lead to a different set of questions and answers. In other words, rather than foregrounding the way sf extrapolates current scientific facts into future plots, this book searches out objects which resist incorporation into any past, present or future scientific understanding. Such objects are key for speculative realism because they indicate an independence from human thought or perception.

Yet ambiguity is not only an element of the fictional part of sf, but of the science part. Science involves both searching for axiomatic truths (deductive reasoning) and following the evolution of a subject from the variation of observation and measurement (inductive reasoning) (DeLanda 2016: 87). In *Science in Action*, Bruno Latour foregrounds the ambiguity involved in scientific practice by examining the 'uncertainty, people at work, decisions, competition, controversies' (Latour 1987: 4) which comprise messy science in the making, rather than only looking at the proven results and the ready-made conclusions published in academic journals. Going 'through the back door of science in the making' means choosing the more ignorant face of science rather than more knowing one (Latour 1987: 4, 7). The effect of Latour's approach to science is to map the network of human and non-human actants that makes up the scientific process, focusing on the way these actants function rather than on the results they produce. In other words, Latour foregrounds the network of production involved in doing science.

Karen Barad, citing Latour's resistance to the too pure stance of 'critique' (Dolphijn and van der Tuin 2012: 49), has a similar approach. She identifies a scientific 'diffractive methodology' in *Meeting the Universe Halfway: Quantum Physics and the Entanglement of Matter and Meaning*. Instead of taking different disciplines as separate or opposed to each other in critique, Barad remains 'rigorously attentive to important details of specialized arguments within a given field without uncritically endorsing or unconditionally prioritizing one (inter)disciplinary approach over another' (Barad 2007: 93). Both Latour and Barad aim to complicate the way that science is both made and understood. This complication expresses some of the ways ambiguity plays a role in science. It also has implications for the definition of the genre of sf.

John Rieder applies the mapping of actants to his reading of how the genre of sf is made. For Rieder, sf is a fluid set of signs which depend on historical context and varied use. The five main theses he develops for sf are similar to the way that Latour examines scientific process rather than scientific product:

1) sf is historical and mutable;
2) sf has no essence, no single unifying characteristic, and no point of origin;
3) sf is not a set of texts, but rather a way of using texts and of drawing relationships between them;
4) sf's identity is a differentially articulated position in a historical and mutable field of genres;
5) attribution of the identity of sf to a text constitutes an active intervention in its distribution and reception. (Rieder 2010: 193)

The third point can be used to develop Rieder's general thesis. Texts do not belong to genres because of the elements they contain, but rather because of the ways they are used. On the one hand, Samuel Delany claims that 'He turned on his left side' can be read in a sf manner (he switched on the left side of his mechanical body) because linguistic ambiguities are exploited. However, Rieder insists that the sf potential of such a sentence is found in the expectations readers bring to a text, in the 'reader's familiarity and use of sf conventions – in particular here, the expectation that the distinction between organism and machine is going to be blurred or violated' (Rieder 2010: 197). While Latour locates ambiguity in the way that science is made, and Barad locates it in the question of which method applies to interpretation, Rieder sees the reading process itself as creating a historically contingent set of signs which make up the different ideas of the genre of sf for different groups of people in different contexts of creation and reception. This book gathers together texts which, at moments, leave the ambiguous unresolved, rather than coding it into a world of the to-be-discovered. The texts include the more standardly literary (Cormac McCarthy), fantasy (Neil Gaiman, Doris Lessing), weird (China Miéville, Kim Stanley Robinson) and hard sf (Paolo Bacigalupi, Kim Stanley Robinson).

China Miéville makes a similar claim for genre ambiguity in his essay 'Cognition as Ideology: A Dialectic of SF Theory'. Miéville argues that the criticisms that fantasy suffers, such as being anti-cognitive and anti-rationalist, actually undermine the supposed superiority of sf (Miéville 2009: 233). SF is supposedly aligned with the logic of the scientific method, while fantasy is a genre of the impossible (Miéville 2009: 234). As shown above, science incorporates ambiguity. However, the manner in which sf assumes authority over its themes is what makes it different from fantasy. As Miéville says, following the thought of Gwyneth Jones, sf is not about accuracy but about the appearance of accuracy. This appearance is developed through persuasion, and traditional sf is successful as far as this persuasion is successful (Miéville 2009: 238). Both the sf and the more fantastic texts in this book were chosen because of the way they question such strategies of persuasion, replacing them with strategies of ambiguity and darkness. However, the strategies themselves are not ambiguous, but sharply defined.

Quentin Meillassoux's differentiation between sf and extro-science fiction also suffers from reducing science to the study of the solvable, rather than seeing it in the more complex light of Latour, Brand and Rieder. However, Meillasoux's concept of extro-science fiction can be used, though not unproblematically, to foreground the role of the impossible, which is being used as the definition of what is sf in this text. For Meillassoux, every sf implicitly maintains the following axiom: in the anticipated future it will still be possible to subject the world to scientific knowledge. Science will always exist (Meillassoux 2015: 5). Extro-science fiction worlds are not those before or after scientific knowledge, but rather worlds where,

> *in principle, experimental science is impossible* and not unknown *in fact*. Extro-science fiction thus defines a particular regime of the imaginary in which structured – or rather destructured – worlds are conceived in such a way that experimental science cannot deploy its theories or constitute its objects within them. The guiding question of extro-science fiction is: what should a world be, what should a world resemble, so that it is in principle inaccessible to a scientific knowledge, so that it cannot be established as the object of a natural science? (Meillassoux 2015: 5–6)

Thus, according to Meillassoux, events which, no matter how strange, are potentially explainable by a science-yet-to-come are science fiction, while strange events that are destined to be forever bereft of explanation, that do not have and are not expected ever to have a scientific explanation, are considered to be extro-science fiction. What the above discussion of both science and sf shows, however, is that there is no need to go outside science or sf in order to come into contact with the unexplainable: in fact, the impossible forms an important and fundamental condition of both.

The Sounds of Space

Contrary to Meillassoux's claims, one opportunity to explore his ideas about ambiguity is through science itself, through the recording of actual sound in space. The traditional view of space is that it is silent. The reason for this is that sound travels via vibrating molecules, but in the near vacuum of space there are no molecules to vibrate, and thus no sound is possible. Garrett Reisman, an American astronaut who was on numerous missions to the International Space Station, has an interesting observation on the silence of space. He discusses how a change in environment can first be indicated by an auditory clue rather than a visual one.

Speaking of watching a fellow crew member leave the station for a spacewalk, Reisman says:

> One interesting thing that happens is that when you put your crewmates in the airlock to perform an EVA and then shut the hatch, at first you can hear a bunch of clanging as their metal tools softly strike the other equipment, handrails, or the hull of the small airlock. Then as you depress the airlock it still looks exactly the same through the hatch window. But now the clanging sound is gone. You can see their equipment bumping into stuff as before, but now it is silent. (Reisman 2013)

From this perspective the silence of space is a real phenomenon. Yet many times sf ignores this fact, with the sounds of lasers and explosions in space being only some of the most obvious offenders. On the other hand, sometimes sf films do take the silence of space into account, as can be seen in the tagline for original *Alien* film (1979, Ridley Scott): 'In space, no one can hear you scream.' Thus when sf consciously engages with the silence of space, there are usually two main ways of doing so; either 1) to contrast the complete silence of space with the noisy interior of a spaceship, or 2) to focus on inner space (Ballard 1996: 197) by foregrounding the sounds of the body of the astronaut, such as breathing and the pulsing of blood.

However, the idea that there is no sound in space is empirically wrong; science is actually much stranger than that. Sounds, or sound-like objects, have been recorded, and with a variety of instruments. While it is true that sticking your ear out in space will result in a silent (and deadly) experience, there are other ways of listening that involve other sound-carriers than sound waves, and other listening instruments than the human ear. For example, in August 2014, the European Space Agency's Rosetta probe unexpectedly detected a certain kind of 'sound' when it approached Comet 67P/C-G during the first landing of a satellite on a comet. The comet's magnetic 'song' was recorded by the probe's magnetometer. The instrument was not intended to record any kind of sound, but rather to monitor how the comet interacted with the solar plasma emitted by the sun. Scientists in no way expected it to record sounds in space, but as the probe approached the comet they picked up oscillations in the magnetic field of the comet's environment. Although inaudible to the human ear, when increased by a factor of approximately 10,000, low oscillations could be heard. Scientists at the time were not exactly sure what was happening with the recording. Karl-Heinz Glaßmeier, head of Space Physics and Space Sensorics at the Technische Universität Braunschweig, admitted as much, saying that 'This is exciting because it is completely new to us. We did not expect this and we are still working to understand the physics of what is happening' (Kramer 2014).

The situation with sounds in space is that while sf works to represent the silence of space, space is being understood as noisy, not silent. However, the concept of noisy space is not as new as is being presented here. Pythagoras saw the known solar system in terms of a musical scale, or a 'Harmony of the Spheres', in which the planets were related to each other in terms of musical intervals (Koestler 1963: 31–2); yet only Pythagoras himself was master enough to ever hear this, just as Socrates was the only one with peace of mind enough to be attuned to the advice of his *daimonion*. However, hearing the sounds of the sky was not limited to the Ionian philosophers. Einstein claimed that gravity moves in waves, and apparatus have been built on earth to detect this, and have done so. As Doris Lessing put it in her afterword to Olaf Stapledon's novel *Last and First Men* (1930), when she looked up at the stars as a child in southern Rhodesia (now Zimbabwe), the cosmos seemed full of sound:

> After an hour or so of lying back in a deck chair, staring up, eyes drenched with starlight, it was evident that space was far from soundless, and you felt all you had to do was to take a running step or two and then you'd be off, not into immense silences and emptiness, but into a universe alive with sound and movement. (Lessing 2009: 295)

Put briefly, there are two main ways in which Einstein's actual sound-like objects have been found in space: one is by *the recording of plasma oscillations*, the other by *the recording of gravitational wave oscillations*. Although the way in which these sounds happened was not fully understood at the time, it was expected that they would fall into scientific understanding in the future. The recording of the sounds of space is therefore just one more step in confirming a science of a noisy cosmos, as Craig Hogan explains:

Einstein's theory of spacetime tells us that the real universe is not silent, but is actually alive with vibrating energy. Space and time carry a cacophony of vibrations with textures and timbres as rich and varied as the din of sounds in a tropical rain forest or the finale of a Wagner opera. It's just that we haven't heard those sounds yet. The universe is a musical that we've been watching all this time as a silent movie. (Hogan 2006)

The strangeness of the sounds of silent space have a long history of scientific anticipation, research and recording (Bartusiak 2000). The LIGO (Laser Interferometer Gravitational-Wave Observatory) was set up by MIT in Louisiana to 'listen' to the gravitational wave-sounds of space. The expectation of recording sounds has been so strong that, despite not recording any gravitational waves from 2002 to 2010, a new and more sensitive observatory was constructed which detected its first waves during the time of the writing of this book (early 2016).

This observatory, along with the eLISA (Evolved Laser Interferometer Space Antenna) planned to be launched into solar orbit by the European Space Agency in 2034, are what Meillassoux would call two real-world manifestations of sf in that a scientific apparatus is being built around the unheard and the unexplained. Although Meillassoux's too-simplistic reading of both science and sf make the terminology of extro-science fiction problematic, the outline of what he is looking for remains. For while sf might attempt to represent space as silent, real-world sounds are actually being recorded. However, the actual sounds recorded in space sometimes end up being what could more accurately be called axiomatic sf, because they are something unexplainable which can be or is expected to be explained by science. For example, even though the sounds picked up by the Rosetta probe were recorded accidentally and the mechanisms for their production are not understood at the moment, the sounds are expected to fall into the understanding of science some time in the future. This indicates something that this book is not concerned with: sf in the traditional sense. Meillassoux reads sf in a traditional way in order to set his own concept outside of it. However, there is nothing 'extro' about these ambiguous aspects of sf. Instead, this book aims to locate actual moments of the inexplicable in sf, since that is where the problematic human representations of non-human organisations of knowledge take place.

The Zug Effect I

In this book, organisations of knowledge that elude explanation are gathered under the name 'the Zug effect'. This concept is taken from a reading of Damon Knight's 1964 novel *Beyond the Barrier*, which originally appeared a year earlier in a number of instalments with the title 'The Tree of Time'. The novel tells the story of physics professor Gordon Naismith, who can only remember the last four years of his life. He slowly finds out that he is from 20,000 years in the future; he has been sent back in time to 1980, his memory erased, as a punishment. In his past future, Naismith was a Shefth, the only kind of creature that could kill a Zug. The Zugs are fearsome monsters that feast on humans, and a barrier has been constructed to keep them confined to a single area. However, one Zug is found to have escaped 'beyond the barrier'. People have been sent back to 1980 to retrieve Naismith and return him to the future in order to kill the outlying Zug. Of course, at the end of the novel all is revealed to Naismith: '*He* was the one surviving Zug; he himself was the monster he had been sent to kill' (Knight 1970: 133).

Beyond the Barrier is not a good book in the traditional sense, by which I mean that its qualities do not lie in deft characterisation nor in innovative structure. And the book is filled with offensive passages, such as when Naismith tests the English of a woman from the future by asking 'Do you know that you are a dirty little slut?' (Knight 1970: 106). The writing is also at times laughable, as when the Naismith-Zug creature unfolds its giant wings as it splits open the human host that it has been hiding in, and finds that it is a bit peckish: 'so he made a light snack from the food he found in the corridor' (136), the term 'light snack' making a grotesque contrast with the horrific nature of what is being consumed, the corpse it has just crawled out of.

However, more importantly for our purposes, Knight's novel is sf in a non-axiomatic sense. Meillassoux was quoted earlier as defining sf as a genre in which something inexplicable takes place within a scientific context that can eventually make sense of the event. This reading is based on Darko Suvin's famous definition of sf as an estranged genre. For Suvin, estranged and naturalistic genres can be differentiated 'according to whether they endeavour to faithfully reproduce textures, surfaces and relationships vouched for by human senses and common sense, or turn their attention to empirically unknown locations for the new relationships shown in the narration' (Suvin 1988: 34). Suvin defines the genre, in part, as containing empirically unknown elements. Meillassoux, on the other hand, is interested in fiction which contains empirically unknowable elements, meaning elements that can never be subsumed into scientific knowledge. The only mistake Meillassoux makes is to locate these elements outside sf.

Some of the elements of the world constructed in *Beyond the Barrier* are unknowable. For example, when Naismith is eventually brought back 20,000 years into the future, he is confronted by a scene that is either virtual or not: the issue is never resolved. Naismith is brought into the future by Liss-Yani, who in typical Knight style is wearing 'total-access clothing' (Knight 1970: 109), although nothing sexual seems to happen between them. A shimmering disc appears before Naismith, showing a room beyond:

> the disk turned transparent, and they were looking into another room, darker and even more enormous that the one they were in. In the vast space myriads of tiny shapes were moving: some were human, some were the symmetrical forms of machines – boxes, sarcophagi, vase shapes. As Naismith's vision adjusted to the scene, he began to make out serried ranks of dark objects, not visibly connected to one another, among which the human and robot forms came and went . . .
> 'This is the Barrier control network,' the girl's voice explained, 'They've been working on it for five years. It's almost finished.'
> 'Is this an actual entranceway into that room,' Naismith asked, fumbling for words, 'or a – a viewscreen?'
> Prell looked at him curiously, 'What's the difference?'
> Naismith realized, in confusion, that there was no difference, in the question as he had asked it: the two phrases . . . were almost identical.
> (111–12)

In this scene the question of whether the view into the Barrier control network is virtual or real is never resolved. Naismith enters the room, interacts with its occupants, and the issue of virtuality is never raised again. This scene is not sf in the axiomatic sense, because its estrangement is unknown to epistemology; the situation will forever remain strange.

One key to the manner in which this unknowability functions in the scene is found in Knight's mention of 'ranks of dark objects, not visibly connected to one another, among which the human and robot forms came and went...' These 'dark objects' can be related to what Levi Bryant calls dark objects in *Onto-Cartography*. Bryant delineates different types of objects and the ways in which they are open and closed to the inputs and outputs of other objects, thus attempting a cartography of all the entities in an environment. In this schema, dark objects are entities (or what Bryant calls 'machines') which are not connected to any other object at all, and thus are only theoretically possible since they could never interact with any other object.

> An absolutely dark object would have to meet two criteria. First, they would have to be so thoroughly unrelated to other machines that they would receive no inputs generating local manifestations. Second, their powers or operations would have to be *dormant* such that they generated no inputs from within themselves. Because such objects would receive no inputs from other machines, nor produce any inputs from within themselves, they would thus undergo no local manifestations. They would be there in the world without appearing or manifesting themselves in any way. (Bryant 2014: 199)

The dark objects are perceived by Naismith, and are thus not absolutely dark according to Bryant's definition (he calls such objects of minimum connection dim or relatively dark). However, the manner in which Knight describes them as being 'not visibly connected to one another' in a scene in which they are connected to at least one other object (Naismith) is significant; this is mirrored by the scene being both virtual and non-virtual: the issue is not resolved.

In other words, the dark objects Naismith sees are, paradoxically, signifiers of unknowability, and thus are a moment of unknowability within knowability. They fit into a more useful concept developed by Meillassoux, which he calls a Type-2 world. A Type-1 world is one in which unknowable events have no effect on cognition, because they are too rare or are simply dismissed (like reports of ghosts or alien abductions); thus Type-1 worlds feature unknowable events which do not challenge knowability in any way (Meillassoux 2015: 34). Type-3 worlds consist solely of unknowable events, and thus are not worlds at all since both science and consciousness are absent (Meillassoux 2015: 40). Type-2 worlds are non-axiomatic worlds because their 'irregularity is sufficient to abolish science, but not consciousness' (Meillassoux

2015: 36). In such a world randomness reigns: 'Laboratory experiments would start in their turn to produce the most diverse results, abolishing the possibility of constituting a science of nature' (Meillassoux 2015: 36). As a result, in a Type-2 world no predictions can be made; instead it is 'A world in which we could only *chronicle* things' (Meillassoux 2015: 36). This is where the non-connectedness of Bryant's dark objects comes into play, for a perverse way of reading them is not that they are simply connected to anything, but rather that they are connected to anything, but in unpredictable ways. This is why such objects can only be chronicled rather than experimented upon, for they are outside of science, and thus of sf, at least in the narrow sense. As Meillassoux says, 'we can only record variations of behaviour that very diverse theories (which are valid each time for determinate times and places) can potentially describe' (Meillassoux 2015: 37).

The removal from reality in *Beyond the Barrier* has been noted before. Artist Robert Smithson has compared the novel to Kasimir Malevich's 'non-objective world' in which images bear no relation to the real world, although they are perceivable. Smithson compares Malevich's idea to the 'null structures' of the City of the Future, where buildings are designed according to the conditions of perception rather than being predicated on classical ideas or action and reaction (Smithson 1996: 14). Smithson compares this idea to a scene from Knight's novel:

> In Damon Knight's Sci-fi novel, 'Beyond the Barrier,' he describes in a phenomenological manner just such surface-structures: 'Part of the scene before them seemed to expand. Where one of the flotation machines had been there was a dim lattice of crystals, growing more shadowy and insubstantial as it swelled; then darkness; then a dazzle of faint prismatic light-tiny complexes in a vast three-dimensional array, growing steadily bigger.' This description has none of the 'values' of the naturalistic 'literary' novel, it is crystalline, and of the mind of virtue of being outside of unconscious action. This very well could be an inchoate concept for a work by Judd, LeWitt, Flavin, or Insley. (Smithson 1996: 14–15)

Smithson foregrounds the way in which description in Knight's novel can sometimes not be understood. In other words, it does not offer single new elements which can be subsumed into an otherwise understandable world (what Suvin calls cognitive estrangement).

As Anthony Vidler says in a comment on the above quote from Smithson, the artist is interested in Knight's unpredictable use of space, for 'Smithson's purpose was, with the limited means available to him as an artist, to break into and shatter the pervasive and all-dominating rule of the spectacle, to reflect or deflect vision (mirror play) to reassert the power of space in the epoch of the "fading of space"' (Vidler 2001: 249). Not all of the descriptions in *Beyond the Barrier* are of this kind. But there are some, and there is no rule as to when the accepted rules of reality are going to be subverted. Yet this is not an argument against 'realism' in any form: in fact, as Graham Harman says, 'I hold that *only* realism, *only* a model of individuals with real constitutions outside our interactions with them' can defeat the idea that our universe is ultimately rooted in persons (Harman 2013: 11). At the same time, Harman argues for a kind of dark object realism, in which 'Realism is not realism if the reality it describes can be translated without energy loss into human knowledge, or indeed into any sort of relation at all' (Harman 2013: 12). The loss of energy in the description above is seen in the way in which it does not translate into human experience without asperity. It is this asperity which makes the novel an example of a Type-2 world (although Harman also holds the necessity of sufficient reason [2013: 14]).

The polar opposite of *Beyond the Barrier* is Hal Clement's *Mission of Gravity* (1953). On the one hand the novel attempts a description of extreme difference, describing the planet Mesklin, which is shaped like a discus and has a gravitational force between 3 and 700 times greater than on Earth (Clement 1962: 13). The differences between life adapted to such an environment and life on Earth is the focus of the novel. For example, the main Mesklin character, Barlennan, is 'fifteen inches long and two in diameter' (Clement 1962: 20), has 18 legs and is scared to fall from any height whatsoever, since such extreme gravity means that even the smallest drop is fatal. Describing the differences between Mesklinian and Terrestrial physics is one of the main purposes of the novel (and is also indicated in the title of one of the novel's sequels, the short story 'Lecture Demonstration').

Mission of Gravity falls into the genre of hard sf. The categorisation of 'hard science fiction', meaning work that 'displays an especially heightened concern for, and an especially heightened connection to, science' (Westfahl 2005: 187), was originally coined to describe Clement and John Campbell as writers (Stableford

2007: 11). As Thomas Disch says, *Mission of Gravity* shows 'the author's zeal for the scientific process' (Disch 2000: 205), which not only means that events receive axiomatic scientific explanations, but also that all questions raised by the contact of people from one world with another are resolved: there are no mysteries in the novel whatsoever, nor any descriptions which, no matter how fantastic, are not meant to be as realistic as possible.

For example, at one point the main human character, Lackland, is out on the Mesklin surface with Barlennan, trying to extract a sample of tough flesh from a large dead creature they have found. They both hear an explosion coming from Lackland's vehicle, a 'tank' (Clement 1962: 37). Because the Mesklin natives have no knowledge of explosives, Barlennan is interested in the phenomenon and says, '"I take it you were carrying some explosive in your tank ... Why did you not use it to get the material you wanted from this animal? And what made it act while it was still in the tank?"' Lackland responds, saying that '"You have a genius for asking difficult questions... The answer to your first one is that I was not carrying any; and to the second, your guess is as good as mine at this point"' (Clement 1962: 38). Although Lackland can think of no logical explanation for the explosion, he only cannot think of one 'at this point': he fully expects to do so in the future. This is sf as Meillassoux understands it, meaning that unknown elements will still be subject to scientific knowledge in the future (Meillassoux 2015: 5). And of course Lackland does eventually understand what happened:

> 'As nearly as I can figure out about the tank, the floor partition between cockpit and engine compartment wasn't airtight. When I got out to do some investigating, Mesklin's atmosphere – high pressure hydrogen – began leaking in and mixing with the normal air under the floor. It did the same in the cockpit too, of course, but practically all the oxygen was swept out through the door from there and diluted below danger point before anything happened. Underneath – well, there was a spark before the oxygen went.' (Clement 1962: 41)

The novel is filled with such strange events followed by their eventual scientific explanation. However, while Disch says that such a structure is what makes the novel 'the best account of alien life on another planet that I'd ever read' (Disch 2000: 204), the crux of speculative realism and sf is the representation of unknowable events within the knowable that indicates 'alien' organisations of knowledge when compared with our own. Tracing the manner in which such events are represented in a literary form, along with the consequences of their appearance, is what is called 'the Zug effect', and is the focus of this work.

Speculative Realism

Let us revisit Darko Suvin. The novum, according to Suvin, is a *'novelty, innovation ... validated by cognitive logic'* (Suvin 2010: 67, italics in original). The way the novum works at first seems similar to Meillassoux's Type-2 world because both logic and illogic, at least for a moment, coexist; in other words, the novum functions through the setting of *'one thing by the side of another'* (Suvin 1988: 142, italics in original). However, a difference between Suvin and Meillassoux appears in how validation by cognitive logic takes place when the novelty is eventually explained, just as Lackland came to understand how the explosion happened in his tank after thinking about it for a while. As discussed in Chapter 5, Samuel Delany has developed an alternative to the novum which attempts to capture the essence of what is here being called the Zug effect. In order to differentiate his idea from the separation inherent in setting one thing by the side of another, Delany calls his concept *inmixing*. Delany provides an example in a reading of a term from Frank Herbert's *Dune* (1965):

> What is significant about an *ornithopter* is not how it is *like* either a helicopter or a bird. What is significant about it is that, when we focus our mind's eye at the joint of wing and fuselage, we can *see* the hydraulic pistons, when we open up the wing-casing, we can *follow* the cables and pulleys inside, we can *hear* the bearings in the bearing case around the connective shaft – which joints, pistons, cables and bearings are *foreign to both* birds and helicopters but without which our ornithopter *would not fly*. (Delany 2009: 141, italics in original)

In this passage Delany stresses that it is not that two terms which are not usually thought of together are set next to each other (in this case, helicopter and bird). Rather, what is essential to the ornithopter is foreign to both birds and helicopters. In other words, cognition does not resolve the difference between the two terms (as it does with the novum); rather cognition is stymied by what does not fit either term. It is from the lack of resolution between the two that the Zug effect can take place.

With the ornithopter, Delany indicates a difference between the essence of the thing and its qualities. The essence of the ornithopter is different from its qualities of a helicopter or a bird. Yet the ornithopter is not just different from these qualities, it is also, somehow, connected. The way in which, according to Delany, essence and qualities are connected is through *seeing*, *following* and *hearing* what is going on in the text.

It is at this point that an important difference arises between the thought of Meillassoux and Harman. This difference can be used to initiate an overview of the philosophical field of speculative realism in general, with a focus on how it relates to the arguments developed herein. The term 'speculative realism' was coined by Ray Brassier to describe the approach of a group of philosophers who gathered at a workshop at Goldsmiths College, University of London, in April 2007 (Harman 2011b: 77–81). Brassier, Graham Harman, Iain Hamilton Grant and Quentin Meillassoux gathered because they all took the idea of correlationism as their enemy. As succinctly defined by Meillassoux, correlationism means that 'we can't know what the reality of the object in itself is because we can't distinguish between properties which are supposed to belong to the object and properties belonging to the subjective access to the object' (Meillassoux, cited in Harman 2011b: 81). Or, as Meillassoux put it in *After Finitude*, correlationism is 'the idea according to which we only ever have access to the correlation between thinking and being, and never to either term considered apart from the other' (Meillassoux 2009: 5). These philosophers differ in the way that access to objects features in their thought. Brassier takes a 'scientist's' approach in which following the rules of science functions as freedom from subjectivity, or what he calls 'compulsive freedom' (Brassier 2013). Grant devises a 'non-eliminative Idealist' reading of Schelling in which the Ideal is not a framework of nature, but rather a part of it (Niemoczynski and Grant 2013).

Meillassoux and Harman also both think about correlationism in different ways. For Meillassoux, correlationism is upended by the inclusion of the impossible within the possible (a Type-2 world), while for Harman it is the withdrawn nature of the essence of objects that takes on this task. These positions are ontologically different, for as Meillassoux argued in a talk given in Berlin in

2012, access to objects takes place without subjectivity; he claims that Harman reschedules this subjectivity into objects themselves (Meillassoux 2012a: 7). Harman, on the other hand, argues that Meillassoux 'essentially reprises the old Cartesian ontology' when he divides objects into human subjects and dead matter. Instead, Harman argues against giving ontological superiority to any object whatsoever, without of course denying some of the special properties of human subjects (Harman and Cogburn 2015). Both thinkers can be joined in describing the Zug effect, however, since it involves dark objects which are withdrawn from understanding (Harman), yet whose withdrawal is experienced through the non-sensical (Meillassoux).

Meillassoux's division of objects into subjects and lifeless matter can be seen in his description of ancestrality in *After Finitude*. The earth is 4.5 billion years old, while humanity, in the form of *Homo habilis*, first existed between 2.8 and 1.5 million years ago. For Meillassoux,

> contemporary science is in a position to precisely determine – albeit in the form of revisable hypotheses – the dates of the formation of the fossils of creatures living prior to the emergence of the first hominids, the date of the accretion of the earth, the date of the formation of stars, and even the 'age' of the universe itself. (Meillassoux 2009: 9)

This means that the world existed before thought, and therefore that thought is part of the world, rather than the other way around, as correlationism would have it (Meillassoux 2009: 13). The same argument is offered for an awareness of one's own death, for 'I must grant that my possible annihilation is thinkable as something that is not just the correlate of my thought of this annihilation' (Meillassoux 2009: 57). Thus the ontological difference between thought and dead matter provides an escape from the correlationist circle.

Harman, on the other hand, sees all objects as ontologically equal. All objects, not just dead ones, provide access beyond correlationism. This happens because all objects withdraw. In *Weird Realism: Lovecraft and Philosophy*, Harman develops a reading of withdrawn essence, separated qualities and indirect connections in his reading of 100 passages from H. P. Lovecraft. He states that Lovecraft's primary stylistic theme is 'the separation of an object from its qualities' (Harman 2012: 113), and it is the technique with which Lovecraft is able to represent the alien in literature. And in *The Quadruple Object*, Harman indicates the difference between an object's essence and its qualities thus:

> The ocean remains the same though its successive waves advance and recede. A Caribbean parrot retains its identity no matter how exactly its wings currently flap, and no matter what curses or threats it now utters in the Spanish language. The phenomenal world is not just an idealist sanctuary from the blows of harsh reality, but an active seismic zone where intentional objects grind slowly against their own qualities. (Harman 2011a: 26)

In this passage Harman indicates two things: first, the separation between essence (i.e. identity) and manifest qualities; second, a connection between qualities and essence in the 'grind' that takes place between the two.

The separation between an object and its qualities is seen in the way that, no matter in how much detail an object is described, the description never actually becomes that object: there is always a distance between a gathering of the qualities that an object has and the object itself (Harman 2012: 3). In other words, a parrot is still a parrot whether its wings flap in one way or another.

Here we come back to Delany's reading of the ornithopter. The essence of the ornithopter is what is withdrawn from its comparison to both birds and helicopters. Yet the ornithopter is not simply different from these two, as would be a sticking plaster or a bout of depression. It is also connected to them, and it is this combination of connection and difference which makes the ornithopter a relatively dark object, and thus a figure of the Zug effect.

The identity of the ornithopter can be experienced, just not by a direct explication of all of its qualities (since all of the qualities of the ornithopter will never actually be the ornithopter – there is always a difference). Instead, Harman indicates that *indirect* access to the essence of objects exists, albeit through allusion and misdirection: 'This indirect access is achieved by allowing the hidden object to deform the sensual world, just as the existence of a black hole might be inferred from the swirl of light and gases orbiting its core' (Harman 2012: 238). Non-axiomatic sf is the deformation of the sensual world in the sense that the scientific, testable experience of the world is disrupted; it is through this disruption that 'something' else can be said to exist. On the one hand this something is never resolved, its essence is never captured by descriptions of its qualities (it is never incorporated into the understanding of a future science). Yet at the same time this essence can be experienced, but only indirectly; one of the main tasks of this book is to lay out a number of narrative strategies in sf texts for indirectly representing such an essence. In Harman's reading of Lovecraft, indirectness takes place through the way his style 'involves allusions in depth to indescribable realities withdrawing from all linguistic, perceptual, and even cognitive access' which is mixed with the way his descriptions can also 'generate perplexity on the fully accessible plane of empirical sensory data' (Harman 2012: 162). It is the combination of the withdrawn essence of objects and some of their accessible qualities which interests Harman in Lovecraft, and which also leads to an experience of the Zug effect.

Joanna Russ's 1970 novel *And Chaos Died* is noted (and more often than not derided) for containing many such descriptions of withdrawn objects. Steven Shaviro, undoubtedly the leading figure in thinking about speculative realism and sf together, singles out Russ's short story 'What Did You Do During the Revolution, Grandma?' (1983) as the only example he can think of for Meillassoux's extro-science fiction (Shaviro 2015a: 80). This is because of the way in which a series of parallel universes are similar to Meillassoux's Type 1–3 worlds. However, *And Chaos Died* is a more sustained example of the Type-2 world that Meillassoux describes. For example, this description: 'The big one was obviously one of those epoxy-and-metal eggs produced by itself – the Platonic Idea of a pebble turned inside out, born of a computer and aspiring towards the condition of Mechanical Opera.' This is a description of a spacecraft – 'It was a big, discreet, muffled luxury liner' (Russ 1970: 93) – but it is hard to know exactly what the ship looks like. This is because the description is almost entirely made of the 'invisible' connections the spaceship has with other objects; in other words, this is a representation of the dark side of an object, although only a relatively dark side. Rather than describing the ship through connections between more easily known qualities (height, length, volume, orientation), withdrawn aspects of the ship are compared to withdrawn aspects of other objects. Compare this to a description of an unknown object in Clement's *Mission of Gravity*. At the beginning of the novel an inhabitant of the high-gravity planet is using a communication device given them by the Earthlings. Only its qualities are described, but none of its qualities are in any kind of tension whatsoever with essence:

> It was an apparently solid block three inches long and about half as high and wide. A transparent spot in the otherwise blank surface of one end looked like an eye, and apparently functioned as one. The only other feature was a small, round hole in one of the long faces. The block was lying with this face upward, and the 'eye' end projecting slightly from under the shelter flap. The flap itself opened downwind, of course, so that its fabric was now plastered tightly against the flat upper surface of the machine. (Clement 1962: 9)

This description is different from Russ's because it uses familiar extensive qualities (height, length, volume) to describe an unfamiliar object. The goal of this passage is understanding. With Russ, the goal is different: not an understanding of what the object looks like, but rather an exposure of its 'hidden' qualities. This is why, on the same page, the main character Jai Vedh 'had attacks of wishing to get outside it and cling to the skin, so the thing's vanity might be satisfied by being seen from the outside; it was unnatural to make a beautiful outside for no one' (Russ 1970: 93). Seeing objects from the inside is simply another way of seeing the 'dark' connections between objects that are always there, but are sometimes impossible to see. It is like seeing an eye from the inside, from behind the lens, and describing its potential to register ultraviolet light, although it seems impossible to see at the time.

This inside-out approach is not confined to this single passage of Russ's novel, but is found throughout. It is also explicitly stated as a descriptive function. Later in the novel, Jai Vedh comes into contact with a number of odd creatures who are not only described in an inside-out manner, but are described as *being* inside out:

> Inside them something flowed and gibbered like the specter of a big-headed monkey: the ghosts of fingers, the ghosts of buttocks, glowing ectoplasmic bellies, skin, ears, ribbed knuckles, little bits of fur. The ghost in the machine. Trying to shake its way out, grabbing the cage.
> *You've turned yourselves inside out*, he said. (Russ 1970: 112–13)

Samuel Delany, in a review of Russ's novel, describes such difficulties in understanding as problems of narration rather than style.

> The difficulty is in the narrative structure itself. At no time does Jai, the protagonist, think about any of the concerns in the novel as an explicit problem he wishes to solve and to which a sizable proportion of his subsequent actions would be directed.
>
> When a writer does employ such a convention, immediately a vast amount of mental house-keeping is facilitated for the reader. When we read a novel employing such a narrative convention, certain actions are immediately subordinated to certain others; primary, secondary, and even tertiary levels are established almost at once. The novel is much easier to read.
>
> When a writer does not employ this convention, the reader is bereft of this prestructured organization. *All data are equal until they link up with other data that put them into a pattern*: it is harder reading, and more demanding. (Delany 1979, emphasis added)

Delany indicates that what is structurally difficult about the novel is not that new qualities are being invented and attached to objects (which would be the case with fantasy, or Meillassoux's Type-3 world), but rather that the qualities of an object are no longer being filtered (like having the eye lens removed). While 'all' data can never be represented (and we should not assume that Delany is actually saying so), describing objects from the inside-out is one way of describing previously dark qualities that all objects actually have.

Russ is concerned with this narrative strategy of representing the unknowable, and one of the references that she provides for her narrative is the work of H. P. Lovecraft, the same writer that Harman uses to draw out his reading of weird realism. In her short essay 'On the Fascination of Horror Stories, Including Lovecraft's', Russ sets herself in opposition to both Darko Suvin and Damon Knight (Russ 1995: 59); however, in the context of this discussion, Russ's technique of describing things inside-out is closer to Knight than Suvin. In relation to Lovecraft, Russ calls horror a 'fiction of extreme states' (Russ 1995: 61) which attempts to represent 'the destructive, the irrevocable, the terrifying, and the demonic' which is otherwise often ignored (62). In other words, work like Lovecraft's attempts 'to give the subjective, undiluted, raw, absolute, global experience-in-itself of these basic human issues' (63). The undiluted, raw absolute experience that Russ mentions here is simply illuminating the existence of the dark corners of objects. In other words, she is interested in representing the withdrawn aspect of objects through a description of Type-2 worlds.[1]

The Zug Effect II

The reason that Damon Knight is being used as an initial focal point for this discussion is because the Zug is both a figure of withdrawal and of connection. The first time Naismith hears the term, before he is aware that he is a time traveller and a Zug himself, the word 'had an unpleasant sound, somehow; it made a shudder of distaste run up his spine' (Knight 1970: 9). The Zug is described as a 'mutated ortholidian', a 30-foot flesh-eating monster (24–5). The first time Naismith encounters one is in a dream; the Zug has 'an impossibly fluid reptilian motion, and looked at him with tiny red eyes' (21). This 'impossibility' underlies the traits of Zugian motion, indirectly describing the essence of the Zug while separating that essence from its qualities. This is a similar technique to that which Harman finds in Lovecraft's story 'The Call of Cthulhu', whose impossible application of adjectives endows nouns with an almost 'psychic potency' (Harman 2012: 76–7).

However, the Zug is not only a figure of separation, but also of connection. In fact, the similarity of the Zug to humanity is the most frightening thing about it. One confrontation between Naismith and a Zug begins by stressing difference: 'Two little red eyes started at him, and there was a faint rattle of bony plates.' Yet as the creature becomes more visible it becomes more similar to Naismith, and thus more terrifying: 'It was a shape of tremendous animal power, armored and clawed, many-limbed ... but the most frightening thing about it was the look of intelligence, or merciless, ancient wisdom in its eyes ...' (Knight 1970: 86).

Presenting the Zugs as figures of difference and then of similarity happens again in the novel. When Naismith returns to the future from which he originated, he is sent to meet the head of the community, her Highness, because an alarm sounds to indicate that a Zug has been detected outside the barrier and Naismith, who is the only Shefth around, has been sent to kill it. He is provided with a helmet which is fitted with a 'shimmering disk' in front of his eyes. The disc is 'for illusions', for '"The Zug may appear in some confusing shape, but look through that, and you will be able to see its real aspect"' (Knight 1970: 123). And when the Zug does appear, it is first in the form of the divine, which only appears as terror after Naismith looks through the disc:

> Naismith's hand slapped his chest instinctively, came up with the cool metal of the gun, even as his mind registered the incongruity of what he was seeing. The thing that was now hurtling toward him with incredible speed, winged, glittering, was no Zug – it was an angel.
>
> Naismith had an impression of blazing eyes, a manlike face of inhuman beauty, powerful arms outstretched.
>
> In that frozen moment, he was aware of the passengers in the bubbles, all facing around, bright-eyed, intent, like spectators at a boxing match. He saw the gnome's bubble begin to move. Then his jaw clenched, and the view-disk sprang into being in front of his face. The angel disappeared, in its place was a many-legged monster, red-eyed, clawed and hideous.
>
> 'Zug!' shouted the voices around him. Then the beast was upon him. (126)

Naismith fires and kills the Zug, but this is not the end of the story. There is still another Zug remaining beyond the barrier, and this time it is Naismith himself.

The Zug effect combines both separation and similarity, both withdrawal and essence. While a human, Naismith really is a Zug. Yet after breaking out of his human host shell, the Zug finds himself much more Naismith than expected. At the same time, this new creature is not a stranger to the Zugness that he now embodies. For example, when first seeing his new Zug-reflection in a mirror, Naismith finds his new body already familiar:

> He paused to examine his reflection in the silvery disk of a mirror. It was strange, and yet perfectly natural, to look at himself and see this pale, unearthly figure, with its blazing eyes in the inhuman mask of the face. He flexed his great arms, and the smaller grasping members; then, the tail, watching the sharp sting emerge. (136)

It seems quite hard to accept that these Zug qualities are still to be connected to the essence of Naismith, but on just the next page an insistence on this is found: 'Every thought, every feeling that Naismith had had during the months their minds were linked together was recorded in his brain. It was not merely that he remembered Naismith: he *was* Naismith. He was a member of the race of conquerors; and he was also a man' (137). In this sense the Zug effect is not about abandoning the human condition, but rather about locating the human condition within the conditions of others, including other objects, forces, fantasies and ideas. This is the force of the image of the Zug in Knight's novel, and why it ends with the future rejoining of Zug and humanity, into a new kind of being:

> It was pleasant to think that in a thousand years, or ten thousand, Zug and Man might meet again, and this time blend their powers into something greater. It would take that long, or longer; Naismith and his kind could afford to wait.
> For God is not born in a day. (142)

The figure of the Zug thus brings together three main points that will be developed throughout this book: a separation of the essence of an object from its qualities, or what Harman calls *fission* (Harman 2012: 243); the joining together of an object to qualities which seem 'unnatural' to it, or what Harman calls *fusion* (240); and the tension created out of such moments of separation and gathering. It is believed that a focus on non-human objects is one way for such separation and gathering to be represented in fiction. Knight is the proper place to start this discussion because of his tendency to write fiction which is both science fiction and not-science fiction.

Knight is better known as an editor of sf than as a writer of it. And his own attempts at defining the genre are filled with the same conjunction of separation from and similarity to more traditional ideas of what the genre entails. At times, Knight is less concerned with the manner in which a novum is incorporated into either science or cognition than he is interested in the way that the fantastic is represented, no matter the consequences. As James Gunn states:

> I remember an excellent debate between Damon Knight and me in my classroom in which Damon maintained there was no significant difference between fantasy and science fiction, and I insisted there was.
> An immediate complication: do the words we use have the same meaning for us both? If Damon considers everything irrelevant except the fantastic elements (or for that part of the fiction that is contrary to things as we know them), then I never will convince him that there is a meaningful difference. (Gunn 2005: 6)

However, at least on a conscious level, Knight's definition of sf as 'speculative' is not as unwieldy as Gunn claims. *In Search of*

Wonder, Knight's collection of sf criticism from the first half of the 1950s, contains the following definition of sf:

> Science fiction is speculative; but so is every work of fiction, to some degree; historical and exotic fiction particularly so.
>
> These are convenient standards, and it's inevitable that librarians and critics will use them – but there must have been a time when stories about India or Alaska or the South Seas were 'outlandish,' 'weird,' 'unbelievable,' 'unheard-of' and so on. Such stories have gained mass acceptance simply by being around long enough to become familiar; and we may expect that science fiction will do the same. (Knight 1967: 14)

For Knight, extinguishing a sense of wonder is only a matter of time: science will catch up with the strange things we find in fiction. In fact, in perhaps the most famous essay in the collection, 'Cosmic Jerrybuilder A. E. van Vogt', Knight attacks van Vogt's novel *The World of Null-A* (1948) for its dream-like structure and lack of linear narrative. Although it seems as if Knight is arguing against his own work, really he is not. Instead, he is arguing against sf as Meillassoux too simply defines it. In the examination of outlandish, weird, unbelievable and unheard-of moments in literature, a number of texts discussed below, including Neil Gaiman's novels and Doris Lessing's *The Cleft* (2007), are not sf in Meillassoux's sense, but rather provide scenes of weirdness un-reified within an otherwise logical context.

The Anthropocene

The purpose of the Zug effect is, in what seems like a paradox at first, to represent non-correlationist worlds. This is necessary because our correlationist world is destroying the planet. Popularised by chemist Paul Crutzen (who won the Nobel Prize in 1995 for work on the ozone layer), the concept of the Anthropocene denotes 'the current epoch in which humans and our societies have become a global geophysical force' (Steffen, Crutzen and McNeill 2007: 614). It is a phase during which humanity affects the world-system on a global rather than just a local scale, and in which these effects are becoming unmanageable. In other words, 'The human is no longer that figure in the foreground which pursues its self-interest against the background of a wholistic, organicist cycle that the human might perturb but with which it can remain in balance and harmony, in the end, by simply *withdrawing* from certain excesses' (Wark 2015: xii).

Crutzen et al. take the year 1800 as the start of the Anthropocene, as this date marks the rise of industrialisation in the Western world. More specifically, the authors take the increase of CO_2 in the atmosphere as their key indicator of humanity's influence on the planet. More specifically still, they see a rise of around 25 ppm of CO_2 from 1800 to 1945 as the first clear indicator of the Anthropocene, which exceeds the margins of error for such studies (Steffen, Crutzen and McNeill 2007: 616). Thus they are able to use CO_2 measurements to divide the Anthropocene into three stages: Stage 1, from 1800 to 1945; Stage 2, the Great Acceleration, from 1945 to 2015, during which the Earth entered its sixth great event of extinction (617); and Stage 3, from 2015 onward, which is characterised by the fact that policymakers are starting to take the Anthropocene into consideration (618–19). Although the timing of Stage 3 was premature (the article was published in 2007, and thus perhaps includes a bit of wishful thinking), the concept of the Anthropocene has been widely discussed as a division from the Holocene (the name for our current time, thought to have started around 12,000 years ago).

Yet setting 1800 as the start-date for the Anthropocene is also problematic. This is because fixes for current problems are then traced back to chemical emissions caused by the industrial revolution. In other words, using CO_2 (and other emissions) as the marker for the rise of the Anthropocene leads to thinking of the minimising of CO_2 emissions as a 'fix', rather than addressing the kind of thinking that was behind such a relationship to the environment. In *Capitalism and the Web of Life* Jason Moore makes a similar point when he argues that basing the Anthropocene on the rise of the use of steam and coal 'makes for an easy story. Easy, because it does not challenge the naturalized inequalities, alienation, and violence inscribed in modernity's strategic relations of power and production. It is an easy story to tell because it does not ask us to think about these relations *at all*' (Moore 2015: 170). In other words, limiting the problem to that of industrialisation also limits possible alternatives to those born from industrialisation: 'to locate the origins of the modern world with the steam engine and the coal pit is to prioritize shutting down the steam engines and the coal pits (and their twenty-first century alternatives)' (Moore 2015:

172). Instead Moore posits locating the start of the Anthropocene in 1450, with the rise of capitalism rather than of industrialisation (182–7). This change foregrounds strategies of 'global conquest, endless commodification, and relentless rationalization' which, instead of focusing on coal and steam, can 'prioritize the relations of power, capital, and nature that rendered fossil capitalism so deadly in the first place'. As Moore summarises, 'Shut down a coal plant, and you can slow global warming for a day; shut down the relations that made the coal plant, and you can stop it for good' (172).

Moore then suggests the term 'Capitalocene' to replace Anthropocene, in order to stress the original relations which have led to the situation where, in the words of Roy Scranton, 'the changes wrought by global warming will affect not only the world's climate and biodiversity, but its very geological structure, and not just for centuries, but for millennia' (Scranton 2015: 18). The main issue, as Donna Haraway indicates, is 'when do changes in degree become changes in kind, and what are the effects of bioculturally, biotechnically, biopolitically, historically situated people (not Man) relative to, and combined with, the effects of other species assemblages and other biotic/abiotic forces?' (Haraway 2015: 159). In order to stress the nature of the Anthropocene to foreground the connectedness between all of the objects and ideas in an environment, Haraway has coined a new term for the current period, the 'Chthulucene', based on H. P. Lovecraft's superhuman monstrosity Cthulhu, although Haraway changes the spelling slightly (adding an extra 'h') in order indicate a difference between her thought and Lovecraft's racism and misogyny (Haraway 2015: 160), which S. T. Joshi and David Schultz see as beginning in the poem 'De Triumpho Naturae: The Triumph of Nature over Northern Ignorance' (1905) – written when the author was 15 and which argues that freeing blacks from slavery was a mistake – and continuing throughout his life (Joshi and Schultz 2001: 134). The focus of Haraway's concept is both the intra-connectedness of things in the world and a sense of mourning for connections and things which are now lost:

> 'my' Chthulucene ... entangles myriad temporalities and spatialities and myriad intra-active entities-in-assemblages – including the more-than-human, other-than-human, inhuman, and human-as-humus ... Chthulucene is to join forces to reconstitute refuges, to make possible partial and robust biological-cultural-political-technological

recuperation and recomposition, which must include mourning irreversible losses. (Haraway 2015: 160)

In other words, the Chthulucene is an awareness of the connectedness of objects and their qualities in both space and time. The focus of this book is to foreground narrative strategies for putting such moments in focus.

A number of concepts introduced by Haraway in the above quotations will recur throughout this book, especially assemblages (through Gilles Deleuze and Manuel DeLanda) and Harman's reading of Lovecraft. However, one direct reference Haraway makes leads to a number of concrete literary examples of the Chthulucene in action. Among the references to alternative titles for the Anthropocene, Haraway cites Kim Stanley Robinson's sf novel 2312 (2012), which uses the term 'The Dithering' for what Crutzen et al. describe as Stage-1 Anthropocene. As Robinson writes, the generations of the Dithering 'had heedlessly pushed the climate into a change with an unstoppable momentum to it, continuing not only into the present but for centuries more to come, as methane clathrate releases and permafrost melting began to out-gas the third great wave of greenhouse gases, possibly the largest of them all' (Robinson 2012: 360–1). While the Dithering is only the initial time period mentioned in the novel (it is followed by the Crisis, the Turnaround, the Accelerando, the Ritard and finally, the Balkanization, the period in which the novel takes place) (277–9), one of the strategies Robinson suggests as an alternative to the problems of the period is similar to what Haraway suggests, meaning a foregrounding of entanglement.

Just as dark objects functioned in *Beyond the Barrier* to foreground connections outside of science, Robinson foregrounds the manner in which objects, environments and ideas are entangled in what Moore calls 'double internality', meaning that humanity and nature are *co-produced* through each other, rather than humanity merely affecting the background of nature (which would then allow humanity to 'rescue' nature by no longer acting upon it) (Moore 2015: 9). One of the key ways for double internality to be represented in literature is through a disturbance in vision, which is the focus of the first two chapters of this book. In Knight's novel, this disturbance is indicated in the 'darkness' of the objects encountered by Naismith. In Robinson's *2312*, a similar effect of the dark takes place.

Alex, who has recently died, was part of a small group of people mapping the power structures of both humans and computers throughout the inhabited solar system. Alex's grand-daughter, Swan Er Hong, has been roped into taking Alex's place in the small group. Swan was a terraria designer, meaning that she developed the terraforming direction of the inside of asteroids converted into spaceships. Now she is a performance artist who makes both goldsworthies and abramovics (Robinson 2012: 5). On various ships used during her journey from Mercury to Jupiter's moon Io, Swan encounters two of the designs she created in her previous life; however, on a trip from Io to Earth, she catches a ship of someone else's design, a blackliner. Rather than being designed for relaxing on a beach or delving into sexual variations, the blackliner is completely dark inside so that the passengers' other senses are heightened.

'Inside the blackliner, darkness reigned. It was as black as could be, the black one would find inside a deep cave inside the earth' (Robinson 2012: 88). With Bryant's dark objects, the darkness represents the manner in which an object is not connected to any inputs or outputs of any other object. Yet if an object cannot receive or generate contact with other objects, what could it ever be good for (Bryant 2014: 199–200)? This would be an example of an absolutely dark object; yet a relatively dark object would only be invisible to some objects, but not to others (Bryant 2014: 200). For example, ultraviolet light, meaning light with a wavelength below 400 nanometers, is invisible to the human eye because it is absorbed by the eye lens in order to reduce its harmful effects. Yet those suffering from aphakia, or an absence of the eye lens, can see what is usually considered invisible. Or, as Bryant argues:

> The concept of dark objects reminds us not to reduce the world to the machines that we happen to encounter in the world. As we seek to understand the behavior and actions of other machines, including other humans, it reminds us that they might be responding to agencies that we ourselves don't register. In this regard, we ought not jump to the conclusion that mysterious behavior indicates irrationality or madness, but ought to hold open the possibility that perhaps agencies are at work that we ourselves do not register. (2014: 200–1)

This leads to two other aspects of dark objects: that every object has a bit of 'darkness' in it (the withdrawn nature of objects, according to Harman) and that objects are not static, that they can change, and this change is due to the connections which are part of the unexploited darkness which may come forth when new situations arise (Bryant 2014: 201). The Zug effect is what needs to take place for the unexploited darkness of one object to 'connect' to the unexploited darkness of another. Unexpected connections are essential for the Anthropocene because environmental damage cannot be undone by turning back (meaning to stop doing harm) but rather only by going forward, making new connections rather than revitalising old ones. As Scranton says in *Learning to Die in the Anthropocene*, 'For humanity to survive in the Anthropocene, we need to learn to live with and through the end of our current civilization. Change, risk, conflict, strife, and death are the very processes of life, and we cannot avoid them. We must learn to accept and adapt' (Scranton 2015: 22). The manner of this adaptation takes many different forms, but one is through what Patrick Trevor-Roper calls 'the blunting of sight', meaning that a lack of focus can blur the edges of one object and another, allowing the withdrawn to come forth (Trevor-Roper 1970). One method for such blunting is through an experience of darkness. The reason sf is a privileged genre in this regard is that the sense of wonder that it posits does not necessarily have to be resolved; it can remain weird. And as Nick Srnicek and Alex Williams state at the end of *Inventing the Future*, it is the wonder of sf which can offer alternatives to the strategies for living that have led to the Anthropocene:

> We must expand our collective imagination beyond what capitalism allows. Rather than settling for marginal improvements in battery life and computer power, the left should mobilise dreams of decarbonizing the economy, space travel, robot economies – all the traditional touchstones of science fiction – in order to prepare for a day beyond capitalism. (Srnicek and Williams 2015: 183)

In *2312* the blackliner is a mechanism through which connections are made between an object and qualities which do not belong together. This is not just where relative black objects can be seen, but it also illustrates the difference between Type-2 and Type-1 worlds: in the former, there is no attempt to make the connections between objects fit into a scientific (or future scientific) understanding, while in Type-1 worlds, unexpected connections remain weird between objects, but it is implied that one day they will become expected. One of the ways to allow such not-fitting connections is through disruptions of vision. Swan starts to feel that without any qualities to anchor her, there would be too many connections between things to process:

> No face to cling to with one's gaze, nothing at all to see – her memory and imagination would run riot, her starved senses left to spin hungrily, making things up – nothing but her unhappiness for company. Pure being, unadulterated thought, revealing what the phenomenal world could hide but not change: the blank at the heart of things. (Robinson 2012: 90)

The 'blank at the heart of things' is the withdrawn nature of any object, which makes every object a (relatively) dark object. The strategy of the blackliner is simply to make this dark nature of every object more visible through dimming the dominance of vision.

One consequence of Swan's experience of the Zug effect is a memory that she is faced with: in the past she ingested the Enceladan suite of aliens, which permanently merged with her being in continuously unpredictable ways (Robinson 2012: 89–90). Although Swan has undergone many other internal and external bio-modifications, it is the merging of herself with the aliens that causes the most shocked reactions from others who learn of it. And in the blackliner Swan herself is confused, asking 'Infecting herself with an alien, was it wise? No, it was not! Crying out then as if poisoned, trapped in a kaleidoscope, a roaring in her ears, exclaiming over and over, *But I was – I was Swan – I was – I was Swan –*' (90). Although this scene will be picked up later in the final chapter of this book, here it can be used as one indication of the way in which dark objects are not only about being removed from understanding, but are relative objects which foreground the slipperiness between an object and its qualities. The focus of the Zug effect is the need to recognise this slippage, just as Swan does in this scene. As Scranton says, 'The enemy isn't *out there* somewhere' in the form of big oil, neoliberal politics or Wall Street oligarchs; rather, 'the enemy is ourselves. Not as individuals, but as a collective. A system. A hive' (Scranton 2015: 85).

In Knight's novel the dark objects were not completely removed from any understanding whatsoever, but were relative, and thus functioned as gathering points between objects which were usually invisible to each other; the reason that this novel is used as a focal point for this book is that the objects which were invisible to each other were actually one and the same object: Naismith, who was also the Zug. This is similar to the end of van Vogt's *The World of Null-A*, which Knight disparaged. In *Null-A*, logic is often thrown to the winds ('null-A' means non-Aristotelian) and the main plot of the novel is that the protagonist Gosseyn is searching for his enemy, only to find, in the final sentence, that when confronting his foe, 'The face was his own' (van Vogt 1948: 190). What both novels have in common is that an object which was once considered completely transparent (Naismith, Gosseyn) is now found to have an opaque element: they are in fact the enemy for which they have been searching. As Paul Gilding, the former head of Greenpeace, says, 'This is no longer an environmental issue. How we respond now will decide the future of human civilization. We are the people we've been waiting for. There is no one else. There is no other time. It's us and it is now' (Gilding 2008).

The thing to understand about the Anthropocene is that the time for intervention is over, the planet has been changed to such an effect that the damage is done. So what is needed is to come at the problem sideways, from a completely unexpected angle. This leads to the Zug effect, which is really two things: a kind of vision that sees relatively dark objects and a way to imagine worlds in which such objects exist. The Zug effect is irrational, weird and unanticipated; but is also reality because it draws its power from the withdrawn nature of objects, their dark side, rather than from a rule-less Type-3 world of fantasy. The consequence of the Zug effect is that unexpected connections are made between objects. The consequence of these unexpected connections is that non-Anthropocene futures have the potential to be invented.

This chapter has discussed a number of different topics related to both speculative realism and sf. The Zug effect has been defined as moments of ambiguity within sf. Contra Meillassoux, such moments are seen as essential to sf itself, rather than as something outside of it in the form of extro-science fiction. Although Meillassoux argues that sf assumes that the unknown will always be subsumed within future scientific knowledge, the actual recording of the sounds of space was seen as one example of real-world scientific ambiguity. However, Meillassoux's Type-2 world is seen as a powerful description of the Zug effect, in which a connection of both similarity and difference occurs.

The Zug effect is essential to understanding the connection between speculative realism and sf because it indicates a deformation of the sensual world, in which axiomatic science is disrupted, through which something else can be said to exist. This deformation takes place through the combination of both separation and similarity, which is captured in the role of the monster in *Beyond the Barrier*. It is there that speculative realism, sf and the Anthropocene come together. You are the monster you were sent to destroy. This notion captures this tension between relation and non-relation, between the way an object relates to other objects and the monstrous, weird, withdrawn nature of its darkness.

Notes

1. In another example, Kyle Muntz's novella *Green Lights* (2014) also illustrates the difference between science fiction and extro-science fiction. The novel tells the story of a pair in love, a city which never ends and changes colours, and an old man with a cane in the shape of a snake who eats children. This surreal story bounces back between that which is unknown, but knowable, and that which is completely unknowable.

   In the first chapter, entitled 'Green', the main protagonist meets Mr B, who claims that everyone is sick and that there is no one to take their temperature: '*We're freezing. The ice is coming soon*' (Muntz 2014: 30) – earlier M makes a similar claim to being incurable, saying that he was bitten by the old man's snake cane and that there was no doctor in the world who could provide the antidote (23). Thus the novella sets up the notion of being cold, and sick, and incurable, meaning that it is outside medical understanding, in other words, it is extro-science fiction. When the next section begins with 'The world froze' (31), it seems as if it will continue in this vein. However, it eventually becomes clear that the phrase can be understood in the world-logic of the reader, for it is just the onset of winter that is meant; the narrator continues with 'Every morning, when I got up, I would open the window to knock the icicles away; then I would make breakfast, and drink coffee. Ice had taken over the world. Brushing my teeth was nearly impossible' (31).

   Green Lights therefore seems to flirt with the line of extro-science fiction, containing some elements that are meant to be taken metaphorically, such as Mr B's comments regarding sickness and the coming of winter, which are then reined in to reality by the narrator stating that winter is actually coming. This reading is supported by details from the next section, such as 'On the streets, I saw a big group of people, all wearing thick coats with fur lining their faces, pulling treasure chests attached to heavy chains' (31). All these details might be estranged at first, but are soon understandable in terms of people wearing furs and carrying purses.

Yet this flirting with sf is quickly dispensed with. The narrator states that he got a job 'carrying a flamethrower around the neighborhood, melting people. My coworkers treated me like shit' (32), which seems impossible to understand except in a literal and illogical sense. The same is true of a passage closely following, where the narrator sees 'someone', and 'Behind him, I saw the flaming skeleton of an animal, hideously thin, extending its claws; and above that, yes – its eyes glowing green, drool frozen around its mouth – the head of a bear. No mammoth sounds of it; there are fields in this country. Each field we pass smells of sewage and cranberries' (33).

In one sense *Green Lights* is surreal, because anything could happen, and thus it fits into Meillassoux's derided Type-3 world, which is totally random. Yet when coupled with the tension of sf in the novella, as seen in the way that actual winter is described, although in somewhat poetic terms, Muntz's novella is a prime example of the insertion of incongruous elements within a functioning story world. What the novella misses are the consequences of the insertion of extro-science fiction within sf, something which the rest of this book means to draw out.

2

Divine Paraphrase: Cormac McCarthy

Not all strangeness shows.
Samuel Delany, *The Jewels of Aptor* (1962)

Impoverished World

In Cormac McCarthy's post-apocalyptic novel *The Road* (2006), which won the Pulitzer Prize for fiction, a boy and his father struggle to survive in a world decimated by an unspecified catastrophe. The entirety of the story, apart from a few flashbacks, revolves around their travelling a desolate road south, trying to avoid being eaten by the few other remaining humans. The boy was born into this world, while the father was born before; this difference is represented by the language they use.

When coming across things, whether natural rocks and trees or human-made boats, the father uses specific vocabulary pertaining to what they find. This can be seen throughout the novel, but an exemplary case is in a paragraph which describes the father's exploration of a sailing boat just off a beach:

> He swam the length of the steel hull and turned, treading water, gasping with the cold. Amidships the sheer-rail was just awash. He pulled himself along to the transom. The steel was gray and saltscoured but he could make out the worn gilt lettering. Pájaro de Esperanza. Tenerife. An empty pair of lifeboat davits. He got hold of the rail and pulled himself aboard and turned and crouched on the slant of the wood deck shivering. A few lengths of braided cable snapped off at the turnbuckles. Shredded holes in the wood where hardware had been ripped out. Some terrible force to sweep the decks of everything. He waved at the boy but he didnt wave back. (McCarthy 2006: 239)

In this description, unusual vocabulary is used: *amidships, sheerrail, transom, saltscoured, davits, turnbuckles*. These are specific words from a particular domain: boats. Such linguistic specificity is a part of much of McCarthy's oeuvre, as can be seen in a passage from his third novel, *Child of God* (1973), when the necrophiliac murderer Ballard comes to get his axe sharpened, and is given a long lecture by the smith on the best way to dress it (McCarthy 1993: 70–4). This stylistic feature of McCarthy's writing has been noted before (Collado-Rodríguez 2012; Hardwig 2013; Kunsa 2009). In *The Road* the use of such vocabulary has a particular function: survival. It is the end of the world, and such language is about to disappear; the father seems to be the only person left alive who speaks it, and his health is failing. Saving the language means saving the world.

The boy is different; he is a figure of language lost. The difference between the boy and his father can be seen in the end of the boat passage: the father looks for the boy, as if to confirm that he is a part of the father's world, meaning the world of the boat that is being described, but the boy is unresponsive: he does not wave back. Perhaps he has nothing to say in the face of such a wordstore. If nothing else the boy is not a part of the father's world of the names of things. However, it is more accurate to say that the boy is not a part of the world at all.

The boy is not a part of the world because the world has ended. Post-apocalyptic America is described as a dark place, as the opening of the novel shows:

> When he woke in the woods in the dark and cold of the night he'd reach out to touch the child sleeping beside him. Nights dark beyond darkness and the days more gray each one than what had gone before. Like the onset of some cold glaucoma dimming away the world. (McCarthy 2006: 1)

The dimming away of the world is mirrored by a loss of the usefulness of things. Rain is not potable because it absorbs ash on its way down. Trees no longer bear fruit because they are dry to the core, surrounded by 'The cold relentless circling of the intestate earth. Darkness implacable' (138). The loss of the use of things is mirrored in the way the father's language is connected to 'Things no longer known in the world' (139), as seen in the passage about the boat quoted above.

Earlier, Damon Knight's *Beyond the Barrier* was used to develop Levi Bryant's idea of objects (or what he calls machines) which are relatively dark. Such objects remind us 'not to reduce the world to the machines that we happen to encounter in the world', that 'machines are defined not by their qualities but by their powers, capacities, or abilities' and there are always 'hitherto unknown powers residing in machines that only manifest themselves when the machine is perturbed in the right way' (Bryant 2014: 200–2). In *The Road*, the post-apocalyptic world is dark, but relatively so because it is perceivable. The pre-apocalyptic world, as represented by the language of the father, is different. The father's world is full of objects which are known and useful. The father's world is a place of light and speech, while the boy's world consists of darkness and silence. This is illustrated in a dream the father has. 'He'd been visited in a dream by creatures of a kind he'd never seen before. They did not speak.' When the father wakes from the dream he connects it to his son. 'He turned and looked at the boy. Maybe he understood for the first time that to the boy he was himself an alien. A being from a planet that no longer existed. The tales of which were suspect' (McCarthy 2006: 163). However, rather than reading the post-apocalyptic world as one of loss, its darkness is taken as a sign of potential. While this interpretation goes against the grain of most of the novel, it is supported by the repeated figuration of the boy as God, as developed below.

The idea that the world is made up of useful things can be understood within the context of Martin Heidegger's idea of world as a context in which things make sense:

> What we encounter as nearest to us, although we do not grasp it thematically, is the room, not as what is "between the four walls" in a geometrical, spatial sense, but rather as material for living ... A totality of useful things is always already discovered *before* the individual useful thing. (Heidegger 1996: 64)

For Heidegger, world is that from within which things become available to us: 'beings are accessible in the surrounding world which in themselves do not need to be produced and are always ready at hand' (66). It is this concept of the shell in which we make contact with things that the figure of the boy in *The Road* challenges; the father is still locked in this shell while the boy is located within a darkness which represents the end of use, the end of sense, or as McCarthy puts it, 'The ponderous counterspectacle of things ceasing to be' (2006: 293).

To understand the world of the boy, two trains of thought that take world beyond (yet through) Heidegger will be used: Eugene Thacker's notion of a world-without-us and Timothy Morton's notion of the end of the world. With *In the Dust of This Planet*, Thacker delineates three types of world: the first is 'the world that we, as human beings, interpret and give meaning to, the world that we relate to or feel alien from, the world that we are at once a part of and that is also separate from the human' (Thacker 2011: 4). This is the world of the boat described above, because it can be a part of the father's world, yet alien to the father's current experience, since the boat no longer has the same function as before. Yet at the same time, the world can be resistant to our understanding of it; things do not work or they challenge our experience of things. In this sense 'the world is some inaccessible, already-given state, when we then turn into the world-for-us' (Thacker 2011: 5). This is the role of the boat for the boy, because he has not seen a boat before; in this sense the boat is an example of *the world-in-itself* which the boy then turns into world-for-us by seeing it as a storage chest of potential life-saving food and supplies rather than a luxurious means of putting about on a Saturday afternoon.

But Thacker is mainly interested in his third type of world, which he calls the world-without-us, meaning 'the world if we as human beings were to become extinct . . . the world-without-us is the subtraction of the human from the world' (Thacker 2011: 5). In *The Road* Thacker's third type of world is found in the notion of things that exist in excess of the human use of them. The end of the world is found in this excess. When the father and the boy finally reach their goal, the ocean to the south, they find it is not the Promised Land they just barely hoped it might be. The beach is littered with objects, but objects seemingly without use: 'Glass floats covered with a gray crust. The bones of seabirds. At the tide line a woven mat of weeds and the ribs of fishes in their millions stretching along the shore as far as eye could see like an isocline of death. One vast salt sepulcher. Senseless. Senseless' (McCarthy 2006: 237).

Yet we need to tread carefully here. It is not that these objects are broken and thus reveal a deeper meaning than they had when used properly. Like the dusty glass floating on the surface of the ocean, these objects have no depth. As Bill Hardwig argues, the desolate world of *The Road* is not a lament 'primarily for the natural world, ruined by a calamitous event'; instead 'there exists in *The Road* a profound tenderness for the artificial, for the human-made objects that for most of the rest of his oeuvre McCarthy has tried to pry away in order to get to something more substantial' (Hardwig 2013: 44). In the post-apocalyptic world of *The Road*, objects are not pried away to see what is underneath, but rather there is an exploration of the weird qualities that all objects actually already have. The 'exhaustion of the world' in the Anthropocene (Bonneuil and Fressoz 2015: 193) makes these unusual qualities more visible, but it is not necessary. The functional keyboard I am using to write these words is just as apocalyptic as the millions of fish ribs spread along the shore.

In *Hyperobjects: Philosophy and Ecology after the End of the World*, Timothy Morton reads the world's end as a way to formulate the removal of the Heideggerian context within which things become visible: 'It is the end of the world, since worlds depend on backgrounds and foregrounds. *World* is a fragile aesthetic effect around whose corners we are beginning to see. True planetary awareness is the creeping realization not that "We Are the World" but that we aren't' (Morton 2013a: 99). The lack of foreground and background that Morton mentions is, as Thacker puts it, the loss of a human-centric world-for-us in which a world-in-itself becomes the background. For example, a conversation about the weather once formed a pleasant social background for human interaction; now, because of the threat of global warming, even a seemingly innocent comment such as 'It looks like rain' is ruined by an often unexpressed fear that the weather is no longer as regular as it once was (Morton 2013a: 102–3). This ruination is the loss of background, or the loss of world. Such an event is apocalyptic in that it can *'lift the veil'* of givenness that the world assumes; however, such lifting events 'do not catapult us into a beyond. Rather they fix us more firmly to the spot, which is no longer an embeddedness in a world' (Morton 2013a: 144). Or, as Thomas Ligotti puts it in his horror short story 'The Journal of J. P. Drapeau',

> But is there really a strange world? Of course. Are there, then, two worlds? Not at all. There is only our own world and it alone is alien to us, intrinsically so by virtue of its lack of mysteries. If only it actually were deranged by invisible powers, if only it were susceptible to real

strangeness, perhaps it would seem more like a home to us, and less like an empty room filled with the echoes of this dreadful improvising. To think that we might have found comfort in a world suited to our nature, only to end up in one so resoundingly strange! (Ligotti 2015: 232)

In a series of lectures given at the University of California, Irvine, in May 2015, and published under the title *Dark Ecology*, Morton traces the development of the concept of world as use through the rise of farming, or what he calls *agrilogistics*. The machinery of agriculture is bigger than the Anthropocene for Morton, because the effects of agriculture are more pervasive than those of steam or oil (Morton 2016: 42). The problem with agriculture is use: 'it is a technical, planned, and perfectly logical approach to built space' (42). This kind of logistics approach to the world 'promises to eliminate fear, anxiety, and contradiction – social, physical, and ontological – by establishing thin rigid boundaries between human and nonhuman worlds and by reducing existence to sheer quantity' (43). Although Morton simplifies agriculture as much as Meillassoux does sf, his point is about the approach of agrilogistics rather than the actual logistics of agriculture. Most important for this discussion, however, is the way Morton connects agrilogistics with Heidegger's concept of world:

> The very concept of 'world' as the temporality region suffused with human destiny emerges from agrilogistic functioning. World, as Heidegger knew, is *normative*: the concept works if some beings have it and some don't. When, like Jakob von Uexküll, you start to realize that at least all lifeforms have a world, you have begun to cheapen the concept almost to worthlessness. The concept reaches zero when humans realize that there is no 'away,' that there is no background to their foreground despite the luxury holiday ads, a lack of a stage set on which *world* can perform, a lack that is evident in the return of culturally (and physically) repressed 'pollution' and awareness of the consequences of human action on nonhumans. The end of the biosphere as we know it is also the end of the 'world' as a normative and useful concept. (46)

Although the rise of industrial agriculture finds a more direct representation in McCarthy's *Border Trilogy* (Monk 2016: 81), the end of the world in *The Road* is the end of foreground and background, it is the end of a frame in which objects make sense. This is what is meant when the post-apocalyptic world is described as 'The frailty of everything revealed at last', in which 'The last instance of a thing takes the class with it' (McCarthy 2006: 28). The removal of the class in which to make sense of the thing is the concept of world reaching zero.

However, the post-apocalyptic world of *The Road* is still understandable. It is not just nonsense; if this were the case, it would be the Type-3 world that Meillassoux describes:

> the third type of universe devoid of necessary laws would no longer be a world: it would be a universe in which disorderly modifications are so frequent that, following the example of chaos described by Kant in the objective deduction, the conditions of science as well as those of consciousness would be abolished. (Meillassoux 2015: 40)

One of the clearest examples of a Type-3 world in recent sf can be found in Cixin Liu's *Three-Body Problem* trilogy. The title is taken from a problem in physics, based on Isaac Newton's realisation that he could predict the future positions of two bodies in motion around each other, but could not when a third body was included (Diacu 1996: 67). Although a number of different types of solutions have been discovered for the problem, no general solution to all permutations has been found (Cartwright 2013). Liu uses this problem as the basis for his trilogy: an alien race is subject to the randomness of the three-body problem because their planet has three suns (Liu 2014: 193). Because of this, these 'Trisolarans' are unable to plan for periods of drought and thus they decide to take over the Earth, with its predictable relationship to its single sun. They have a 400-year journey to get to the Earth. In order to decrease the chance that the Earth's inhabitants will develop technology to a high enough level to defend themselves from invasion, the aliens turn the Earth into the same kind of Type-3 world they are subjected to: a world without rules where scientific thought is impossible.

The aliens are able to manipulate the radioactive background to the universe, and they use it to signal a countdown. Scientists are unable to rationalise this anomaly and they commit suicide in droves. The laws of physics seem to have been randomised. Referencing Isaac Asimov's short story 'The Billiard Ball', which is the same story that Meillassoux discusses in *Science Fiction and Extro-Science Fiction*, a scientist in *The Three-Body Problem* says:

> high-energy particle accelerators raised the amount of energy available for colliding particles by an order of magnitude, to a level never before achieved by the human race. Yet, with the new equipment, the same particles, the same energy levels, and the same experimental parameters would yield different results. Not only would the results vary if different accelerators were used, but even with the same accelerator, experiments performed at different times would give different results. Physicists panicked. They repeated the ultra-high-energy collision experiments again and again using the same conditions, but every time the result was different, and there seemed to be no pattern. (Liu 2014: 70)

The result of these experiments is that '"It means that laws of physics that could be applied anywhere in the universe do not exist, which means that physics . . . also does not exist"' (71). This is a description of a Type-3 world, which is actually not a world because neither scientific thought nor consciousness (as shown by the suicide of many of the world's top scientists) are possible.

The world of *The Road* is different. It is not the absence of meaning but rather the withdrawal of objects from the qualities usually assigned to them, and the fusion of objects with qualities usually foreign to them. Graham Harman calls these two techniques fission and fusion (Harman 2012: 237–43), and they are taken up in detail below. However, the main question that *The Road* poses is in what kind of world is the fission and fusion of objects and qualities possible? It is a dark world in which the shadowy withdrawn nature of all objects becomes visible, as seen in the boy not having the use-filled language of the father. In one scene near the end of the novel, the father 'got up and walked out to the road. The black shape of it running from dark to dark. Then a distant low rumble. Not thunder. You could feel it under your feet. A sound without cognate and so without description. Something imponderable shifting out there in the dark' (McCarthy 2006: 279). The source of the sound is never revealed. As with the Zug effect, something unknown is allowed to remain unknown. At the end of the world, as Morton says, 'The haunting, withdrawn yet vivid spectrality of things means that there can be sets of things that are not strictly members of that set . . .' (Morton 2016: 74).

This is what is meant in *The Road* when it is stated that 'The frailty of everything revealed at last', in which 'The last instance of a thing takes the class with it' (McCarthy 2006: 28).

What kind of world is this? Although the novel does not directly tackle the social and political issues of climate change (Giggs 2011: 202), it is a description of the Anthropocene. There is a lack of a solid background on to which a world can be built. The trees of the forest are literally so dried out that they are cracking and falling all around (McCarthy 2006: 101–2). 'There could be a cow somewhere being fed and cared for. Could there? Fed what? Saved for what? Beyond the open door the dead grass rasped drying in the wind' (127). When Morton says that there is now 'a lack of a stage set on which *world* can perform' (2016: 46) he means that the agrilogistic approach to the world as one of use is becoming less tenable. This is not an escape out of one world for another. Rather, humanity is becoming fixed 'more firmly to the spot, which is no longer an embeddedness in a world' (Morton 2013a: 144). This is not the end of the world, but a challenge to seeing the world in terms of what is useful and what is not useful. A different approach is needed.

Graham Harman's expansion of Heidegger's reading of the 'broken hammer' develops what it means to be fixed to the spot of the world's end. Briefly, when we use a hammer in its fully functioning state we experience its unpoetic 'handiness' (*Zuhandenheit*) (Heidegger 1996: 67) in the world-for-us, meaning that we engage with a hammer in all of its banality, which does not include its irony or ambiguity in the sense that it does not challenge the user to think. However, for Heidegger a broken hammer is different: 'When we discover its unusability, the thing becomes conspicuous. *Conspicuousness* presents the thing at hand in a certain unhandiness [*Vorhandenheit*]' (Heidegger 1996: 68). However, the thought of Harman shows that it is actually in the banal handiness of objects that weirdness becomes apparent. In other words, it is in the banal language of the apocalyptic world itself, as exemplified in the boy, that worldlessness takes place. Or, as Levi Bryant puts it, 'there is no "super object," Whole, or totality that would gather all objects together in harmonious unity' (2012: 33).

In *Tool-Being* Harman aims to show how the strength of Heidegger's reading of the hammer does not lie in the way in which the broken hammer reveals something about toolness, but rather in the way that the everyday hammer is not merely a hammer. This

Heideggerian 'mere' [*bloß*] is what makes even everyday objects resistant, a central tenet of Harman's object-oriented ontology: 'The idea of an object-oriented philosophy is the idea of an ontology that would retain the structure of Heidegger's fundamental dualism, but would develop it to the point where concrete entities again become a central philosophical problem' (Harman 2002: 49).

The valorisation of everyday objects takes a number of forms in Harman's thought, from foregrounding the way that technology is not as negative as it seems in Heidegger (Harman 2010) to a critique of Quentin Meillassoux's use of mathematics as a privileged point of access to the world beyond human thought (Meillassoux 2011: 147–9). While aspects of both of these arguments are taken up below, what is of interest here is the way that in *Weird Realism*, Harman develops a reading of the withdrawn nature of all objects through two strategies: the fission of an object from qualities usually associated with it (vertical tension) and the fusion of an object with qualities not usually associated with it (horizontal tension). In other words, vertical tension is that between 'unknowable objects and their tangible qualities' while horizontal tension is that 'between an accessible object and its gratuitous amassing of numerous palpable surfaces' (Harman 2012: 31). An example of a vertical tension would be between a hammer we hold in our hand and the hammer revealed by its unhandiness. An example of horizontal tension would be between the hammer we hold in our hand, the hammer we write about in a poem and the hammer we study under a microscope. A tension arises from this latter example because none of these 'unbroken' experiences of the hammer exhaust its being; in other words, the hammer is always more than we can experience, even if we experience it in a multitude of ways, exposing qualities that the hammer is not usually associated with. The strength of Harman's argument lies in his foregrounding of the fact that the ways these various approaches fail to capture an object indicate how an object is more than all of these approaches. Thus everyday experience can indicate the way that objects are not 'merely' what they are, although in an indirect rather than direct fashion, since objects are approached from various sides rather than by direct description or understanding (Willems 2010: 89–94). In the following reading of *The Road*, the divine nature of the boy is read as the excess of objects in their unreachable perfection, and paraphrase as one of the means of indirect access to this world-without-us.

In the example of the boat provided at the beginning of this chapter, the father related to the boat by a vertical gap, while for the boy it is a horizontal one. This can be seen in the language that surrounds the boy in a later scene where he discusses the boat's owners with his father:

> Where do you think the people went, Papa?
> That were on the ship?
> Yes.
> I don't know.
> Do you think they died?
> I don't know.
> But the odds are not in their favor.
> The man smiled. The odds are not in their favor?
> No. Are they?
> No. Probably not.
> I think they died.
> Maybe they did.
> I think that's what happened to them.
> They could be alive somewhere, the man said. It's possible. The boy didnt answer. They went on. (McCarthy 2006: 258–9)

At first it seems that the boy's use of the cliché 'The odds are not in their favor' is an example of a Heideggerian reading of the broken hammer rather than a Harmanian one. The use of the cliché points to a gap between an object as it is used normally and an object out-of-context. In the pre-apocalyptic world the use of the cliché would not arouse comment, while in the broken world of *The Road* its use is conspicuous, thus causing the father to think about it.

True as this might be, what is of more interest is the other language the boy uses, the non-cliché language, the language that does not arouse any kind of thought in the father. Banal phrases that the boy uses such as 'No. Are they?' and 'I think they died' are what capture the strange atmosphere of the novel, not the periodic use of phrases from a past world. The boy speaks in a language that mirrors what Ian Bogost calls the 'alien everyday', meaning a sense of wonder about everyday objects rather than extraordinary ones (Bogost 2012: 133). On the other hand, the father's rich use of vocabulary represents the agrilogistic world which has passed. So do the clichés the boy uses. However, it is in the everyday phrases that make up most of the boy's speech that a new approach to the world is to be found. The boy's language is an example of a horizontal gap, or the fusion of an object with qualities not usually associated with it. With the boy, it is the fusion of banal everyday language with the end of the world.

The Heresy of Paraphrase

A classic essay which rails against the ineptitude of everyday language is Cleanth Brooks's 'The Heresy of Paraphrase' from 1947. Brooks locates his essay near the end of *The Well-Wrought Urn*, in which he provides a number of close readings of classic literary texts in order to bring out some of their ambiguities and ironies. Brooks is interested in 'the resistance which any good poem sets up against all attempts to paraphrase it' (1947: 196). Paraphrase is seen as being unworthy because it smooths over the ambiguity of a poem by reducing the structure of a text to a vehicle to carry meaning: 'For the imagery and the rhythm are not merely the instruments by which this fancied core-of-meaning-which-can-be-expressed-in-a paraphrase is directly rendered' (197).

The reason that paraphrase is unable to contain the multiplicities of ambiguity is because it is based on content rather than structure. The problem with content is that one content cannot be absolutely more poetic than another. For example, a schoolroom is not poetic or non-poetic, which is also true for a baby or a devil: 'The "content" of the poems is various, and if we attempt to find one quality of content which is shared by all the poems – a "poetic" subject matter or diction or imagery – we shall find that we have merely confused the issues' (Brooks 1947: 193). Paraphrase is connected to diminished space because it attempts to restrict the meaning of a text to its content ('this poem means that . . .'). Content is problematic because it cannot be said to be poetic or unpoetic. Being poetic means allowing expressions full of ambiguity and irony to take place rather than a direct expression of fact. In other words, 'What poetry seems to be *about* is . . . irrelevant to its value' (Kermode 2002: 151).

Yet in *The Road*, the worldlessness of the post-apocalyptic setting is being argued to be 'best reflected' in the banality of the boy rather than the linguistic richness of the father. Here we diverge from Brooks, for he privileges a *poetically* ambiguous and ironic text (Brooks 1947: 202–3). In other words, ambiguity and irony differentiate the structure of poetry from the structure of prose.

However, the point of *The Road* is that ambiguity is found in everyday expression, rather than poetry. It is at this point also that Harman, in *Weird Realism*, takes Brooks to task. But first Brooks enters Harman's thought as one of his main references in arguing for 'the inherent stupidity of all *content*' (Harman 2012: 12). This means that the multiple ways of engagement (content, paraphrase, the world) will always be exceeded by an object. For Harman, content is stupid because no matter how many times and in how many different ways you engage with an apple, for example, these multiple engagements will never *be* an apple. Yet Harman also critiques Brooks because all objects exceed all other objects, not just poetic ones; 'Irony and paradox cannot be local peculiarities of literature, then, but are an ontological structure permeating the cosmos' (Harman 2012: 248). Thus, excess is everywhere, even in banality. For Thacker, this excess of things was indicated in the world-without-us, for Morton, in the end of the word. *The Road* posits another location: the divinity of the boy.

The Divine *Infans*

Harman argues that objects in their essence, or perfection, are always in excess of the multiple ways we come into contact with them (Harman 2013: 27–9). In McCarthy's novel this excess arises from the fusion of two elements: the youth of the boy and the divine nature of his being.

Divinity is seen in an obvious sense in that the boy is taken to be the second coming of Jesus Christ; as his father says of him, 'If he is not the word of God God never spoke' (McCarthy 2006: 3). This statement is a marker of the divine because *divine* simply means *of God*. In addition there are many other religious references. A snowflake expires 'like the last host of christendom' (15), the boy and his father are described as looking 'like medicant friars' (133) and most importantly, in a scene looked at below, the boy makes his father pray when they come across a large stash of preserved foodstuffs (154–5). One of the main signs of the boy's youth is the fact that he was born into the new world, while the father was born into the old one. The boy's lack of language to describe, or paraphrase, the post-apocalyptic world is consciously foregrounded in a passage (quoted above in part) describing the road on which the father and son are travelling, which I have divided into three sections:

He [the father] got up and walked out to the road. The black shape of it running from dark to dark. Then a distant low rumble. Not thunder. You could feel it under your feet. [1] A sound without cognate and so without description. Something imponderable shifting out there in the dark. The earth itself contracting with the cold. It did not come again. What time of year? What age the child? He walked out to the road and stood. The silence. [2] The salitter drying from the earth. The mudstained shape of flooded cities burned to the waterline. At a crossroads a ground set with dolmen stones where the spoken bones of oracles lay moldering. No sound but the wind. What will you say? A living man spoke these lines? He sharpened a quill with his small pen knife to scribe these things in sloe or lampblack? At some reckonable and entabled moment? [3] He is coming to steal my eyes. To seal my mouth with dirt. (279–80)

What 'A sound without cognate and so without description', 'Something imponderable' and 'The silence' all have in common is that they represent a resistance to world: things are either unknown or left unsaid. Throughout the novel this worldlessness is called the 'nameless dark' (8); a 'blackness without depth or dimension' (70) which can be related to the divine in that 'The divine is dark because we have no concept of it' (Thacker 2011: 136). Or, as Harman puts it, 'Perhaps God is not the most alert of all beings, but rather the most oblivious' (Harman 2010: 71). This first section is a description of the post-apocalyptic world of the novel, which is the natural habitat of the boy. This is not the world of the father, as seen in his confusion when he asks 'What time of year? What age the child?'

That this silent and dark world is the boy's world reflects what Meillassoux describes as the *infans*: '*the child* (or *infans*, the Latin term that suggestively designates the unborn child, or a child who does not yet speak)' (Meillassoux 2011: 225). The child is an important figure for Meillassoux for two main reasons: it does not take power seriously (abandoning it quickly after use), and it sees itself as equal to all, thus showing that it is essentially human. Thus as a representation of negation of use, the child is a figure which 'assures the impossibility of any religious vision of the advent [of something new in the world]' (Meillassoux 2011: 225). However, the boy is not simply a figure of uselessness, but rather he is in language (the world-for-us), but uses speech in a reduced, or weak, form (the world-in-itself, represented through the brokenness of language); this comes about through a narrative strategy which allows both language and loss to become present.

This strategy can be found in other readings of the *infans*. In *Infant Figures: The Death of the 'Infans' and Other Scenes of Origin*, Christopher Fynsk does not shy away from the apparent paradox of locating the *infans* both before speech and as the condition for such speech to arise; instead he argues that the *infans* enacts an ethical '"yes" of responsibility, sufferings that occurred [. . .] before their death' (Fynsk 2000: 130). This ethical dimension of the language-weak boy in *The Road* can be seen, for example, near the end of the novel. The father and the boy have their goods stolen from them while the father is out on the boat. Eventually they catch up with the thief whom the father strips of clothes and goods and leaves for dead. The boy asks the father to give the man back his clothes and feed him. The father is upset and tells the boy 'You're not the one who has to worry about everything', to which the boy poignantly replies, 'Yes I am [. . .] I am the one' (McCarthy 2006: 277).

Another reading of the *infans* can be found in Giorgio Agamben's *Infancy and History*, in which he asks a similar question to Fynsk about the 'wordless' human: '*is there such a thing as human in-fancy? How can in-fancy be humanly possible? And if it is possible, where is it sited?*' (Agamben 2007: 54, italics in original). Agamben argues that approaching infancy through language (an idealist approach in which humanity is defined by language) is challenged by a more fundamental understanding of infancy as the site of an experience of removal (56, 58). Agamben locates this removal in the rupture between the language which all animals have and the speech which is a human-only trait (59): thus what is human is a continuous falling away (or excess) from infancy/experience and into language (60). For Agamben, this rupture is important because the movement from infancy into language has the ability to transform language itself. Thus this rupture is a site of the new, and as Agamben argues elsewhere, the contemporary dissolving of this gap is detrimental to human experience (Agamben 2011). Thus the figure of the boy is further clarified, for he functions as a linguistic representation of the falling away from speech; this is because he is the end of the world.

On the other hand, section 2 of the quote from *The Road* reflects the father's linguistically full universe. The words *sloe* and *lampblack* are being used here for the last time in the history of the earth. The word *salitter* was used by the seventeenth-century Christian mystic Jakob Böhme to describe the stuff from which paradise is made. A *dolmen* is an ancient tomb, a *sloe* a kind of plum. These things are to disappear from the earth as soon as the father is not around to remember them. In this sense the useful vocabulary of the father also functions as a 'falling away' in its ephemerality.

At the same time it is section 3 that offers a more concrete insight into the mechanics of worldless excess. The person coming to steal eyes and stuff throats is the man who is using the language of section 2. This is the father. At the same time it is the father who is speaking these lines in free indirect style; thus it is the father who is both using this language and who is the cause of the language's demise. The father is the monster he is meant to destroy. This is a moment of what Harman foregrounded as the 'mere', because both a resistance to representation and its effluence are represented in the same figure. This is a horizontal tension which is usually connected with the boy, but now it is seen also to be connected with the father, a feature that emerges in the 2009 film adaptation of the novel by John Hillcoat, discussed below.

Horizontal tension in *The Road* actually comes about on its first pages, through the figure of the animal which is in language but removed from speech. As quoted in part above, this animal comes forth in a dream sequence:

> And on the far shore a creature that raised its dripping mouth from the rimstone pool and stared into the light with eyes dead white and sightless as the eggs of spiders. It swung its head low over the water *as if* to take the scent of what it could not see. Crouching there pale and naked and translucent, its alabaster bones cast up in shadow on the rocks behind it. Its bowels, its beating heart. The brain that pulsed in a dull glass bell. It swung its head from side to side and then gave out a low moan and turned and lurched away and loped soundlessly into the dark. (McCarthy 2006: 2, emphasis mine)

At first it seems that the creature is merely a figure of loss, as it is sightless, without speech, existing in the dark. In other words, it could be suggested that there is a similarity between the animal of the dream and the boy in the sense that both are removed from an access to the world mediated by calling things by their specific name; this argument could then go on to contrast this figure with the father, who is 'rich' in speech.

However, there is another narrative strategy present which indicates quite a different link to the boy: the *mere*. The animal swings its head over water *as if* to smell something invisible. In this sense the creature both makes a gesture and does not. The creature does move its head, since it is stated that 'It swung its head low. . .' However, this gesture is not completed, or is interrupted by the 'as if'. What is the difference between the creature swinging its head to take in the scent of something it cannot see and the creature swinging its head *as if* it were doing so? It is a representation of a 'falling away'. The importance of such moments has been highlighted by Harman in his work on H. P. Lovecraft. In *Weird Realism* Harman provides exactly 100 examples of similar moments of the 'as if' from a few of Lovecraft's stories. The details of his argument are not as important here as his main thesis. Although he agrees with what can briefly be called the 'idealist' argument that objects cannot be accessed directly (the first interpretation provided of this scene from *The Road*), he disagrees with the idea that objects can never be accessed. Instead, he argues that objects can be accessed *indirectly*: 'This indirect access is achieved by allowing the hidden object to deform the sensual world, just as the existence of a black hole might be inferred from the swirl of light and gases orbiting its core' (Harman 2012: 238). This swirl of light and gases has already appeared in this chapter under the aegis of *paraphrase*; in other words, the 'tension between accessible sensual objects and the inaccessible qualities that are of structural importance for them' (Harman 2012: 243). What this means for the 'as if' from the passage above is that the image of the creature is not accessible through direct statement but rather through the distance between the creature and such a direct statement, that is, through the ambiguous disruption of indirect representation. The creature thus foregrounds some important features of the boy that otherwise might not be seen, for although the boy is meant to be a concretisation of the word of God, and hence the second coming, he is also a figure for the loss of the word, for a removal from language. In this sense, as Stefan Skrimshire says, *The Road* is a novel 'of a tortuously open future, the absence of referents for forging new values, new rules and new duties' (Skrimshire 2011: 5). In other words, the novel is not about redemption through preservation or order, but rather about a future world brought about through the loss and disfunction of falling away.

In *The Road* 'Everything uncoupled from its shoring. Unsupported in the ashen air' (McCarthy 2006: 10). This is a description of the post-agrilogistic world. It mirrors the *infans* because it is an image of silence and darkness. On the other hand, this world is divine not because it references another level of being through transcendence, but because everyday banality is seen to contain the weirdness of withdrawn objects. This reading is supported by comparing a scene from the novel and the same scene in its film adaptation.

About half-way through the novel, the father and son find an oasis from starvation in the form of a bomb-shelter which is full of untouched supplies. Before eating their first proper meal, the boy tells the father that they need to thank the people that left this food. The boy is unsure how to do it but the father encourages him to try:

> The boy sat staring at his plate. He seemed lost. The man was about to speak when he said: Dear people, thank you for all this food and stuff. We know that you saved it for yourself and if you were here we wouldnt eat it no matter how hungry we were and we're sorry that you didnt get to eat it and we hope that you're safe in heaven with God. (McCarthy 2006: 154–5)

When taken on its own, this scene could be said to argue that holiness is innate: the boy has never observed prayer in his life, but he is reproducing it here. However, when taken in conjunction with the film version, a more complex reading surfaces.

In the same scene from John Hillcoat's 2009 adaptation of the novel, the boy (Koki Smit-McPhee) is sitting on a bunk-bed above the father (Viggo Mortensen), who is sitting in a chair on the ground. The boy gives thanks first, putting his palms together in a sign of prayer and asking his father, 'like this?' The father nods agreement and the boy gives a short prayer. However, in an addition to the novel, the boy then looks at his father and says 'Your turn.' The father then gives a slight grunt before putting his hands together and offering his short prayer: 'Thank you, people.' The father looks to the boy to see if this is enough, to which the boy gives his assent. When the boy is shown in prayer his hands barely fit in the frame. However, when the father prays, another sort of iconography is presented. His hands are fully in the frame and his unkempt beard and longish hair, coupled with his robe-like hoodie, give him the simplistic appearance of Christ. This image is further supported by the halo-like lamp of the shelter casting its circular glow behind the father's head.

In the novel, it is the boy who is figured as Christ. For example, when carrying wood he is called 'God's own firedrake' (McCarthy 2006: 31); the father's last words are 'Look around you, he said. There is no prophet in the earth's long chronicle who's not honored here today' (297); and at the end of the story, the mother of the boy's new family says of the boy that 'the breath of God was his breath, yet through it pass from man to man through all of time' (306). The father, on the other hand, is never represented as Christ, the closest being that both father and son are compared to 'mendicant friars sent forth to find their keep' (133), because of their raggedy clothes. In this sense it could be argued, as Thomas Schaub does in 'Secular Scripture and Cormac McCarthy's *The Road*', that the religious aspect of the novel is found in the love the father has for his son (Schaub 2009: 153–4). However, in the film the father becomes the Son of God in the image of his praying, and the son becomes the Father up high on his bunk-bed, overlooking his father and giving approval to the adequacy of his prayers. Thus the operation of the exchange of roles is foregrounded rather than the roles themselves. In other words, in this moment of tension between book and film, father and son are removed from their roles in the world and given new ones. This moment is not one of the world-in-itself turned into the world-for-us but rather a figure of the end of the world, in that both father and son are 'falling away', or in excess of the context in which we have come to know them. Falling away simply means that objects express qualities that have hitherto been hidden both by use, because then objects seem limited in scope, and by lack of use, because withdrawn qualities remain dark. Divinity is the state in which the withdrawn nature of all objects becomes an issue, as it does in this scene from the novel and film.

It is not that humans are 'in' divinity *even* in their fallen state, but that they are so *only* in such a state. It is in the state of falling, or the worldlessness between *infans* and speech, that humanity now exists. The second question is addressed by the film adaptation of *The Road*. Here, divinity comes forth through a gesture of withdrawal. This can be seen in the way in which the boy stops being Christ, and the father stops being the Father: 'We see that we are *weak,* in the precise sense that our discourse and maps and plans regarding things are not those things. There is an irreducible gap' (Morton 2013: 133). It is in their states of removal from Christ/Father that the Holy Spirit is born. In this sense it is the change from Christ to the Father that is divine. This goes beyond what Skrimshire sees in *The Road* as an 'admission by all characters of a destabilising uncertainty about that road that lies ahead' (Skrimshire 2011: 11). Instead what is being constructed is a similar moment to that traced by Meillassoux's reading of Stéphane Mallarmé's poem *Un coup de dés*, in which a text negates itself by both offering a possible interpretation and disrupting that interpretation; this represents a moving away from '*being*' and into the '*perhaps*' (Meillassoux 2012b: 212), which is a strategy for a site of divinity to erupt at the end of the world. It is the 'God still to come' (Meillassoux 2009: 268).

The Road represents a darkness. The father's pre-apocalyptic world is one of agrilogistics; it is known and useful, as seen in the vocabulary that he uses. The boy represents the worldless, meaning a place of darkness and silence which signals the end of use, of 'The ponderous counterspectacle of things ceasing to be' (McCarthy 2006: 293). Yet this is not a novel about absence, but rather excess, and when things are in excess of the human use of them the world ends, becoming 'Senseless. Senseless' (237).

The end of the world in the novel is the removal of background and foreground, the removal of the context in which things make sense. It is the removal of the class in which knowledge can be formed, the removal of a stage on which, as Morton tells us, the world can perform for us. Fission and fusion are the strategies through which the end of the world takes place, and they will be a central part of all the discussions of the novels throughout this book. However, *The Road* shows that the end of the world is not an escape from the world. Instead, it is a novel about becoming more firmly rooted to the world around us, but a world removed from the anthropomorphic use which has given rise to the Anthropocene.

The boy, read as a figure of the *infans*, falls away from the world of the father in his lack of useful language. Yet this falling away is read as divine because it figures the withdrawn, dark, removed nature of all objects, not just those of a post-apocalyptic setting. The novels of Neil Gaiman, discussed in the next chapter, continue to develop narrative strategies of falling away. However, they do not describe a falling away of language so much as a falling away of vision.

3

Double-Vision: Neil Gaiman

It's the basic condition of life, to be required to violate our own identity.
            Philip K. Dick, *Do Androids Dream of Electric Sheep?* (1968)

Stupidity, Animality, Multiplicity, Inability

A number of works by Neil Gaiman include incomprehensible elements within a comprehensible story. Such inclusion in sf is here called the Zug effect. This effect appears in Gaiman's work when diachronic events are represented synchronically. In his novel *Anansi Boys* (2005), Gaiman calls these events moments of 'double-vision' (Gaiman 2005: 151). These moments consist of the co-presencing of the changed and the unchanged within a single being at one moment in time. In other words, a Type-2 world is developed in which both the knowable and unknowable appear together. While change is everywhere around us, in germination, growth and decay, the term 'double-vision' indicates the potential of seeing more than one side of a transformation simultaneously, thereby presenting a moment of stasis within change. One of the important consequences of Gaiman's double-vision is that the movement of change then becomes easier to see.

The images seen in double-vision make no sense, and thus mirror the role of unknowability within the known world that Meillassoux foregrounds. These images do not make sense because they function as relatively dark objects whose outputs do not match the traditional inputs of an environment, and thus they spill over the context in which they appear. Spilling over means that the images are different from what is expected, but it does not mean that they can be anything at all. This is used to develop the difference between modulation and metamorphosis. The images examined in Gaiman's novels do not morph from one to another, but rather form modulations of the same essential object. Such modulation becomes present through what Ian Bogost calls 'dismantling', meaning the way in which objects take on new life when their given connections to other objects are disturbed. Double-vision involves disturbing vision, which leads to the appearance of weird, multiple and contradictory qualities. Yet these different qualities appear all at once, and not one after the other, as Meillassoux insists.

While Gaiman is best known for writing the *Sandman* series of comics (1989–96), here I will be looking at three prose works: two novels, *American Gods* (2001) and *Anansi Boys* (2005), and the short story 'How to Talk to Girls at Parties' (2006). Gaiman's novel *American Gods* tells the story of a pantheon of deities who were carried to America by their believers' thoughts and deeds and who are now dying out because of a lack of worshippers and their sacrifices. These 'old gods' decide to go to war with the new gods of technology, consumer culture and media, whose worshippers abound. In this sense, as Gaiman has stated in a *Rain Taxi* interview, the novel is political in that it is about immigration and 'the way that America tends to eat other cultures' (Dornemann and Everding 2001). At the centre of the novel lies Shadow, to whom the world of the gods is initially invisible. He eventually learns that he is the son of Mr Wednesday, who is actually the god Odin, among many other incarnations. Mr Wednesday enlists Shadow into the fight between the old gods and the new.

The first experience of double-vision that Shadow undergoes happens at the roadside attraction of The House on the Rock. Mr Wednesday has attempted to gather as many of the old gods as possible in an attempt to rally the troops. Among the exhibition rooms Shadow meets a number of Mr Wednesday's acquaintances, although none of them seem to have any god-like qualities. The transformation of these men into gods takes place on an indoor carousel. As the carousel spins, Shadow begins to see things differently than usual: 'The images that reached his mind [1] made no sense: [2] it was like seeing the world through the [3] multifaceted jewelled eyes of a dragonfly, but [3] each facet saw something completely different, and he was [4] unable to combine the things he was seeing, or thought he was seeing, [1] into a whole that made any sense' (Gaiman 2004: 144). This quote presents four elements of double-vision: 1) a lack of making sense; 2) animal vision; 3) multiplicity; and 4) not-doing.

The experience of the carousel is framed at the beginning and end by the destruction of understanding [1]. The images that reach Shadow's mind 'made no sense' at first, and in the end he is 'unable' to make the images into a whole which 'made any sense'. This is what Meillassoux defines as the unknowability found in a world of knowability, or Type-2 worlds. Being unable to combine what is seen into a whole which makes sense, and merely being left to record such an experience, is what Meillassoux means when he argues for the need to decompose the knowable 'by tilting the world toward extro-science and pursuing this enterprise of degradation toward a less and less inhabitable world, making the tale itself progressively impossible, until we isolate certain lives that are tightened around their own flow in the midst of gaps' (Meillassoux 2015: 57). Such a tilting has traditionally been taken up from a number of perspectives: the voice of the animal, madness and what Žižek calls the kernel of trauma resistant to symbolic reification. Such a refusal finds another theoretical counterpart in Avital Ronell's *Stupidity*, which traces the unthought of puerility throughout a number of literary and philosophical sources. Stemming from both Deleuze's call for stupidity as the adequate determination of thought in *Difference and Repetition*, and from Samuel Beckett's claim to his distinction from Joyce, in that 'Joyce tended toward omniscience and omnipotence as an artist, but I'm working with impotence, ignorance' (cited in Ronell 2002: 32–3), Ronell's investigation of stupidity takes the form of a double-figure that both opens up structures of knowledge to change and traces these structures' oppressive dismissiveness:

> Whether in the precincts of the literary or the psychological, stupidity offers a whirligig of imponderables: as irreducible obstinacy, tenacity, compactedness, the infissurable, it is at once dense and empty, cracked, the interminable 'duh' of contemporary usage. A total loser, stupidity is also that which rules, reproducing itself in clichés, in innocence and the abundance of world. It is at once unassailable and the object of terrific violence. (Ronell 2002: 38)

Thus stupidity is a mechanism for the way the unknowable can become visible. Another word for this mechanism is 'not-doing' sense (part [4] in Gaiman's quote above).

In the first chapter of this book, objects that do not do anything were called dark objects. Such objects are out of communication with each other, and were found in *Beyond the Barrier* both in the way dark objects were actually seen and also in the way some descriptions of the world had no connection with realistic narrating techniques; such descriptions were not used to form unusual pictures of the world through Darko Suvin's estrangement, but were rather used to communicate the incommunicability of other worlds. In order to describe this lack of communication between objects, Levi Bryant used the word 'dormant': 'Second, their powers or operations would have to be *dormant* such that they generated no inputs from within themselves' (Bryant 2014: 199). This term is used to stress that dark objects are not characterless objects, but rather objects whose characters (potential outputs and inputs) do not match any other objects in the environment, and are thus invisible to them.

The term 'dormant' is a reference to what Graham Harman calls the 'dormant object', meaning an object that does not communicate with the human domain, although nonetheless it is something to which we have access:

> Yet there may be other objects that do have real parts that make them real things, but still have no relation to anything further; precisely for this reason, they will currently have no psyche. We might call them 'dormant objects,' a notion excluded in advance by every relationist philosophy. The dormant is the sleeping, and though perfect sleep may be impossible for dreamers like us, nightly sleep is our closest approach to the freedom from relation in which we are most ourselves. Perhaps God is not the most alert of all beings, but rather the most oblivious. (Harman 2010: 71)

The nightly sleep that Harman suggests as a possible mode of apprehension for dormant objects is what is called 'double-vision' in this chapter. Another name for this mode is stupidity.

In the quote above, Gaiman provides another metaphor for both dormant objects and sleepy vision: the animal. The second element [2] of the quote from *American Gods* indicates that the visual experience Shadow is undergoing is like the 'multifaceted jeweled eyes of a dragonfly'. While the tens of thousands of lenslets of a dragonfly eye actually allow it to see in a radius of 360° rather than in any sort of fractured sense (Handwerk 2005), which is perhaps indicated by Gaiman's use of 'like [. . .] but' in this quote, the metaphorical use of insect vision indicates the possibilities of seeing. As I have argued elsewhere, a powerful example of this metaphor of insect vision can be found in the artwork of Diana Thater, whose *Knots + Surfaces* (2001), for example, provides a representation of the discovery made by mathematician Barbara Shipman that when a schema of a six-dimensional object is turned into a two-dimensional one, the curves produced are similar to the pattern that bees produce when dancing. Thus Thater created an installation in which the multiple vision of the 'quantum bee' is represented through multiple projections ([4] above) on multiple planes of a gallery-articulated space (Willems 2009b: 94).[1] In other words, what Gaiman and Thater are trying to do is to represent 'not doing' the knowable of one world by inserting the unknowable of another into it.

A classic description of the unknowability of the animal world is Jakob von Uexküll's concept of the *Umwelt*, otherwise known as a *function-circle*. As von Uexküll describes it in his *Theoretical Biology*, the function-circle of the animal consists of responses to stimuli, which then affect the outer world, which then influence the stimuli. Such a periodic circle is the function-circle of the animal: 'For each individual animal, however, its function-circles constitute a world by themselves, within which it leads its existence in complete isolation' (von Uexküll 1926: 126). Function-circles lead to dormant objects, for all animals, human and non-human. In fact, one of the most important contributions of von Uexküll is in disregarding the superiority of the human's function-circle when compared to the animal's: both are seen through their 'limitations'.

In *Facticity, Poverty and Clones*, I considered the way that Heidegger uses the concept of the animal as a figure for which the world itself is unknowable (Willems 2010: 24–5, 35, 130). I will briefly revisit the argument here. In *Being and Time*, Heidegger describes the way beings relate to the world in terms of how they relate to death. He calls the end of biological life *perishing* [*Verenden*] (Heidegger 1996: 291). Both humans and other animals can *perish*, but humans have a particular relationship to their own death, or facticity, which Heidegger says is *to demise* [*Ableben*] (291). Humans come '*face to face* with the "nothing" of the possible impossibility of its existence' (310). The experience of the potential of the end of one's life is called *dying* [*Tode*], which stands for 'that *way of Being* in which Dasein *is towards* its death' (291). Only humans demise, or, as Stuart Elden puts it, 'humans, in their being, realize that their being is in issue' (Elden

2006: 276). However, Heidegger is not so much interested in the event of death (*perishing*), but rather in the *experience* of being-towards-death [*Sein-zum-Tode*], or of how the awareness of one's being is an issue.

For Heidegger, animals also have a relationship with death, but a lesser one, which he calls a relationship of *poverty* [*Armut*] (Heidegger 1995: 192–5). Access to the possibility of one's demise implies a second-order level of consciousness[2] that has been assumed to set humanity apart from other animals, allowing human beings alone to appropriate what Heidegger calls 'being there' or *Dasein* (Willems 2009a: 81–2). However, the crossed-out relationship of poverty that the animal has to the world, which is one of both knowing and not-knowing, can function as a metaphor for the way that humans have access to objects in general. As Simon Critchley argues, Heidegger's description of the crossed-out being of the animal is 'an attempt to render Being invisible that simply makes it more visible' (Critchley 1997: 17). Therefore an impoverished access to world is the more accurate one, as the boy showed in *The Road*. Or, as Floyd Merrell claims, using the language of von Uexküll, 'Within each organism, along the functional cycle or information-conveying loop, external signals enter and become internal signals, having been processed in the transition according to our particular capacities' (Merrell 2003: 266).

However, Gaiman's use of animal vision indicates an opening up to the unknowable rather than a closing off of the knowable. Giorgio Agamben provides a similarly 'open' reading of von Uexküll in *The Open*, seen in how the threads of a spider web

> are exactly proportioned to the visual capacity of the eye of the fly, who cannot see them and therefore flies toward death unawares. The two perceptual worlds of the fly and the spider are absolutely uncommunicating, and yet so perfectly in tune that we might say that the original score of the fly, which we can also call its original image or archetype, acts on that of the spider in such a way that the web the spider weaves can be described as 'fly-like'. (Agamben 2004: 42)

Thus the mutual development between fly and spider is both an example of being-with and distance, as they are dormant to each other and 'uncommunicating', an aspect that forms a key point in the discussion of speculative realism because it indicates a presence of something beyond the givenness of perception.

The Diachronic in the Synchronic

The scene under discussion from *American Gods* takes place in front of a carousel. The circular nowhere of the carousel mirrors the manner in which Mr Wednesday's human friends turn into gods – through a metamorphosis-within-stasis. The description of Shadow's actual experience of double-vision takes place as he observes Mr Nancy (who is the father of the two 'Anansi boys' in Gaiman's follow-up novel of the same name).

> [Shadow] was looking at Mr Nancy, an old black man with a pencil moustache, in his check sports jacket and his lemon-yellow gloves, riding a carousel lion as it rose and lowered, high in the air; and, *at the same time, in the same place*, he saw a jeweled spider as high as a horse, its eyes an emerald nebula, strutting, staring down at him; and *simultaneously* he was looking at an extraordinarily tall man with teak-colored skin and three sets of arms, wearing a flowing ostrich-feather headdress, his face painted with red stripes, riding an irritated golden lion, two of his six hands holding on tightly to the beast's mane; and he was *also seeing* a young black boy, dressed in rags, his left foot all swollen and crawling with black flies; *and last of all, and behind all these things*, Shadow was looking at a tiny brown spider, hiding under a withered ochre leaf. (Gaiman 2004: 144, emphasis mine)

Shadow experiences multiple stages of a historical timeline all 'at the same time' and 'in the same place'. Shadow experiences all of the changes of Mr Nancy simultaneously, the instantiations of what he once was and what he now is, which includes spiders, a boy and various gods. Although Mr Nancy has taken on many forms during his life, his past forms are not left behind. However, he is not some kind of shape-changer either. He is not sometimes a spider and sometimes a small boy. He is all of these things at once. Shadow's experience is of the diachronic within the synchronic and it indicates a double-vision not of metamorphosis, which would involve the complete transformation of one object into another, but of modulation (Shaviro 2010: 13).

Complete transformation involves a disconnection between what came before and what comes after. Such metamorphosis in effect consists of two different objects, one before and one after, which have nothing to do with each other once the moment of change is over. This is not what happens in Gaiman's novel. It does not describe the change of one shape into another. Instead, it is about multiple manifestations of the same shape. As Shaviro puts it, modulation is different. It 'requires an underlying fixity, in the form of a carrier wave or signal that is made to undergo a series of controlled and coded variations' (Shaviro 2010: 13). The fixity in the above scene is Mr Nancy. The spider, tall man and young boy do not come after, or before, Mr Nancy. Rather there is a tension between Mr Nancy and these other images.

Modulation 'resists the very transformations that it also expresses' (Shaviro 2010: 13). In literary terms, modulation is a figure of metaphor. It expresses both difference and similarity. A metaphor does not work if the two terms connected are unrelated in every way. *A song is like a bicycle* does not have any immediate metaphorical value because the terms are too disparate. At the same time, *A song is like a tune* also does not work because the terms are too strongly connected with each other to engage any kind of metaphorical thought (Harman 2016: 102–3). Modulation only works when there is a combination of relation and non-relation between terms. At first it seems that the connection between Mr Nancy and a tall man is too strong to generate a metaphor. This is why Gaiman distances the tall man from Mr Nancy through a number of odd qualities: the man is extraordinarily tall, has three pairs of arms and has a face painted with stripes. In the opposite manner, when Mr Nancy is compared to a spider the two terms are too distant to create a metaphor. This may be true with the first description of the spider, which is jewelled, huge and has emerald nebulas for eyes. The second spider metaphor works better, however, because the spider, which is strange enough already, is not made more strange through odd qualities. It is just brown, and small, hiding under a leaf. This second spider is not too odd to form a metaphorical relation with Mr Nancy. Its ratio of relation and non-relation is better.

The importance of modulation for speculative realism is that it shows how relations between objects, or between an object and its qualities, are asymmetrical (Harman 2016: 101–2). A symmetrical relation would mean that two objects either relate to each other equally, or do not relate to each other equally. Thus a metaphor could not be made. Symmetrical relations are a part of assemblages and networks, taken up in the next chapter. The reason that Harman argues that objects are asymmetrical is because there is a part of them that remains fixed. The part that remains fixed is the withdrawn aspect of an object, defined below as its essence. What is important here is that Mr Nancy does not change into the different beings in this scene, but modulates into them. This is because Mr Nancy remains, forming asymmetrical relationships to the old man, young boy and plain brown spider.

Modulation is also a key trope in sf. As Shaviro argues, sf imagines the extremes of what might be possible, in the weirdest senses, while remaining connected to realism through the process of extrapolation:

> The method of science fiction is emotional and situational, rather than rational and universalizing. Philosophical argumentation and scientific experimentation both endeavor to *prove* and to *ground* their assertions, however counterintuitive these may seem to be at first glance. Science fiction also proposes counterintuitive scenarios; but its effort is rather to work through the weirdest and most extreme ramifications of these scenarios, and to image *what it would be like* if they were true. Where philosophy is foundational, science fiction is pragmatic and exploratory. And where physical science seeks to settle upon predictable and repeatable results, science fiction seeks to unsettle and singularize these results, and provide us with unrepeatable histories. (Shaviro 2015a: 9, italics in original)

One technique for the wild speculation of sf is modulation. However, Gaiman's novel modulates by showing various unrepeatable histories in the same object at the same time.

An argument could thus be made for using *American Gods* to add a new chronotope to those Mikhail Bakhtin laid out in his famous essay 'Forms of Time and Chronotope in the Novel' – perhaps the 'chronotope of the carousel' in which multiple events that are diachronically distant become simultaneously represented in story-time, although needing to be represented one-after-the-other on the page. However, a more fruitful approach is to understand why Bakhtin sees new forms of the representation of time in the novel as important. Towards the end of his essay, Bakhtin asks:

> What is the significance of all these chronotopes? What is most obvious is their meaning for *narrative*. They are the organizing centers for the fundamental narrative events of the novel. The chronotope is the place where the knots of narrative are tied and untied. It can be said without

qualification that to them belongs the meaning that shapes narrative.' (Bakhtin 1981: 250)

Thus scenes of double-vision, because they posit an unusual representation of time in narrative, can be seen as a locus for deriving meaning from the novel. They can also be moments of vision, for in the chronotope, 'Time becomes, in effect, palpable and visible' (Bakhtin 1981: 250).

At the same time, there is something more complex going on in this quotation from *American Gods*, and this has to do with an element of difference within this modulation. For although Shadow is seeing these multiple forms of Mr Nancy at the same time and place, he also is not. At the beginning of the passage it is stated that he is seeing everything 'at the same time, in the same place'; however, at the end of the quotation there are markers of both time and space: 'and last of all, and behind all these things' there lies the figure of a tiny brown spider, indicating its status as the primary or original manifestation of Mr Nancy. This is not a contradiction, but rather a manner in which to map space within the novel, and thus bring out the significance of the figure of the carousel. For if there is merely the multiple without any kind of difference contained, then what is being described is Meillassoux's Type-3 world, meaning a correlationist or relational structure which then becomes trapped in its own self-reflexivity. But what the carousel actually does is to represent both the diachronic (in the *at the same time*) and the synchronic (in the *last of all and behind all things*) together. Assuming a clockwise rotation, the structure of the carousel can be represented as shown in Figure 1.

Although *American Gods* does not provide a map of the movement of the carousel per se, the inscription of space within time in the apparently contradictory statements in this passage adds another element to representation – but of what? Of course, space plays a great role in Bakhtin's essay, from public squares to landscapes (Bakhtin 1981: 248–9; Bachelard 1994: 27), but, as Franco Moretti argues in *Graphs, Maps, Trees*, there are no maps included: 'Take Bakhtin's essay on the chronotope: it is the greatest single study ever written on space and narrative, and it doesn't have a single map' (Moretti 2007: 35). The figure of a carousel provides a structure through which we can trace the relation of the diachronic and the synchronic of double-vision (and indeed, in Moretti's chapter on maps he is more interested in narratives

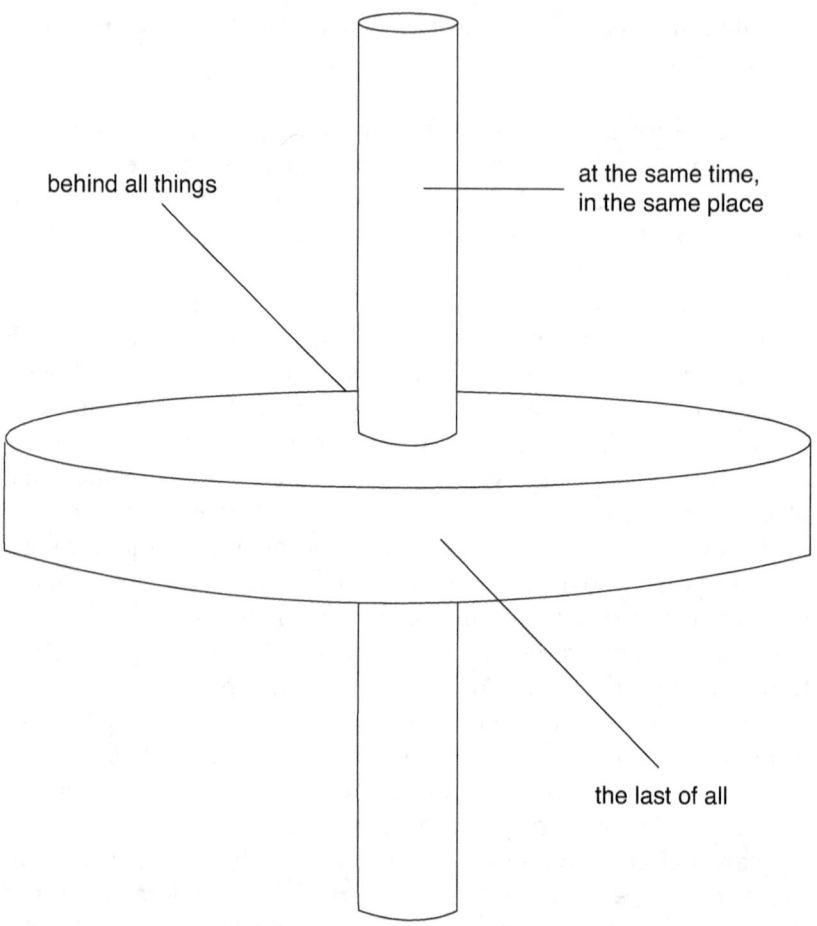

Figure 1

that one can actually map, such as Mary Mitford's *Our Village* (1824–32), rather than narratives that actually provide maps).[3] The reason that mapping is important here is simple: just as the simultaneity of double-vision makes time palpable, the mapping of space foregrounds force: as Moretti says, 'As in an experiment, the force "from without" of large national processes alters the initial narrative structure beyond recognition, and reveals the direct, almost tangible relationship between social conflict and literary form. Reveals form as a diagram of forces: or perhaps, even, as *nothing but force*' (Moretti 2007: 64).

In one sense the novel resists describing what this force might be. For while there are other examples of this kind of multiple-seeing in *American Gods* (Gaiman 2004: 151, 262), the mechanics of this vision are never specifically laid out. Such a refusal to stipulate the rationale behind an experience is the prerogative of literature in general, but perhaps especially of the genre of the fantastic, in which, as Tzvetan Todorov argued in his classic and problematic study, strange events remain unexplained (Todorov 1975: 25). In the scene with Mr Nancy, the narrator merely states that 'Shadow saw all these things, and he knew they were the same thing' (Gaiman 2004: 144). However, in another moment of double-vision in the novel, a possible clue is provided. It is implied that these moments are connected to a shift, or a blurring, of vision. For example, in one scene Mr Wednesday lays his hand on Shadow's shoulder. This causes Shadow to experience 'a *dizzying* moment of double-vision' (262, emphasis mine) in which he sees Mr Wednesday simultaneously as the man he currently is as well as 'hundreds and hundreds of winters' and as a grey man. While the term 'dizzy' is not medically precise, it is often connected to a distortion of vision, which then leads to a lack of balance. Such a distortion of vision, however slack, provides a gateway into understanding the force at work in the relationship between sight and non-sight, or what here comes under the aegis of double-vision.

Such distortion can be thought of as what Ian Bogost calls 'dismantling' (Bogost 2012: 127). Taking apart a video game system exposes new, unseen objects that were there all along. Microprocessors and signal encoders take on a new life when the mastery of the overall system is removed. Dismantling makes the connections between objects more visible by removing the assumptions that certain connections are given, while others are impossible. Objects become worthy of wonder because of what they are, and what they do, rather than because of the systems they fit into. Dismantling allows one 'to acknowledge the real object that isolates, while refusing to hold that it must always connect to any other in a network of relations' (Bogost 2012: 129).

Dizziness dismantles vision. It allows the parts that make up Mr Nancy to be seen on their own. In this sense dizziness is destructive, as Catherine Malabou sees it, in that it is a form of apoptosis, or the 'cellular suicide' that allows for the creation of new things such as the empty space that allows fingers to separate from one another during fetal development (Malabou 2012: 4–5). At the same time dismantling allows what Shaviro calls 'the universe of things' to be seen. Shaviro takes this idea from an sf short story by Gwyneth Jones of the same name. In the story, the technology of an alien culture is alive, in distinction from the inanimate technology used on Earth. When a terrestrial mechanic has visions of the alien culture, he sees his own world populated by tools and machines that have suddenly been imbued with life. Thus the story 'encourages us to think about the liveliness of objects and about the ways that they are related to us. The story suggests that even when we have shaped things into tools and have thereby constrained them to serve our own purposes, they still have independent lives of their own' (Shaviro 2014: 47–8).

Light-headedness, dizziness and blurred vision all indicate a removal from the world shaped into tools, which in Gaiman's novel is represented as a removal from the world of sight. However, this is not a leaving of the world, but rather a dismantling of it, of seeing it through a skewed perspective. This is a description not only of a Type-2 world but also of 'the world through blunted sight' which Patrick Trevor-Roper traced as essential to art in his book of the same name. In his opening chapter, entitled 'The Unfocused Image', Trevor-Roper, an ophthalmologist by trade, makes the argument that skewed or otherwise distorted vision (myopia, astigmatism, and so on) has been at the root of many of the new visions provided by literature and the fine arts over the decades (Trevor-Roper 1970: 17–66). In his analysis of the work of Modigliani, Trevor-Roper argues that it could have been the artist's astigmatism that accounts for the manner in which the figures in his paintings tend to lean to the left:

> Thus it could just be argued that the oblique astigmatic, whose retinal images are sloping, but who straightens his percepts, since his touch and intellect tell him that the objects are in fact upright, may overcompensate when he paints them on his canvas, and the result of this could be that the picture we see is sloping in the opposite direction. (Trevor-Roper 1970: 89–90)

It is not passing out or fainting, which would be to leave the world completely (even if just for a moment, a Type-3 world moment); rather it is having one's vision disrupted, although still in use (thus Type-2). Martin Jay, who examines thought from the Greeks to the poststructuralists in order to trace alternatives to the primacy of vision in *Downcast Eyes*, concludes that what is necessary is not a turning away from vision but an emphatic Nietzschean 'yes' to the multiplication of vision based upon a dialectic model:

> Indeed, it is precisely the proliferation of models of visuality that the antiocularcentric discourse, for all its fury against the ones it distrusts, tacitly encourages. Ocular-*ec*centricity rather than blindness, it might be argued, is the antidote to privileging any one visual order or scopic regime. What might be called 'the dialectics of seeing' precludes the reification of scopic regimes. Rather than calling for the exorbitation or enucleation of 'the eye,' it is better to encourage the multiplication of a thousand eyes, which, like Nietzsche's thousand suns, suggests the openness of human possibilities. (Jay 1994: 591)

The structure of the carousel combines the thought of Trevor-Roper and Jay: there is the multiplicity of vision enacted in the 'at the same place, in the same time' of the middle bar of the diagram above. This aspect of double-vision is found in how Shadow sees the multiples of Mr Nancy, for example, all at once. But at the same time there is a disturbance to his vision, represented by the two edges of the disc in the diagram, seen in the 'last of all' and 'behind all things'. Here we have both a temporal and a spatial disruption to multiplicity, a disruption that the work of Trevor-Roper connects to a 'weakness' of vision, and that Gaiman connects to dizziness or blurred vision. Thus the force that the map of the carousel indicates is that of a dizzifying-multiplication, or what will be called below 'pure presence'.

A final example of double-vision from *American Gods* makes the connection between blurred and multiple vision explicit. In this scene Shadow dies, although he is shortly to return to life. As Shadow is being ferried across the river Styx, a smoking oil lamp hanging at the front of the boat causes a blurriness of vision. Then Shadow is able to see the psychopomp boatman (whom he knew as Mr Ibis in real life, when he was alive) in his multiple incarnations: 'The smoke stung Shadow's eyes. He wiped the tears away with his hand, and, through the smoke, he thought he saw a tall man, in a suit, with gold-rimmed spectacles. The smoke cleared and the boatman was once more a half-human creature with the head of a river-bird' (Gaiman 2004: 522). Although Mr Ibis does not appear as both creatures at once in a strict sense, he does lecture Shadow on the prevalence of simultaneity: '"You people talk about the living and the dead as if they were two mutually exclusive categories. As if you cannot have a river that is also a road, or a song that is also a color"' (523). Gaiman's sequel-of-sorts to *American Gods*, the novel *Anansi Boys*, develops the concept of double-vision by including the manner in which double-vision is represented, which is storytelling, or the word.

The Word of God

Anansi Boys first sets up the 'poetic word' at the heart of change and double-vision, then displaces language with style, which can also be called a way of seeing, referred to as blurriness in the preceding section. *Anansi Boys* tells the story of two sons of Mr Nancy (the character in *American Gods*): Fat Charlie, who lacks self-confidence in all he does, and Spider, who can influence almost any person or object in the world on command. Eventually it is found that both sons used to be one person, although they were split at a young age. Thus multiple entities being 'at the same time, in the same place' is central to the novel, although this is also disrupted. The disruption, at first, takes the form of the word.

The function that the word, or storytelling, has in the novel is that it is the means by which Spider exerts his magical influence on the world. For example, when he meets Fat Charlie's fiancée Rosie, he convinces her that he is actually Fat Charlie simply by telling her so, although there is really no physical resemblance (Gaiman 2005: 102). He also gets Fat Charlie to leave the apartment while he brings Rosie over just by telling him to go, which overrides any will Fat Charlie has to stop Spider's seduction (125). These are just two among many examples. However, the importance of the poetic word in enacting moments of metamorphosis is developed when Spider is captured by an enemy and tied spread-eagled, face down, to four stakes in the ground. In addition, in order to curb his magic, his tongue is cut out. To try and save himself he attempts to create a spider out of mud. Eventually he is able to get one of his hands free enough to form the spider, but the problem is making the word which would breathe life into his creation: he has no tongue.

> The word, that would be the hardest part. Making a spider, or something quite like it, from blood and spit and clay, that was easy. Gods, even minor mischief gods like Spider, know how to do that. But the

final part of Making was going to prove the hardest. You need a word to give something life. You need to name it. (312)

Life is given by naming, though not the kind of naming the father gave in *The Road*. Rather, the kind of language Spider uses is closer to that of the boy. The divinity of the boy's language was connected to the worldlessness in which it was spoken. The world was dismantled, as Bogost would put it. And when things become dismantled wonder happens. This is because, when the world falls away, 'Each thing remains alien to every other, operationally as well as physically. To wonder is to respect things as things in themselves' (Bogost 2012: 131). This is the universe of things that Shaviro describes, where inanimate objects are seen to have life. The life of things simply means that objects have qualities that they were not expected to have. The main character of Ann Leckie's *Ancillary Justice* (2013) mirrors this idea. Breq is a woman who used to be a spaceship. 'Nineteen years, three months, and one week before I found Seivarden in the snow, I was a troop carrier orbiting the planet Shis'urna' (Leckie 2013: 9). Much of the novel is about the dismantling of the spaceship, not so much in a literal sense, but in how assumptions about how spaceships work are challenged by the way that Breq functions in the world.

The boy in *The Road* has a similar function to Breq because both are figures of dismantling. However, while Breq is the dismantling of a ship, the boy is the dismantling of language. With Spider, magic is given when a word is provided. This seems the antithesis of what is being discussed here. Spider is a figure of linguistic dominance rather than dismantling.

However, Charlie is different. He taps into the magic of the universe of things in another manner than Spider. Charlie's story revolves around his trying to claim the power of the poetic word that his brother Spider has for himself. Eventually he is able to do so, although his power does not rest in his brother's medium of the word but rather in a more 'natural' domain: song. This can be seen the first time the meek Charlie makes a stand for himself, deterring a man with a gun by singing 'Under the Boardwalk' in a restaurant (Gaiman 2005: 320–1). Charlie uses song to tap into the same powers that Spider has through the word. The reason that song is an important counterpoint to the word is that as a figure of territorialisation/deterritorialisation it opens what is described below as a *speculative* manner with which to experience the non-human world within the human world. The way in which song relates to the territory has been mapped out by Deleuze and Guattari in their work on the refrain in *A Thousand Plateaus*. Here they argue that song is that which can put up a border between ourselves and the outer world:

> A child hums to summon the strength for the schoolwork she has to hand in. A housewife sings to herself, or listens to the radio, as she marshals the antichaos forces of her work. Radios and television sets are like sound walls around every household and mark territories (the neighbor complains when it gets too loud). (Deleuze and Guattari 2005: 311)

As Brian Boyd argues, the marking of territory is one of the main functions that song has for birds (Boyd 2009: 76–7), or, as Deleuze and Guattari put it, 'The role of the refrain has often been emphasized: it is territorial, a territorial assemblage. Bird songs: the bird sings to mark its territory' (Deleuze and Guattari 2005: 312). The reason that song can striate space is because of rhythm, which both divides and joins; rhythm 'ties together critical moments' (Deleuze and Guattari 2005: 312). However, just as song can territorialise, and thus eventually become an expression of knowledge, the use of song within the symbolic deterritorialises because rhythm (a representation of the unknowable) is reinserted into expression (the knowable) (Willems 2011).

Gaiman indicates the importance of song in the opening of *Anansi Boys*, where he states that it is song that can create something new in the world:

> It begins, as most things begin, with a song.
> In the beginning, after all, were the words, and they came with a tune. That was how the world was made, how the void was divided, how the lands and the stars and the dreams and the little gods and the animals, how all of them came into the world.
> They were sung.
> The great beasts were sung into existence, after the Singer had done with the planets and the hills and the trees and the oceans and the lesser beasts. The cliffs that bound existence were sung, and the hunting grounds, and the dark.
> Songs remain. They last. The right song can turn an emperor into a laughing stock, can bring down dynasties. A song can last long after

the events and the people in it are dust and dreams and gone. That's the power of songs. (Gaiman 2005: 1–2)

Gaiman indicates both the territorialising and deterritorialising natures of song. Song territorialises because it divides: it is how 'the void was divided' and it sings 'the cliffs that bound existence' into presence. However, song also deterritorialises, it disrupts the structures that it creates: it brings down rulers and dynasties. In the novel this dual nature of the song is represented in moments of double-vision, although the previously determined categories of 'dizziness' and 'double-vision' never actually appear together.

In one example, the 'dizziness' seen in *American Gods* can be found in *Anansi Boys* when a ritual is enacted to transport Fat Charlie into the backstage world of the gods:

In Fat Charlie's mind all *the sounds began to blend into one strange sound*: the humming and the hissing and the buzzing and the drums. He was starting to feel *light-headed. Everything was funny*. Everything was unlikely. In the noises of the women he could hear the sound of wildlife in the forest, hear the crackling of enormous fires. His fingers felt stretched and rubbery, his feet were an immensely long way away.

It seemed then that he was somewhere above them, somewhere above everything, and that beneath him there were five people around a table. Then one of the women at the table gestured and dropped something into the bowl in the middle of the table, *and it flared up so brightly that Fat Charlie was momentarily blinded. He shut his eyes, which, he found, did no good at all. Even with his eyes closed, everything was much too bright for comfort.*

He rubbed his eyes against the daylight. He looked around. (Gaiman 2005: 163, emphasis mine)

In this example, an initial aural confusion sets Fat Charlie off balance, which is one of the main effects of dizziness. This confusion is then intensified by actual visual impairment, which, however, does not bring about a moment of double-vision but rather one of Heideggerian unveiling, for although the world of gods is seen to exist 'backstage', it is always accessible although at no point existing in the same time and place as found in moments of double-vision. Or, as Ian Bogost says, 'to see the richness of the one world, sometimes we must make ourselves blind to another'

(Bogost 2016: 233). Another way to express this blinding is to call it the dismantling of vision.

However, in another example, which is taken from earlier in the novel, an experience of double-vision seems to have taken place, but it is tied to storytelling rather than dizziness:

> What's that? You want to know if Anansi looked like a spider? Sure he did, except when he looked like a man.
> No, he never changed his shape. It's just a matter of how you tell the story. That's all. (Gaiman 2005: 45)

In this scene, the narrator addresses the narratee's scepticism regarding Spider's powers. The wording 'he never changed his shape' is the only explicit indication of double-vision in the novel. However, here it is tied not just to a story, but to the way in which the story is told. This indicates that the word in Gaiman is not just connected to a belief in language but to the form in which something is said; in other words, there is a disruption possible within language itself, just as the song of creation remains in creation and can be the engine of its deterritorialisation. In the final work of Gaiman's to be looked at, his short story 'How to Talk to Girls' (2007), both language and dizziness are 'combined' in a coordinate they share: the manner in which moments of double-vision are experienced.

From Prior to Co-present

While the word and the song indicate different mechanisms for change in Gaiman's work, the result of both is the same; an understanding of the change they engender can stem from Heidegger's notion of 'poetic dwelling'. Taking the line '... poetically man dwells ...' from Hölderlin for the title of an essay, Heidegger argues that a poetic relationship to the world exists a priori to the everyday manner in which we dwell in it (Heidegger 2001: 213). Poetic dwelling is a kind of constructing, or thinking, the world (215–16) which was described as being-in-the-world earlier. In this essay too, Heidegger connects this constructing with a measuring of the world, which is based on the kind of dying that is reserved for *Dasein*:

> In poetry there takes place what all measuring is in the ground of its being. Hence it is necessary to pay heed to the basic act of measuring.

That consists in man's first of all taking the measure which then is applied in every measuring act. In poetry the taking of measure occurs. To write poetry is measure-taking, understood in the strict sense of the word, by which man first receives the measure for the breadth of his being. Man exists as a mortal. He is called mortal because he can die. To be able to die means: to be capable of death as death. Only man dies – and indeed continually, so long as he stays on this earth, so long as he dwells. His dwelling, however, rests in the poetic. (219)

Thus a poetic relationship to the world can be said to be twofold: it involves a certain distance from one's world and it involves the ability to change or form that world.[4] The second aspect is dependent on the first in that when a being is enraptured in its environment – like a tick which only responds to light and movement (Agamben 2004: 46–7) – it does not have the distance to observe that environment, to engage in research within it, and thus to name and to change it. Earlier this was described as a lessened relationship to the world, or a relation which is impoverished. Yet this is also a *poetic* relationship. For if poetry (and thus capital-L Literature) is what is removed from everyday language in order to fundamentalise the ambiguities within it (Empson 1966), then philosophy can also be seen not as that which constructs the truth (being enraptured in the world) but as that which shows the way in which truth is constructed. Both aspects involve a distance from the world, a not-participating in it fully, a not-doing (at least not for now).

Poetic dwelling is central to Gaiman's short story 'How to Talk to Girls'. This story features a number of girls from another universe who are apparently the last remnants of a destroyed planet. This story is being looked at here because the girls are girls, but at the same time they are also poems. However, they do not change from one to the other, as in *Anansi Boys* (a kind of metamorphosis), but are simultaneously both, as in *American Gods* (modulation). Nevertheless, a part of the make-up of their multitude is the word, in the shape of a poem. Thus they form a kind of synthesis of the two novels.

The girls have been shot through space not simply to inform others of their now-lost world, but in fact to recreate it. A human, Enn, goes to what he thinks is a normal party where he meets the metrically named Triolet, who says '"If you want. I am a poem, or I am a pattern, or a race of people whose world was swallowed by the sea"' (Gaiman 2007: 250). Although in this passage 'or' seems to indicate a state of metamorphosis, or of different consecutive perspectives, rather than the modulation of a diachronic experience in a synchronic image, when Triolet tells Enn about her background, it is seen that she is actually all of these things, and all of these things at once:

> 'We knew that it would soon be over, and so we put it all into a poem, to tell the universe who we were, and why we were here, and what we said and did and thought and dreamed and yearned for. We wrapped our dreams in words and patterned the words so that they would live forever, unforgettable. Then we sent the poem as a pattern of flux, to wait in the heart of a star, beaming out its message in pulses and bursts and fuzzes across the electromagnetic spectrum, until the time when, on worlds a thousand sun systems distant, the pattern would be decoded and read, and it would become a poem once again.' (250)

Triolet is that poem, beamed out of a star, but at the same time she is a girl whispering this poem to Enn. Here we have another example of the simultaneous multiplicity that Mr Nancy exhibited. Yet why is it that Triolet is able to be many things at once? Triolet seems to take place in space, but not in time, because she can be many things at once, in one place, just like Mr Nancy.

This is an important point in the story because it foregrounds a central point in speculative realism: the role of time and space. For Meillassoux, Triolet and Mr Nancy would illustrate impossible states of contradiction. As he says in *After Finitude*, 'in becoming, things must be this, *then* other than this; they are, *then* they are not' (Meillassoux 2009: 70). This point is taken up in the next chapter. However, here Gaiman's work represents a challenge to Meillassoux's assumption. For Meillassoux, contradiction negates being, since an object cannot be one thing and the other at the same time; it must first be one, then the other. For Meillassoux, the chronology of metamorphosis is the accurate way to describe change. Yet Gaiman's characters are not one thing then another, but one thing and another (and another, and another). These are figures for whom chronology is suspended. The overlap of the figures on top of each other is only possible because of this contradictory dismantling of temporality.

Elie Ayache has read much into the randomness that Meillassoux sees in his Type-2 world, but he also criticises Meillassoux for his insistence on the role of temporality in change. For Ayache, randomness actually only ever takes place in space, and never in time (Ayache 2014: 970–4). Ayache, an ex-stockbroker, locates the impetus for this thinking in the way that pricing is determined in relation to the financial instrument of derivatives;[5] he names this timeless randomness the 'blank swan', in distinction from Nassim Nicholas Taleb's 'black swan', the latter aiming to foreground the strength of predictable oddity (Taleb 2007; Ayache 2010). For Ayache, it is material forces that determine which side of a die will come up at the end of a throw. One throw has nothing to do with the one before. No law of large numbers is applicable here to guarantee that after a sufficiently large amount of throws every number on the die will eventually have come up. Instead,

> The static and timeless *realization* of probability is that it is a distribution of mass, that mass means matter, and that the only matter here – the only reality here – is the fact that a static die lies on a certain unique face, because it was forced to do so by the surrounding matter and the surrounding world – *and that this face could have been different*. (Ayache 2014: 972)

For Ayache, the materiality of space removes randomisation from chronology. This would seem to be in line with the aspect of Meillassoux that holds that it is mathematics that proves that there is knowledge outside of the world of thought (Meillassoux 2009: 117); yet it is precisely at this juncture that Ayache differentiates himself from Meillassoux.

For Meillassoux, the advent of the new is not predetermined in any way. It is random in that no germ of it was contained in what came before, as there was not something contained in the nothing at the gestation of the universe, there is no life contained in non-life, and there is no human consciousness contained in non-humans. All of these changes arose out of nothing, and the next change, if it comes at all, can never be predicted (and thus it could be a God, or the resurrection of all the humans who have ever existed, or it could be anything else).

> God did not create thought, and nothing in the world was thinking before the advent of thought; God did not create the suffering or pleasure found in vital activity, and nothing suffered or enjoyed in

> the world before the advent of life. This indicates in the most striking fashion that if we think advent in its truth, it is an advent *ex nihilo* and thus *without any reason at all*, and *for that very reason* it is without limit ... If advent is immanent, then it is absurd; thus it is capable of anything. (Meillassoux 2011: 176)

Ayache takes from Meillassoux the way that the event makes a complete break with the past. It is absurd, meaning that there is no *arche* that turns the future into a possibility. This is the speculative nature of both speculative realism and speculative materialism which Ayache and Meillassoux share (Ayache 2015: 84). It is this break from chronology that helps explain what is going on in Gaiman's novel, and it is something that Meillassoux seems to reinsert in his thought on non-contradiction. Yet Ayache differs from Meillassoux in his insistence on the materiality of the event. It is the physical properties of the die throw that determine the outcome. In this sense the die 'writes' the result of its throw when it happens (Ayache 2015: 147–8). It is this insistence on materialism that also marks a difference between Gaiman and Ayache. The 'medium of contingency' that Ayache insists on is challenged by the contradiction of the multiple actors in Gaiman – Mr Nancy and the spider and the old man and the boy. Rather than being a figure of materiality, this image shows how objects 'often gain the upper hand over their own constituent pieces, and can even abstain from any action at all' (Harman 2016: 115). Triolet is both a poem and a young woman. Mr Nancy is also many things at once. The multiple appearances of the same object together both signals the removal of the object from time and also its removal from materiality, since all of these manifestations both appear and fail to appear at the same time.

At the same time, in Gaiman's story the whispered poem is not in a language that Enn understands; the only way that Enn can comprehend the poem is to be open to the experience of Triolet herself, meaning that Enn must be open to the unknowable. This opening brings about change, de facto:

> 'You cannot hear a poem without it changing you,' she told me. 'They heard it, and it colonized them. It inherited them and it inhabited them, its rhythms becoming part of the way that they thought; its images permanently transmuting their metaphors; its verses, its outlook, its aspirations becoming their lives.' (Gaiman 2007: 250)

Yet here lies a difference from what has been discussed so far: the openness that Enn must have does not indicate a stillness, or not-doing, as is often associated with potentiality. Rather, the subject is moved. The subject is inhabited, rhythms of thought have changed, metaphors have transmuted, aspirations have been rescheduled. The shifting of the subject is a representation of the imbalance of dizziness.

In Gaiman's story, being and becoming (essence and appearance, or the a priori poetic and the language of a poem) become 'one': Triolet warns Enn that

> Within a generation their children [the children of those who have 'experienced' the poem] would be born already knowing the poem, and, sooner rather than later, as these things go, there were no more children born. There was no need for them, not any longer. There was only a poem, which took flesh and walked and spread itself across the vastness of the known. (Gaiman 2007: 250–1)

Thus the poetic words which are a multiple of double-vision instigate change, and this change is a movement from the a priori of poetic dwelling to an image of 'only a poem', but a poem that dwells in the world through its flesh, which would walk and spread itself. However, in order to develop what the role of noise, or 'motion', in change is, more textual evidence than Gaiman can provide will be needed. Thus a novel from China Miéville is used in order to foreground the role of agitation within double-vision as a means of leading to a discussion of the challenge that speculative realism provides to both the 'co-presencing', and eventually the movement, found in Gaiman's work.

To summarise, this chapter has developed a number of connections and tensions between speculative realism and sf. Strategies for making the withdrawn nature of objects visible have been developed in both philosophy and fiction. Dismantling has been put forward as a mode of freeing objects from the anthropomorphised world they inhabit in order to begin to wonder at the weirdness of the relations they can both have and deny. In sf, dismantling was seen to lead to a universe of things in which seemingly dead objects are actually seen to be alive. While a novel such as Philip K. Dick's *Ubik* (1969) would have provided a more direct representation of such a universe, the focus of this chapter lies on the strategy needed for dismantling the world.

Double-vision is posited as such a strategy, as it involves a challenge to the hegemonic sense of vision in forming a world around subjects and objects. However, the challenge that Gaiman's work poses is that objects in the universe of things are not full of wonder because they can change from one thing into another (from dead to alive, for example), but because they are many things at once. On the one hand this was used as a figure of metaphor, while on the other a challenge to the chronology of metamorphosis was formed. An insistence on the non-chronological aspect of change seemed to locate the discussion in what Ayache calls the medium of contingency, yet double-vision is actually a figure of non-contingency, at least in part. Strangeness and contradiction are essential to Gaiman's vision, and form a challenge to new materialisms.

Yet an important aspect of this chapter remains underdeveloped. Although change has been connected to modulation rather than metamorphosis, its connection to the essence of an object has been glossed over. This is corrected in the next chapter.

Notes

1. However, fracturedness is not to be coupled with totality. See Brian Massumi's history of 'total vision' in *Parables for the Virtual: Movement, Affect, Sensation* (Massumi 2002: 144–52).
2. 'Secondness', according to Charles Peirce's well-known categories of firstness, secondness and thirdness, is the level at which the human is first to be found because it is there that reason initially makes an appearance (Peirce 1991: 180–203).
3. This attention to location recalls Ian Watt's dictum that realism includes a heightened specificity of place (Watt 1971: 32).
4. Regarding the role of distance in the origin of poetic dwelling, Véronique Fóti argues that 'Heidegger himself, stressing that the source, in its de-reivation, exceeds itself and is thus not self-sufficient, characterizes the origin as both excess and lack; yet he seeks immediately to embed the source in its hidden "ground," which, whatever its darkness, stands firm. To show forth (*zeigen*) the origin, he insists, is to establish it firmly and festively (*festigen, festecken*) in its *essential* ground, which is the holy. Such a showing, which renders festive and firm, is what he understands by a poetic founding, which also founds itself by abiding in a nearness to the origin that keeps open the dimension of distance' (Fóti 1995: 58).

5. A derivative can be loosely defined as a future 'bet' made on the anticipated change in value of an underlying asset. Using this financial instrument to safeguard loss in value is hedging, while anticipating a profit is speculating.

4

Subtraction and Contradiction: China Miéville

'We are bound to hurt one another so much, again and again. We are so terribly different.'
'Yes,' he said, 'but the more different, the more lovely the loving.'
Olaf Stapeldon, *Sirius* (1944)

Assemblage and Subtraction

In the previous chapter it was argued that double-vision is a strategy for dismantling the world. Dizziness challenges the hegemony of vision. While vision solidifies the world, when it becomes blurred the world can break down into the universe of things, big and small. Double-vision represents this breakdown because within it, different modulations of a single identity are visible at the same time. Double-vision is thus a strategy which causes the Zug effect. It describes moments in which, due to dizziness or other disruptions, vision becomes disconnected from objects. Or, aspects of objects are represented as remaining dark, or withdrawn from vision. On the one hand, this is a representation of the withdrawn nature of objects foregrounded by Graham Harman and Levi Bryant. On the other hand, it mirrors the way that sf can imbue the everyday world with weirdness, as seen above in the way that Steven Shaviro describes common tools becoming filled with life. Yet the withdrawn nature of objects can also be used to discuss the role of essence among all this change.

China Miéville's second novel *Perdido Street Station* (2000) addresses the idea of essence from three different perspectives which mirror a number of concepts of speculative realism. Briefly, the first character in the novel under discussion is Lin, who is a khepri, which means that she has a human body and a scarab-like head. She is a sculptor who sees with an insectile vision that divides the world into a multitude of fragments which are each comprehended in their uniqueness; thus Lin takes on a similar position in the novel to the multitudinous vision seen in *American Gods*, which was described in a similar fashion. The second character is Mr Motley, a 'remade' human whose name indicates the variety of amalgamated body parts that make up his person. He hires Lin to sculpt his likeness. However, while sculpting her model Lin becomes disoriented because Mr Motley's body parts are not just various, but are also constantly changing. He berates her for not being fluid enough to see him in his constant state of change, claiming that she still has a 'base' image of what he was like before. It is here that the stasis of double-vision begins to be criticised. According to Mr Motley, Lin's problem is that, through her sculpture, she is trying 'to freeze in time a body in flux' (Miéville 2000: 134). Thus he begins to point a way forward to an expansion of the synchronic representation of the diachronic. This way forward is the incorporation of movement into an experience of double-vision. The third character is a Weaver, which is a kind of inter-world spider. One key feature of the Weavers is that they are difficult to understand. They do not dream, which becomes a source of strength when they fight creatures who feed on the subconscious mind.

The main plot of the novel is centred on trying to rein in a group of 'slake-moths' which have escaped. The moths are dangerous because they feed on the inhabitants' subconsciousnesses until their prey is rendered inert: 'The subconscious is their nectar' (457). The Weavers eventually play a key role in this fight. They have no hidden messages, no animal cortex to contradict a symbolic existence. They have no ego, and they are unfathomable to others, thus they are immune to the slake-moths. Yet the Weavers are perceived; they are relative rather than absolute dark objects. These two different characters are representations of the way in which a subject changes when open to an experience of the multitude: Lin represents seeing the many rather than the whole; Mr Motley stresses observing change; and finally, the Weavers question the role of comprehension itself. What these characters have in common is a representation of the effects that double-vision need to have in the subject in order to come about.

Turning to the first figure of the novel, the narrator divulges that Lin is a khepri; her external qualities are presented, yet these qualities are presented 'in pieces', meaning that the connection between one quality and another is minimised. Lin is characterised as hairless, with red skin, and is extremely muscular. In fact, her muscles were 'each distinct. She was like an anatomical atlas' (12). The distinctness of each muscle from the other is, on the one hand, simply a description of a well-defined body; on the other it is the first hint to the way that Lin actually sees the world, which is in a fragmented manner.

Lin's manner of experiencing the world can be seen the first time she is on her own in the story. After having had sex with Isaac, a relationship which is still taboo enough in the city that they cannot be seen out together in public, Lin goes to the khepri quarter to pick up some art supplies. On this outing Lin's seeing things in their fragmentary nature rather than wholeness emerges:

> Lin's bulging mirrored eyes saw the city in *a compound visual cacophony. A million tiny sections of the whole, each minuscule hexagon segment ablaze* with sharp colour and even sharper lines, supersensitive to *differentials* of light, weak on details unless she focused hard enough to hurt slightly. Within each *segment*, the dead scales of decaying walls were invisible to her, *architecture reduced to elemental slabs of colour*. But a precise story was told. *Each visual fragment, each part, each shape, each shade of colour, differed from its surroundings in infinitesimal ways that told her about the state of the whole structure.* (20, emphasis mine)

The way in which Lin experiences the world is through its parts. *A million tiny sections, each minuscule hexagon segment, differentials, elemental slabs of colour.* All of these are seen not as a whole, but rather as a *compound visual cacophony* which focuses both on the manner in which elements are joined and the way they are separate from each other. This line of thought has its best-known theoretical component in the work of Gilles Deleuze on the assemblage, which he has formulated through the equation $(n - 1)$. The assemblage is a gathering of parts which is not necessarily taken as a whole. In a simple example, instead of 'a room' there are chairs, a desk, a floor, gravity, light, plumbing, temperature, design ideals, economic restraints and so on. In the equation $(n - 1)$, the whole of the room is 'taken down' one level and it is the elements of the room that remain. The assemblage

> is not the One that becomes Two or even directly three, four, five, etc. It is not a multiple derived from the One, or to which One is

added (*n* + 1). It is composed not of units but of dimensions, or rather *directions in motion*. It has neither beginning nor end, but always a middle (*milieu*) from which it grows and which it *overspills*. It constitutes linear multiplicities with *n* dimensions having neither subject nor object, which can be laid out on one plane of consistency, and *from which the One is always subtracted* (*n* − 1). (Deleuze and Guattari 2005: 21, emphasis mine)

There is a subtraction from a whole, and what this subtraction makes visible is middles, directions, movement from one-to-the-other rather than the points in between. In the language developed above, this subtraction makes the relative darkness of objects become visible, meaning that the previously hidden ways in which objects connect to each other come to the foreground (as the removal of the eye lens makes the eye's susceptibility to ultraviolet light noticeable). It is a dismantling (Bogost) which makes the multiplicities in the universe of things visible (Shaviro). These multiplicities are what Lin experiences in 'each visual fragment, each part, each shape, each shade of colour', although there is no motion towards other objects attached to these directions as such (each element resides in her experience, rather than passing through). It is movement that the next figure will put into play.

However, first the notion of the assemblage needs to be clarified. It was said earlier that in the assemblage it is the multiplicities that are stressed rather than the whole they make up. One important aspect of multiplicities is that they are in a relation of *exteriority*, in that one element (a colour) can be taken out of one assemblage and put into another, where it carries a different function. As Manuel DeLanda explains in *A New Philosophy of Society: Assemblage Theory and Social Complexity*, 'the exteriority of relations implies a certain autonomy for the terms they relate' (DeLanda 2006: 11). In exteriority, the elements do not relate to each other in terms of what they are, but rather in terms of what they can do:

Relations of exteriority also imply that the properties of the component parts can never explain the relations which constitute a whole [...] In fact, the reason why the properties of a whole cannot be reduced to those of its parts is that they are the result of not an aggregation of the components' own properties but of the actual exercise of their capacities. These capacities do depend on a component's properties but cannot be reduced to them since they involve reference to the properties of other interacting entities. Relations of exteriority guarantee that assemblages may be taken apart while at the same time allowing that the interactions between parts may result in a true synthesis. (DeLanda 2006: 11)

On the one hand, the manner in which the component parts cannot constitute a whole might seem to indicate a similarity to Graham Harman's notion of the withdrawn nature of objects, because according to the exteriority of objects, they can be taken apart. Yet Harman's reading is based on accepting an (always withdrawn) essence to objects which can only be approached indirectly. DeLanda's reading of the assemblage, on the other hand, denies any essence to objects at all. Instead, the manner in which objects function together forms momentary networks of being. As Harman says, DeLanda's world 'is filled with individuals of countless different sizes, and in each case they must be understood through the concrete historical-genetic process through which they appeared, not as instances of an essence shared by many concrete things' (Harman 2008: 370). The difference between DeLanda's view and that running throughout this book is that here objects can be dark objects, meaning that they can exist without any relation to other objects whatsoever (even if only relatively). Meaning is not developed out of the network, but out of indirect experiences of darkness. This difference is reflected in *Perdido Street Station*: the fragmented experience that Lin has of the world is essenceless in DeLanda's sense, and she has trouble in understanding Mr Motley, mainly because he insists on essence.[1]

Contradiction and Crisis Energy

The essence being insisted on here is what is most hidden, strange and fluid; as Harman says, '"essence" simply means that any object has real properties that are not exhausted by their current appearance in the mind or their current impact on other entities more generally' (Harman 2013: 27). The main issue that Lin has in capturing Mr Motley in her sculpture is that she cannot think how to represent essence while seeing his parts in motion. This is because she is a figure of the assemblage, which was called double-vision in the previous chapter. The manner in which the assemblage and essence are connected takes two main forms: what Harman calls fission and fusion, meaning the separation and joining of an object

Subtraction and Contradiction: China Miéville

and qualities. But first, in order to understand the difficulty that Lin has with Mr Motley, the way in which Lin experiences the world needs to be established. In one scene near the beginning of the novel, Lin explains the way she sees the world to Isaac:

> *I see clearly as you, clearer. For you it is undifferentiated. In one corner a slum collapsing, in another a new train with pistons shining, in another a gaudy painted lady below a drab and ancient airship ... You must process as one picture. What chaos! Tells you nothing, contradicts itself, changes its story. For me each tiny part has integrity, each fractionally different from the next, until all variation is accounted for, incrementally, rationally.*
>
> Isaac had been fascinated for a week and a half. He had, typically, taken pages of notes and sought books on insectile vision, subjected Lin to tedious experiments in depth-perception and distance-vision [...]
>
> His interest had quickly waned. The human mind was incapable of processing what the khepri saw. (Miéville 2000: 20-1, italics in original)

Lin's description of the way she sees takes the form of $(n - 1)$, in that Isaac sees the city as a whole, while Lin sees it in the parts making up that whole. Neither sees the city in terms of essence, as that which is withdrawn, or unknowable. However, the unknowable is foregrounded when Lin is contracted by Mr Motley to make a sculpture of him, a contract she will not be able to fulfil because he eventually tortures her nearly beyond repair. As suggested by his name, Mr Motley is a mixture of body parts. Therefore he could be configured as another representative of hybridity (Miller 2010: 39–59) or an assemblage: in short, more parts than whole. However, Lin has a difficult time even looking at him because all the different parts that go to make up his body are not just mixed-up, they are *in flux*: 'The first couple of times she had come here, she had been sure that he changed overnight, that the shards of physiognomy that made up his whole reorganized when no one was looking. She became frightened of her commission' (Miéville 2000: 133). The contrast between her fragmented vision of the world and Mr Motley's diachronic being is the reason she is frightened: it is not because Mr Motley is a mix of scary elements, but rather that the prospect of trying to capture his fluidity in the static nature of her sculpture seems wrong: 'She wondered hysterically if it was like a task in a moral children's tale, if she was to be punished for some nebulous sin by striving *to freeze in time a body in flux*, forever too afraid to say anything, starting each day from the beginning over again' (133–4, emphasis mine). This scene offers an implicit critique of the static nature of the synchronic experience of diachronic events that was found in double-vision.

Lin attempts to cope with the fluctuating body in making her sculpture, but Mr Motley is not satisfied. He critiques her for seeing each of his parts as a fragment, rather than seeing all of his changing parts as himself all at once as an instantiation of his pure presence: Lin still tries to make sense of his configuration by attempting to trace reason and origin in each of his elements. Mr Motley says:

> 'It's so . . . predictable. You're still not looking the right way. At all. It's a wonder you can create such art. You still see *this* – ' he gesticulated vaguely at his own body with a monkey's paw ' – as pathology. You're still interested in what *was* and how it went *wrong. This is not error or absence or mutancy: this is image and essence*.' (140, italics in original)

Mr Motley indicates that the changes his body undergoes are not deviations from a norm, but are rather, in their various forms that make up his modulations, who he is. Mr Motley does not come about as the image of a network, but rather as a mixture of what Harman terms fusion and fission. The projects of Alain Badiou and Quentin Meillassoux can be used as a starting point for thinking about this difference, although the novel eventually goes in a different direction.

In 'Philosophy and Art', Badiou approaches the question of image and essence via Heidegger. He identifies four main strains of Heidegger's thought – the question, the earth, a re-evaluation of the history of philosophy, and poetic-being – and then states that it is only the last which retains any resonance for contemporary thinking (Badiou 2004: 91–2). Badiou then lays out three main strains of Heidegger's thought on the poem: 1) he establishes that a poem is not about knowledge but rather *aletheia*, or the uncovering of truth; 2) he shows how poetry is not necessarily a separate entity from philosophy but can be philosophy; and 3) this leads Heidegger into the 'trap' illuminated by Derrida's critique of non-relation – this 'truth' or philosophy must reside somewhere, and

Heidegger cannot 'escape' locating it in the word itself (Badiou 2004: 98–9; cf. Derrida 1991: 129–36 n. 5).

The next step Badiou takes is the reason he is being considered here. The question he asks is, what has contemporary poetry done to escape the trap of language that Heidegger sets up for himself? Badiou finds a possible path in Mallarmé. Badiou sees 'the separation, the isolation, the coldness of that which is only present insofar as it no longer has any presentable relationship to reality' (Badiou 2004: 98–9) in Mallarmé, meaning that such a poem is 'pure presence' in that it does not refer to anything else, there is no unveilable truth that underlies its language. There is no essence. Badiou sees such poems as mathemes (99). This thesis is, in essence, similar to Meillassoux's argument in his book on Mallarmé, *The Number and the Sign*. Here Meillassoux finds the 'code' to Mallarmé's *Un coup de dés*: by counting the words you come up with the number 707, although other counts are also possible, producing 714, 705 and 703 total words (Meillassoux 2012b: 216). Although Meillassoux finds a variety of meanings in the number 707, the specificity of the count makes the poem an example of an object without essence, for since its structure cannot be incorporated into the canon of verse forms, 'its Meter would belong to it alone' (42).

For Badiou, Mallarmé's work is a poetic figuration of the matheme. Although no pretence is made here at fleshing out the complexities of the role of mathematics in Badiou's thought, a short look at meditation seventeen, 'The Matheme of the Event', from *Being and Event*, brings forth both the doubled structure and the consequences of the matheme for Badiou. Here, the example is the French Revolution. The basic argument is that the event of the revolution included the revolution as one of the terms of its own becoming (Badiou 2005: 180). The matheme Badiou develops for this argument is as follows: S is a situation (the French Revolution); X is the 'evental site' that is presented in S (for example, 'the peasants'); then it can be said that X belongs to, or is presented in S, written thus: $X \subseteq S$; and the event of X (in which the peasants become present in the revolution) is written e_x. This formulation allows Badiou then to express that an event is made up of all the multiples of its site, along with the site itself: $e_x = (x \subseteq X, e_x)$. Thus the matheme indicates '*the mode in which the Revolution is a central term of the Revolution itself*'; that is, the manner in which the conscience of the times – and the retroactive intervention of our own – filters the entire site through the one of its evental qualification' (180). The example Badiou provides of this is the declaration of Saint-Just that 'the revolution is frozen'. In this sense what Saint-Just adds to the revolution, 'that *one-mark* that is the Revolution itself, as this signifier of the event which, being "qualifiable" (the Revolution is "frozen"), proves that it is itself a *term* of the event that it is' (180). Thus, just as the poetry of Mallarmé indicates the 'pure presence' of itself as a singularity, the matheme of the event is the same, in that it is 'the one of the infinite multiple that it is' (180).

The manner in which Lin sees the world lies here. As cited above, Lin describes her vision in the form of $(n-1)$. She says, *'For me each tiny part has integrity, each fractionally different from the next, until all variation is accounted for, incrementally, rationally'* (Miéville 2000: 20). The way she lives her life is similar. Like her vision, her life is made up of component parts. Rather than living in the collective manner of most khepri, Lin says *'I work alone . . . which is part of my . . . rebellion. I left Creekside and then Kinken, left my moiety and my hive'* (49). Her art is also different, not so much because it is better than others' but rather because she *'Tried to make some of the grand figures we all made together a little less perfect . . .'* (49). The figure of Lin is considered here along with the concept of the matheme because, as Badiou puts it, the matheme 'disjoins being from appearing, essence from existence' (Badiou 2005: 125). With Lin's vision *'each tiny part has integrity'*; in Lin's life she works alone; in Lin's art less than perfection is the goal. This is what leads to her inability to see her employer Mr Motley as he wants to be seen: 'She had no clear picture of her boss, only a sense of the ragged discordance of his flesh' (Miéville 2000: 94).

Mr Motley is different. While the matheme disjoins essence from existence, Mr Motley insists on his being an example of existing essence. As quoted above, in describing his own body he says *'This is not error or absence or mutancy: this is image and essence'* (140). Mr Motley is apparently an extreme form of a 'remade' person, which is usually a form of punishment for convicted criminals. A woman who killed her baby because it would not stop crying got a ten-year prison sentence and had her baby's arms grafted on to her face (115). Others crawl on the ground under the weight of huge iron snail shells, while some have had their legs replaced by tank treads. Mr Motley, while perhaps being a remade, is less obviously the fusion of two distinct parts. Instead, the instability of his appearance is foregrounded. As stated above, Lin, upon arriving one day to continue her sculpture, 'had been sure that he had changed overnight, that the shards of physiognomy that made up his whole reorganized when no one was looking' (133). Mr Motley's body is not just remade, but it is in flux. The changes that take place to his body, however, are not visible by direct observation. They take place when no one is looking. They are hidden. They take place in the darkness. At the same time, Mr Motley's body is not understandable via the matheme. 'It felt absurdly prosaic to *count* the razor-sharp shards of chitin that jutted from a scrap of pachyderm skin, just to make sure she had not missed one in her sculpture. It felt almost vulgar, as if his anarchic form should defy accounting' (134, italics in original).

Yet despite Lin's difficulties in sculpting Mr Motley's body, one description of him, given through free indirect speech, provides a different narrative strategy. When Mr Motley enters a room, he is described as 'the chaotic agglutination of flesh that was Mr Motley poised at its centre' (133). Although the 'chaotic agglutination' of Mr Motley's flesh sounds as though it could mirror DeLanda's reading of the assemblage, the location of Mr Motley at his own centre indicates that his insistence on image and essence goes in another direction.

Harman has devoted much energy to reading the way that the unknowable essence of objects can be indirectly experienced. In his reading of 'tool-being' in Heidegger, rather than the broken object revealing the being of a tool in its unhandiness, the everyday functioning of an object is already strange. Another way to say this is that even in the everyday, objects are never present in their totality. As stated in a previous chapter, in speaking of a number of common objects found in a bedroom or office, Heidegger says that 'These "things" never show themselves initially by themselves, in order then to fill out a room as a sum of real things' (Heidegger 1996: 64). A traditional reading of the manner in which such things do become present as such is when their everyday usefulness comes into question, a line of argument which usually follows the motif of the 'broken tool'. In this sense it is in the 'unhandiness' of a broken hammer, for instance, that the hammer as such becomes present (Heidegger 1996: 68). However, as Harman has indicated in his re-evaluation of this concept in *Tool-Being*, 'the visibility of Heidegger's "broken tool" has nothing to do with equipment not being in top working order [...] as ought to be expected, Heidegger teaches us not about smashed-up blades and chisels, but only about beings in general' (Harman 2002: 45). The reason that the broken tool acts as a key point for taking a step beyond Heidegger is that it encapsulates a major aspect of his thought, and that is that authentic being (tool-as-tool) and inauthentic being (tool in use and forgotten) are always tied together through the 'mere' [*bloß*], in that the hammer is not 'merely' a hammer; there is also a more fundamental comportment which has been forgotten through use and which can become experienced through its 'brokenness' (or, as otherwise developed in Heidegger, through anxiety, or boredom). Harman's programme is to retain the dual structure of the 'mere' but to foreground it into an object of pure presence, rather than poetic being: 'The idea of an object-oriented philosophy is the idea of an ontology that would retain the structure of Heidegger's fundamental dualism, but would develop it to the point where concrete entities again become a central philosophical problem' (Harman 2002: 49). Thus when Mr Motley stresses to Lin that, regarding his body, '*This is not error or absence or mutancy: this is image and essence*', he is also asking her to stop looking 'behind' the brokenness of the tool for a veiled truth, but rather to stick to the presence of the object on the surface: it is here that his essence is to be found. This is why Mr Motley can be found in the centre of his own qualities, rather than behind them.

The thrust of Harman's development of an object-oriented ontology can be seen in his similarity and difference in relation to the actor-network-theory developed by Bruno Latour, who is an important figure because of the way in which movement is central to his theory. For example, one of the five major concerns of his theory is with the 'nature of actions', meaning how 'in each course of action a great variety of agents seem to barge in and displace the original goals' (Latour 2007: 22). What is important for Latour here is not that the actor in his theory has some kind of agency that other objects do not have, but rather that they are 'the moving target of a vast array of entities swarming toward it' (46). Thus, in contradistinction to agency, Latour suggests the term *figuration*, stressing that it is not the presence or absence of agency which determines a subject but rather the flow of multiple strands of continually changing influence from other actors in a network which causes a subject to act (53). While at first this might seems like another version of the assemblage as described above – and indeed Latour and Deleuze are like-minded in some ways – it is precisely at this point of necessity of the network of influences as being constitutive of the subject that Harman takes issue with Latour. The way he does it is under the idea of dark or dormant objects.

In his fictionalised chapter 'The Sleeping Zebra', Harman describes a visit to Latour's apartment in Paris. Latour has to leave and Harman is left in the apartment alone, where he dreams of Badiou's take on set theory (Harman 2010: 67–8). This acts as a prelude for Harman's presentation of his concept of a dormant object. As stated above, Harman sets himself apart from Heidegger's tool-beings in that objects do not have a poetic and everyday aspect to them which we can uncover and forget, but rather we interact with objects in the sensual realm. However, this is not the crux of the argument, for Harman goes a step further by arguing that non-human objects relate to each other in the same manner: 'All things, both human and nonhuman, must encounter other things in the form of sensual caricatures' (69). This is not an attempt, as such, to invest objects with a psyche but rather to show how the interaction of one object with another through thought, memory, fantasy or dreaming is only quantitatively and not qualitatively different from when 'dust collides with dirt', since both take place in the sensual realm (69–70).

One of the reasons why Harman sees the everyday use of tools as already strange is that even in the most pedestrian use of a banal object (using a chair for sitting on), all of the aspects of an object are never unveiled. In short, a description of an object, no matter how detailed, never actually becomes that object (Harman 2012: 9–10), and thus objects are always *withdrawn* in some manner. It is this withdrawn element of objects in which the 'weirdness' resides. This is the lesson of Mr Motley's body: he is a figure of the withdrawn, for no matter how closely Lin looks, his body will always be something different next time. It changes when no one is around. Thus Mr Motley claims that the withdrawnness is his essence, a lesson that it is hard for Lin to learn.

The withdrawn element of objects is the darkness or dormancy described above, and it is where Harman differs from Latour: for Latour, objects are defined by the network, while for Harman, they are defined by the weirdness of being withdrawn. Yet such objects are perceivable, as was seen in the dark objects in *Beyond the Barrier* described in the first chapter. The experience of objects takes place in the sensual realm. As Tristan Garcia describes the withdrawn and the sensual, for Harman

> an ontological difference exists between the real object, withdrawn into itself, and the sensual object, internal to perception, there is no need to assume that there is an underlying difference between material or immaterial objects, sensory or non-sensory objects, conscious or unconscious objects. An ontological difference exists for him not between objects and non-objects, nor between object and consciousness, but within the category of object, between real objects and sensual objects. (Garcia 2013: 15)

The difference between real and sensual properties of an object is brought out in an essay Harman wrote which features Miéville. The piece is from the same collection as 'The Sleeping Zebra' (*Circus Philosophicus*) and tells a fable about a time when Harman and Miéville were stranded for 18 hours on an 'Offshore Drilling Rig' (the name of the essay) off the coast of Louisiana, 'a prank on my part' (Beckett 2011), as Harman says in a later interview. In the essay, Harman tells Miéville the myth of an offshore oil rig which is able to throw up all concrete and abstract objects from the past, present and future. This image is used as a way for Harman to describe both the manner in which objects are unknowable (dark, withdrawn) and the way that they affect each other (through sensual qualities).

First Harman images these objects gathered by the oil rig as dark objects: 'We might imagine further that none of these past, present, or future things is capable of any direct connection with its neighbors. They are islands cut off from each other, so that only by means of the rig do they make even indirect contact' (Harman 2010: 46). The reason that the objects pulled up by the rig are dark objects is because they are withdrawn, meaning that they can never be experienced in their totality by the rig, just as a description of an object, no matter how detailed, never becomes that object itself. Thus the objects pulled out of the past, present and future are images of objects, meaning that '"There are as many images of each object as there are rigs that encounter them. Fifty rigs could all siphon the same cat, for instance, and the result would simply be fifty different cat-images, with the cat itself possibly remaining untouched by the exercise"' (48). Earlier, Mr Motley described his body as both image and essence. Essence is taken to be the withdrawn qualities of an object (what Harman calls real qualities) which are dark and unknowable. At the same time Mr Motley is image, meaning that his body is observable, due to its sensual qualities. Although Mr Motley is in flux, he is described. As Lin works on her sculpture different aspects of Mr Motley's body are seen. He is described thus: 'the three-toed reptile claw that was one of Mr Motley's feet' (Miéville 2000: 134), 'the exoskeletal jags, the muscular cavities' (135) and 'the hues of Mr Motley's bizarre flesh were too spectacular, too arresting, not to be represented' (135). It is the interaction of the withdrawn and the present which makes Mr Motley's body fluctuate, for the sensual qualities observed in an object, no matter how many qualities are actually observed, never exhaust that object (this is true for human–object and object–object relations). Lin's sculpture is meant to be a representation of this interaction between quality types, although Mr Motley sees her struggling with the task.

In 'Offshore Drilling Rig' Harman explicitly connects his myth with Miéville's concept of *crisis energy* (Harman 2010: 39), saying that his essay forms its counterpart. In *Perdido Street Station*, Isaac, Lin's lover, is a scientist who is developing his idea of crisis energy and the means to harness it. Isaac's theory aims to capture the energy of urban destruction around him with a 'crisis engine', in the hope of redirecting the negative energy. Crisis energy is a quality of real objects, meaning that, like being withdrawn, it is a part of the essence of every object; as Isaac says, 'Some situations are more crisis-ridden or – prone than others, yes, but the point of crisis theory is that things are in crisis just as part of *being*' (Miéville 2000: 207). Yagharek, who is a Garuda, has come to have his ability to fly restored. After trying to map out various types of animal flying mechanism, Isaac decides to go back to one of his old research threads, crisis energy. Isaac explains that tapping into crisis energy simply involves creating a situation where the energy cannot dissipate, where it gets trapped and starts to feed on itself; in fact, where it turns into a kind of perpetual motion machine:

> 'The vodyanoi can tap crisis energy, I think. In a tiny, tiny way. It's paradoxical. You tap the existing crisis energy in the water to hold it in a shape it fights against, so you put it in *more* crisis . . . but then there's nowhere for the energy to go, so the crisis resolves itself by breaking down into its original form. But what if the vodyanoi used water they'd already . . . uh . . . *watercrafted*, and used it as a constituent for

some experiment that drew on the increased crisis energy ... Sorry, I'm digressing. The point is, I'm trying to work out a way for you to tap into your crisis energy, and channel it to fight. See, if I'm right, it's the only force that's always going to be ... *suffusing* you. And the more you fly, the more you're in crisis, the more you should be able to fly ... That's the theory, anyway.' (207–8)

Yet crisis energy is not only paradoxical in a tiny, tiny way. Contradiction is at the heart of crisis mathematics. In order to get the crisis engine to function, a number of complex calculations need to be made. These calculations are not a part of the matheme of Badiou and Meillassoux because they violate the law of non-contradiction: 'The engine applied rigorous crisis logic to the original operation. A mathematical command had created a perfect arithmetic analogue of a source code from disparate material, and that analogue was simultaneously identical to and *radically different* from the original it mimicked' (773, emphasis in original). A radical difference between a real object (source code, the original) and its qualities (disparate material, mimicry) is essential for the crisis engine to work. In order to function, the engine must reach two different conclusions at once, both $x = y + z$ and $x \neq y + z$. Once both equations are reached a crisis has been created. This operation is 'paradoxical, unsustainable' and features 'logic tearing itself apart' (773).

As discussed in the previous chapter, for Meillassoux, the law of non-contradiction cannot be broken because the identity of an object can never be two things at once. If this were true, then the possibility of identity would be lost:

> real contradiction can in no way be identified with the thesis of universal becoming, for in becoming, things must be this, *then* other than this; they are, *then* they are not. This does not involve *any* contradiction, since the entity is never simultaneously this and its opposite, existent and non-existent. A really illogical entity consists rather in the systematic destruction of the minimal conditions for all becoming – it suppresses the dimension of alterity required for the deployment of any process whatsoever, liquidating it in the formless being which must always already be what it is not. (Meillassoux 2009: 70)

Views on this point lie at the heart of speculative realism. Objects exist independently from thought. But how can this be known if

Subtraction and Contradiction: China Miéville

the only access to them is through human perception? Meillassoux argues that we have access to knowledge about objects which existed in a time before the emergence of humanity (the earth before the evolution of human life). This *'dia-chronicity'* (Meillassoux 2009: 112) is available through science. The validity of scientific statements is not what is at issue in this argument, but rather the basis for validating and falsifying such statements. Even if a complete synchronicity between human thought and the world were found, this would not invalidate objects existing outside human thought, because such a discovery

> would still have been a *discovery* – which is to say that it is precisely insofar as modern science is mathematized that it is capable of *raising* the question of a possible temporal hiatus between thinking and being – of construing the latter as a meaningful hypothesis, of giving it meaning, of rendering it tractable – whether in order to refute it or confirm it. (113)

The law of non-contradiction must remain intact in this scenario, for if a statement can be both true and false at the same time it is not logical, it is not a discovery, it is neither true nor false. In order to access a world outside of human thought Meillasssoux retains the matheme, and in order for the matheme to function in this way contradiction is not possible.

The crisis engine in *Perdido Street Station* works in another way. Its mathematics is one of contradiction. Contradiction is necessary for the production of crisis energy, contradiction is crisis energy. This is a 'paradoxical ontology' (Miéville 2000: 775) which functions differently from Meillassoux's reading of science. But it still relates to the question of objects existing independently of thought. For another way to approach the knowledge of objects outside human thought is to take contradiction as necessary. Objects both are and are not known to human thought at the same time. This is not contradictory per se, but something else. Certain truths are both told and not told at the same time. In Kazuo Ishiguro's novel *Never Let Me Go* (2005), clones are raised to be potential organ donors. Clone-rights activists have been able to bring up a number of young clones in a school environment. The children are not explicitly told their purpose in life until their early teens; however, this does not mean that they are unaware of their fate. Upon being told directly that their organs will eventually be harvested, the children are not surprised, feeling that they have already been 'told and not told' (Ishiguro 2005: 79) about what will happen to them. In another example from the novel, one student constantly teases the other with half-truths in such a subtle way that there was no way to test her statements: 'I hated it when Ruth hinted in this way. I was never sure, of course, if she was telling the truth, but since she wasn't actually "telling it", only hinting, it was never possible to challenge her' (57). In both examples, knowing is a paradox; something is both known and not known at the same time (Willems 2010: 49–50).

In a comment on philosopher Graham Priest's reading of contradiction, Harman says:

> Despite Priest's explicit denial of the fact, there are indirect ways to get at reality, even though direct ones remain impossible. There is no evident contradiction in saying that the enthymeme in rhetoric says something without saying it, that metaphor speaks indirectly in a way that cannot be cashed out in literal terms ... that jokes communicate information in ways that are ruined if these jokes are explained, and so forth. The commitment to thinking the in-itself without thinking it is neither impossible (as per Meillassoux) nor a true contradiction (as per Priest). Instead, it is simply the commitment to *philosophia*, loving something without having it and without ever being able to have it. How exactly this happens is sometimes difficult to determine, but we cannot address the difficulty either by locking ourselves inside the correlational circle and escaping by artificial and idealistic mathematical means, or by claiming that reality itself is contradictory ... Individuals are the root of all contradiction, but are not themselves contradictory. The reason Socrates can be both happy and sad is not because Socrates is *both* happy and sad, but because he is *neither*. The contradiction is grounded in something deeper and non-contradictory. (Harman 2013: 249–50)

Contradiction is found in the fusion and fission of a real object and its qualities. This is the 'deeper' aspect of contradiction that Harman mentions. In the same way, it is something other than being dialectical, as Carl Freedman claims (Freedman 2015: 40–1). It is also the issue that Mr Motley has with Lin. Mr Motley's body is an exercise both in the fusion of unfamiliar qualities to an object, and the separation of familiar qualities from an object through fission. This can be seen in the description of Lin's sculpture during the lattermost stage of its completion. Mr Motley has tortured Lin to such a degree that she can barely work at her sculpture. He believes that Isaac is trying to encroach on his drug trade, although he is not. Mr Motley has tortured Lin in order to get to Isaac. At the end of the novel, Isaac attempts to rescue Lin, but a slake-moth attacks her and sucks out enough of her subconscious to eradicate her sense of self. When Isaac sees the nearly finished sculpture for the first time, he describes it in terms of the fusion of qualities and objects that do not normally belong together. 'It was an incredible multi-coloured thing, a horrific kaleidoscopic figure of composite nightmares, limbs and eyes and legs sprouting in weird combinations' (Miéville 2000: 809). A kaleidoscopic nightmare of limbs and eyes jutting out in strange combinations is a representation of 'the tension between real objects that lie beyond access, and their sensual qualities which exist only when encountered' (Harman 2011a: 103). Mr Motley's body is the expression of the tension between his essence and his image, or between Mr Motley as a real object and the sensual qualities that Lin and Isaac confront.

This is a description of how the crisis engine works in the novel, but not of what it does. The function of the engine is that it can enact any kind of change whatsoever, one of those things being the restoration of flight for Yagharek. As Isaac describes it: '"But to be honest, Yag, this is much bigger than that. If I can *really* unlock crisis energy for you, then your case becomes, frankly, a pretty paltry concern. We're talking about forces and energy that could *totally* change ... everything ..."' (Miéville 2000: 208). Crisis energy is similar to a concept Harman mentions only at the end of 'Offshore Drilling Rig': *allure* (Harman 2010: 51). Allure and crisis energy are similar in two ways. First, allure is born out of fusion: 'allure is a special and intermittent experience in which the intimate bond between a thing's unity and its plurality of [specific qualities] somehow partially disintegrates' (Harman 2005: 143). Secondly, allure is similar to how Isaac describes crisis energy, in that it has the ability to change everything. For Harman, 'Allure is the principle of revolution as such, since only allure make quantum leaps from one state of reality into the next by generating a new relation between objects' (Harman 2005: 244). Crisis energy and allure share a similar structure: the possibility for change is connected to the withdrawn nature of objects. It is this structure that Mr Motley represents, and that Lin struggles to capture in her art. In fact, Lin seems to sense that there is some danger in capturing crisis energy in plastic form, for, although Mr Motley and crisis energy are not directly linked in the novel, Lin knows that she needs to keep the idea out of her mind while in front of model, for although she doubted he had the powers of telepathy, 'she was risking nothing' (Miéville 2000: 252) and feared what might happen if he got a hold of the idea.

In 'Offshore Drilling Rig,' Harman states an interest in Miéville's concept of crisis energy, although he leaves it to Miéville to discuss it in his own words. However, Harman then goes on to create a mythical crisis engine of his own: an offshore drilling rig. The role of the oil rig in the contact of objects with each other is taken up in the next section. What is important here is that the myth of the oil rig foregrounds the tension that objects have with each other in that there is always a darkness involved in contact. This kind of tension is not limited to certain objects or not a part of others: it is a feature of every object. No special crisis engine machine is needed. 'Why not grant *all* objects the power to act as oil rigs, each draining phantasmal energy from all of the others? We can literally imagine all rabbits, monkeys, electrons, acids, and freight trains as equipped with pipes and tubing of their own. All real objects of every size now have the power to interact with all other things, at the price of turning them into images' (Harman 2010: 48). *Perdido Street Station* does not function in this way: crisis energy is limited to the crisis engine.

However, Mr Motley foregrounds another element of crisis energy; the role of movement. Mr Motley insists on Lin seeing his body not in terms of what it was or how it is divergent, but rather in terms of flux and change, of the movement between image and essence. In 'The Sleeping Zebra', Harman also focuses on the role of movement when he says that

> the components of my body change constantly without my always becoming different as a result. It is true that a point may be reached where this change in pieces is sufficient to destroy me. Yet that point must actually be reached; it is not attained automatically with every slight shift in the infrastructure of human and inhuman things. (Harman 2010: 70)

For Harman, this change has two functions. Multiple perspectives function as an indirect strategy for representing essence, and they can also show how dark objects are possible (Willems

2015: 8–9). So when Harman says that 'if an object can exist apart from any specific situation, it can also exist apart from any situation at all' (Harman 2010: 70), he refers to dark or sleeping objects. It is the sleeping or dark aspect of Mr Motley that tricks Lin. She thinks she has problems representing the movement of his parts, but really she cannot formulate his essence because Mr Motley's essence lies in contradiction. Mr Motley insists on being represented as a sleeping object by demanding that both his image and essence be present in the sculpture. Lin struggles to do it. One of the reasons is that she sees the world as an essence-less assemblage.

Mr Motley's body is dark, unknowable. This idea will guide this reading of *Perdido Street Station* into its final phase, a discussion of an experience of non-knowledge, the framework for which is provided by the spider-like Weavers. What is interesting about the Weavers is that they are creatures that are represented as being, in part, removed from understanding. This removal is key because it is what Mr Motley seems to think Lin is missing in her extensive way of seeing the world, although what she is missing is also the essence of herself:

> 'Maybe I'm too hard on you,' Mr Motley said reflectively. 'I mean ... this piece before us makes it clear that you *have* a sense of the ruptured moment, even if your question suggests the opposite ... So maybe,' he continued slowly, 'you yourself *contain* that moment. Part of you understands without recourse to words, even if your higher mind asks questions in a format which renders an answer impossible.' (Miéville 2000: 141)

No Hidden Messages

The crisis engine is not just a machine made of pistons and gears which captures crisis energy, turning it into a kind of perpetual motion machine. The crisis engine is actually a node connecting three different elements that never come into direct contact with each other. In order to get the engine to work, Isaac needs to mediate the three entities: a human being, the construct and a Weaver.

The human is a dying man who is still sound of mind. He is forced against his will to be used as a funnel through which the crisis energy pours in order to attract the remaining slake-moths at the end of the novel, drawing them to their deaths. This man's body is destroyed in the process. His name is Andrej Shelbornek.

The construct is a collection of steam- and oil-powered robots which have gained consciousness. The centre of this collection is an animated bunch of junk in a garbage dump. 'The rubbish was a body. A vast skeleton of industrial waste twenty-five feet from skull to toe' (Miéville 2000: 547). This collection of circuitry, machines, tubes and valves is different from Mr Motley in one important sense: its form is independent of human intervention. 'It was a construct, an enormous construct, formed of cast-off pieces and stolen engines. Thrown together and powered without the intervention of human design' (548). At some points the construct, which is connected to many other smaller individual constructs which have gained sentience throughout the city, is indistinguishable from the garbage in which it lies. 'The Construct Council had sentience, but no feelings' (709). The construct is a collection of inanimate objects fused with animate properties. It speaks to Isaac through a human body fissioned from the properties of life: its brain has been partially removed in order to wire it to the construct. The construct is thus even weirder than Mr Motley because it features both the fusion and fission of objects and properties.

In *Vibrant Matter*, Jane Bennett describes a scene where a number of pieces of garbage come to life. She comes across a glove, pollen, a dead rat, a bottle cap and a stick of wood lying in the street. All of the objects are inanimate: they are dead, junk, debris, similar to the elements that make up the construct. The coming to life of these objects means that they had the ability 'to produce effects' in the viewer (Bennett 2010: 5). One of the strengths of Bennett's book is her argument that the power that things have to affect is 'not entirely reducible to the context in which (human) subjects set them' (5), thus implicating the effects that objects have on each other outside of human observation or thought. However, Bennett still privileges the network or assemblage of objects interacting together, as seen in the collection of debris she sees on the street (Harman 2014: 98). Here is a similar issue as that found in DeLanda: there is no room for essence, the main lesson that Mr Motley provided with his ever-changing form.

One of the ways in which the crisis engine is not a network is the way that its three comprising elements are cut off from each other by a short circuit. The Construct Council agrees to help Isaac because it calculates that once it is connected to the crisis engine it will be able to absorb information about how the engine is made and build one of its own. But Isaac does not want that to happen. He installs a breaker in order to cut the construct off from the information flow: '"That's a breaker," he said, "a circuit-valve. One-way flow only. I'm cutting the Council off from this lot"' (Miéville 2000: 761). The crisis engine is not an assemblage. In fact, it would not work as one. Contradiction lies at the heart of the energy it generates. Part of this contradiction is a cutting off from belonging.

The third creature that makes up the crisis engine, a Weaver, is also a figure of both connection and withdrawal. The Weaver is both described and unknowable. It is understandable and enigmatic. In other words, the Weaver is its own short circuit. The Weavers are the only beings in the novel who are able to defeat the slake-moths unaided. The slake-moths feed off dreams, and the Weavers have no 'hidden' dreams to speak of. They are examples of Harman's reading of tool-being in that nothing lies unveiled in them to uncover, and yet they are considered the strangest creatures in the book:

> The Weaver thought in a *continuous, incomprehensible, rolling stream of awareness*. There were *no layers* to the Weaver's mind, there was *no ego* to control the lower functions, *no animal cortex* to keep the mind grounded. For the Weaver, there were *no dreams at night, no hidden messages* from the secret corners of the mind, no mental clearout of accrued garbage bespeaking an orderly consciousness. For the Weaver, *dreams and consciousness were one. The Weaver dreamed of being conscious and its consciousness was its dream*, in an *endless unfathomable stew of image and desire and cognition and emotion*. (Miéville 2000: 769, emphasis mine)

The way in which the Weavers function is such that there is no tension between a hidden, deep aspect and the manner in which they are experienced. They are described in more detail than any other beings in the novel. They are compared to spiders, they have a teardrop-shaped abdomen, are taut and smooth, have a head the size of a person's chest and pairs of thin and tiny hands besides their more normal spider limbs (401–3). Yet this does not mean that their surface being is completely understandable: they remain creatures that are difficult to know. They are 'utterly alien' beings (402) which are 'objects of beauty disentangled from the fabric of reality itself' (407), thus functioning as relatively dark objects. The Weavers are creatures of what Miéville calls in an essay the high weird, meaning monsters which are 'indescribable and formless *as well as being* and/or *although they are* and/or *in so far as they are* described with an excess of specificity, an accursed share of impossible somatic precision' (Miéville 2008: 105). The key image of the high weird is the tentacle, which is strange but removed from history, being without 'mythic resonance' (Miéville 2008: 105). Yet the tentacle is also an image of reaching out, of connection, and not just separation. Donna Haraway uses the paradox of the connection and separation of the tentacle to discuss the Anthropocene. In 'Tentacular Thinking: Anthropocene, Capitalocene, Chthulucene', Haraway says

> The tentacular are not disembodied figures; they are cnidarians, spiders, fingery beings like humans and raccoons, squid, jellyfish, neural extravaganzas, fibrous entities, flagellated beings, myofibril braids, matted and felted microbial and fungal tangles, probing creepers, swelling roots, reaching and climbing tendrilled ones. The tentacular are also nets and networks, it critters, in and out of clouds. (Haraway 2016)

While the concept of networks has been criticised for its lack of attention to essence in this chapter, Haraway's concept of tentacular thinking is similar to how Harman reads the tool-being of Heidegger in the way that objects are always strange, even in their fully functioning state. Everyday strangeness takes place because all objects are relatively dark objects, in the sense that all objects are withdrawn. The Weavers have no latent content: their dream is manifest. It is this aspect that saves them from the slake-moths. And again, it functions as an illustration of tool-being because two points are illustrated (Harman 2002: 97–8): the Weavers do not represent negation – i.e. ($n - 1$) – but rather the experience of their strangeness is the experience of their everydayness; and secondly, nothing in the Weavers is ever unveiled, in the Heideggerian sense, meaning that there is something that always remains hidden with them (as with all objects); they are not revealed in their totality.

In other words, although the Weavers have no hidden depth, they remain partially unknowable. This point is illustrated in the way the Weavers talk, which has similarities to the descriptive modes of Damon Knight and Joanna Russ discussed in the first chapter. It was stated above that descriptive strategies that made no attempt at realism in the traditional sense illustrated two kinds of tension within an object: the fission of an object from its expected qualities, and the fusion of the qualities of an object with the qualities of another in an equally unexpected way. Fission is a figure of separation, and fusion of joining. The way the Weavers speak is similar, as seen in the following example: 'GOOD GRIEF AND GRACE THE SPILLING SLOSH GROWS MINDFUL BUT MIND IT IS NO MIND ... ONE AND ONE INTO ONE WON'T GO BUT IT IS ONE AND TWO AT ONCE WILL WE WON HOW WIN HOW WONDERFUL ...' (Miéville 2000: 775). Here there is both a separation of words from sense and unexpected connections between one word and another. The way that one word or idea is connected to another, with the alliteration and repetition of 'WE WON HOW WIN HOW WONDERFUL', for example, is more important than any hidden meaning that lies underneath what they are saying, although at times what the Weavers say does become interpretable to the humans listening to them. Yet just as the consciousness of the Weavers is a dream, and their dreams are their consciousness, there is no depth to what they are saying whatsoever: the Weavers are figures of the surface, but of a surface that indicates the impossibility of knowing the Weavers in any kind of totality.

The fission between sense and understanding is similar to what Mr Motley said Lin needed to do in order to see him, to have an experience of his body separate from the words and images she would fit it into. The Weaver is in itself incomprehensible to humanity; this is because the Weaver is all *'image and essence'*, as Mr Motley stated above. However, it needs to be kept in mind that this image and essence is still something that is seen. It is a relatively dark object, meaning that more of the object is withdrawn than is present, and thus the manner in which it is open to unconventional connections with other objects is foregrounded.

This look at Miéville's work has foregrounded a number of aspects of both speculative realism and sf. Lin is a figure of the assemblage because of the insectile structure of her vision. The way she sees the world is similar to the double-vision found in Gaiman's work because the world is dismantled into parts. However, one limit of this approach is that it denies essences to objects, insisting that their being is construed through their position in a network.

Mr Motley, on the other hand, demands that Lin see his body as image and essence, a task she fails to do. The assemblage of her vision is unable to translate his body into a sculpture. Mr Motley's body cannot be calculated, it is not subject to the matheme. Instead it is a figure full of contradiction, a feature that is paralleled in the construction of the crisis engine.

Crisis energy needs contradiction to function. In other words, crisis energy is contradiction. The 'paradoxical ontology' Miéville describes is also found in the figure of the short circuit. The construct is a network of robots which Isaac cuts off from the feedback loop, thus inserting a sense of the withdrawn into his invention. This not only protects Isaac from giving control of crisis energy to the construct, but it also represents the withdrawn nature, or essence, of all objects everywhere.

Yet while a figure like Mr Motley includes change in his body, he does not offer any clues to how change in an object can take place. The manner in which an object can modulate from one phase to another is the focus of the next chapter.

Notes

1. Another way to put it is that for DeLanda, an assemblage/network relates to the new in that it can feature certain emerging properties. For example, in an interpersonal network, the following emergent properties can be described: *density*, or 'a measure of the intensity of connectivity among indirect links'; *stability*, in that there is no tension created between nodes with different attitudes (my friends' friends are not my enemies) and that proximity to other causes similar attitudes to be created; and *solidarity*, although it does not matter what form it takes: 'some members may be motivated by the feelings of togetherness which getting involved in the arrears of the community produces in them, others by altruism, and yet others by strict calculations' (DeLanda 2016: 56–7). However, it is not the specific characteristics that emerge from a network that are the focus here, but rather that in an assemblage there is emergence from parts in a relation of exteriority.

   In other words, what is important about the assemblage is simply the way in which the relation of parts is foregrounded; as Deleuze and Guattari put it: 'There are only multiplicities of multiplicities forming a single *assemblage*, operating in the same *assemblage*: packs in masses and masses in packs' (Deleuze and Guattari 2005: 34).

Assemblages are gatherings of parts in that they can be disassembled and reassembled; or as DeLanda puts it elsewhere, assemblages are both irreducible and decomposable (DeLanda 2011: 185). These features are taken up here in the discussion of Mr Motley and movement along with how Harman expands Bruno Latour's version of network theory. Such plurality is reflected in the world in which *Perdido Street Station* is set, for, as Nicolas Birns argues, in this world 'racial diversity is not plurality leading to a harmonious, diverse multiculturalism, but incommensurability' (Birns 2009: 203). This incommensurability of parts is due to a lack of essence; or, as Jean-Jacques Lecercle has noted (in a discussion of language), there is no 'subject' in relation to the assemblage: 'An assemblage never refers to a subject . . . there is no subject who is the sender of the utterance, no subject whose utterance is reported. The source of the utterance is a collective, whether social, national or political' (Lecercle 2002: 188). In the context of Gaiman's *American Gods*, the assemblage was seen when it was not just, for example, the whole of Mr Nancy that was seen; rather, when double-vision was experienced, the assemblage of all the beings and things that Mr Nancy had ever been became visible, without any essential Mr Nancy lying underneath. In *Perdido Street Station* things are different: Mr Motley insists not just on the assemblage of his parts, but also on the tension they have with the pure presence of his essence.

5

Tension and Phase: Doris Lessing

> How can you love anyone who is a castrated You?
> Joanna Russ, *The Female Man* (1975)

The previous chapters laid out a number of ways in which objects can be surprising. The dismantling of language, vision and the world is one strategy for creating this surprise. In the Anthropocene the world is falling apart around us. If we are to go forward, this falling apart will need to become a part of the solution, meaning part of a vision of a less destructive future.

Up to this point, while the weirdness of objects has been developed, the change weirdness can cause has been relatively ignored. This chapter aims to correct this. Following a number of arguments laid out in Graham Harman's *Immaterialism*, Doris Lessing's novel *The Cleft* (2007) is used to develop the notion of when an object enters a new phase of its existence, and when such change does not take place. The symbiosis of one object and another potentially causes change to occur. However, this only takes place when certain conditions are met. These conditions are similar to the definition of metaphor developed above. In Neil Gaiman's novels, strong metaphors take place when two terms are neither too close nor too distant in meaning from each other. The right balance can create a certain kind of tension which makes a metaphor work. The creation of this tension is essential for a new phase of an object to take place.

The Cleft is about castration and power; the focus of the reading here is on the way in which castration can lead to the separation of an object from its common qualities, thus causing change. *The Cleft* was published the same year Lessing won the Nobel Prize for Literature. It is a fable-like story that presumes that in the beginning of humankind there were only females, who would become impregnated by the moon (Lessing 2008: 11). The novel tells how the first males, called either 'Monsters' or 'Squirts', came about, and it focuses on the changes they wrought on the society of the Clefts. The arrival of the males in the all-female society of the Clefts foregrounds two aspects of the Zug effect noted above: the role of language, as seen in the discussion of *The Road*, and the ability of objects to come together in unexpected ways, as seen in the previous chapters. The manner in which Lessing's novel extends these arguments is to consider how change, seen as movement above, is possible at moments of castration, or of an object in a state of both identification and non-identification with itself, as seen in the failed authority of Horsa at the end of the novel. From a theoretical point of view this reading is performed along with the thought of, among others, Avital Ronell, especially in *Loser Sons* (2012), in which it is posited that the disruptive power of stupidity actually derives from the aporia of authority. In short, this chapter is concerned with the roles of both stasis and change at the heart of the dark object.

Time and Space

When males are first born to females in *The Cleft* they are considered monsters, 'The deformed ones, the freaks, the cripples' (Lessing 2008: 8). The male babies are all disposed of by being left on a high rock to be taken away by large eagles that the females assume use the babies for food (13). Eventually the women learn that the eagles do not eat the boys but rather deposit them some way from where the Clefts live so that they can live their lives as boys and then as young men (15).

The Clefts are impregnated by the moon or the sea. They give birth to both Clefts and Monsters (8). However, the difference between the sexes has no real impact on the Clefts. Although there were males and females, the Clefts did not think in terms of difference or separation: 'We didn't think like that, no, we didn't, that every person had to have a name separate from all the others' (11). Change only became possible after the Clefts started having sex with some of the boys who had been carried away by the eagles. Sex began with a gang rape that ended in the death of one of the Clefts (46–7). There are two major changes caused by this coupling of Clefts and Monsters: it is 'how we became Hes and Shes, and learned to say I as well as we'; and 'some time after that, we, the Clefts, lost the power to give birth without them, the Monsters' (20–1). Giving birth to males is not the decisive change in the life of the Clefts – coupling with them is.

Although Monsters were created at birth, their presence did not change the reality of the Clefts that bore them. It was only when Monsters were born out of sexual union that the lives of the Clefts entered a different phase: they began to think of themselves in terms of sex, they began to differentiate individuals and groups, and, as one of the records of the time puts it, 'I say *think* but did we think? Perhaps a new kind of thinking began like everything else when the Monsters started being born' (8). The change that takes place in the Clefts and the Monsters takes place through symbiosis. At the same time, change does not take place immediately after the first rape and the birth of the first child generated by heterosexual coupling. The change takes a while, but the symbiosis between male and female creates the possibility, dormant at first, for a new phase of life to begin.

In *Immaterialism*, Graham Harman adds a new dimension to object-oriented ontology: change is most likely to arise from a meeting of one object with another (Harman 2016: 46). This change is not necessarily seen in the new things that an object, in this example the community of Clefts, can do, but rather in the new thing they are. This new reality can lie dormant, or be withdrawn from action, as it is for the Clefts immediately after they start having sex with the Monsters. In this sense stasis is the fundamental state of objects. Yet symbiosis with a new person, place or idea can be 'life-changing', meaning that this relationship 'changes the reality of one of its *relata*, rather than merely resulting in discernible mutual impact' (49). However, although Harman provides examples of new phases of reality for his example of the Dutch East India Company, he does not set out a programme for how these new phases can be identified. This will be done by exploring changes in both time and space in the novel.

Time and space are derivative from more fundamental properties of objects in the world. This was developed in the last chapter as essence, meaning how any object has properties that are not exhausted by the way the object currently appears (Harman 2013: 27), or by the ways in which an object interacts with another. This has been seen in the investigation of dark objects throughout this book, where objects are considered to have qualities that are hidden, and that may be revealed by a change in circumstance.

However, they may never be revealed at all, eternally sleeping although no less real; this remainder is what sets Harman's theory off from ideas of the assemblage or the network, where qualities only become real when they interact with other qualities (Harman 2010: 14).

Along with essence, Harman develops both time and space in relation to something more fundamental, the interplay between objects and properties. Time is the tension between a sensual object and its sensual qualities, meaning the way in which an observed tree looks different from different perspectives, but is still a tree (Harman 2011a: 100). Time is about movement, 'shifting features' and the relationship between static and changing qualities. Space, on the other hand, is the combination of relation and non-relation: I am not in my car but I am still connected to it because I could easily walk outside and get in it. Yet at the same time, the object of my car is always withdrawn: even as I drive it down the road I can never exhaust its qualities completely with either knowledge or use. 'Space is the tension between concealed real objects and the sensual qualities associated with them' (Harman 2011a: 100) and it is a large aspect of the definition of dark objects. What is common to both time and space is the way in which tension can be located at the heart of their definitions (108–9). Again, this indicates the problem that Lin had in making Mr Motley's sculpture in *Perdido Street Station*: she could not represent this tension in her work, instead she was looking for a solution to these differences.

New phases arise in *The Cleft* when 'the tension of identity-in-difference' (Harman 2013: 17) becomes an issue in symbiosis. The conceit of the novel is that a historian in Roman times is collating the scattered documents relating to the early period before the advent of males. The first 'historical' document presented by the narrator (although not chronologically the first) initially represents a difficulty with language, then backtracks into a difficulty with thinking. The quote, part of which was cited above, ends by describing a difficulty with time:

> what you don't understand is that what I say now can't be true because I am telling you how I see it all now, but it was all different then. Even words I use are new, I don't know where they came from, sometimes it seems that most of the words in our mouths are this new talk. I say I, and again I, I do this and I think that, but *then* we wouldn't say I, it was we. We thought we.

> I say *think* but did we think? Perhaps a new kind of thinking began like everything else when the Monsters started being born. I am sorry, you keep saying the truth, you want the truth, and that is how we saw you, all of you, at first. Monsters. The deformed ones, the freaks, the cripples.
>
> When was then? I don't know. *Then* was a very long time ago, that's all I know. (Lessing 2008: 7–8, italics in original)

Time is the instability of sensual qualities in relation to a sensual object. In this passage, the speaker foregrounds the difference between the way that events are perceived now and the way they were perceived in the past. The events are sensual objects because they are experienced, in this case, by human perception. The change in sensual qualities is indicated by the way that the words used in the present to describe the event are different from the words used in the past. This difference between present and past descriptions is a tension in time.

Yet there is also a tension in space. The speaker is removed from the event that took place, yet she also has a connection to it through stories handed down over generations. At the same time, the speaker indicates that the Clefts who were alive during the event (the birth of the Monsters) did not understand what was going on completely. When she says 'I say *think* but did we think?' it means at least two things. One is that a new kind of awareness arose with the Monsters, meaning a new phase of life began. At the same time it shows that aspects of the event were withdrawn from the sensual experience of the Clefts. This latter meaning is an indication of a tension in space, which comes about with the contradictory situation of both a relation to the event (they experienced it) coupled with a non-relation to it (parts of it remained unavailable to experience). The combination of tensions in time and space is used here as an indicator that a new phase in the life of the Clefts has begun.

Such tensions are a large part of what separates sf from other genres. As Mark Rose argues, the alienation of sf space arises out of nineteenth-century industrialisation, urbanisation and crises of faith (Rose 1981: 52). In a similar vein, Rose argues that Darwin's evolutionary revolution, which placed humanity as a part of nature, alienated humanity from nature, foregrounding a tension between the timescale of a human life and the geological timescale of nature (98–9). From a materialist point of view,

Ben Woodard argues that the torsions of space found in sf 're-emphasize the unpredictability of a materiality made of powers and flows and not objects, or at least not objects that are anything more than temporary arrests or slowings-down of those powers' (Woodard 2013: 28). Yet as argued in the previous chapter, while the materiality of contingency of Elie Ayache foregrounds the non-chronological role of change, the contradiction that it denies, along with the withdrawn nature of the objects that are changing, puts too much of an emphasis on flux and flow, ignoring the static, sleeping nature of all the objects, material and immaterial, around us. This is important because static withdrawal is necessary in order to create the tension of space and time in Lessing's novel.

Tension and Phase

In *The Cleft*, the paradox of space, meaning the tension of coupling identification and non-identification, takes place a number of times. The same speaker from the passage quoted above provides another example in the shape of her name:

> My name is Maire. There is always someone called Maire. I was born into the family of Cleft Watchers, like my mother and like her mother – these words are new. If everyone gives birth, as soon as they are old enough, everyone is a mother, and you don't have to say Mother. (Lessing 2008: 9)

For the speaker in the historical text, the language used to describe the situation is connected to the rift taking place when the Monsters are born from sexual coupling. There are 'Males, females. New words, new people' (13). This is a different strategy of tension than was found in *The Road*. In McCarthy's novel, the father is a figure of useful language which is part of a world, now lost, while the boy eschews language as a figure of the world lost. In *The Cleft*, language itself is seen as problematic, not just the lack of it. As Maire describes:

> My name Maire is one of the new words.
> We didn't think like that, no, we didn't, that every person had to have a name separate from all the others. Sometimes I think we lived in a kind of dream, a sleep, everything slow and easy and nothing ever

happening but the moon being bright and big, and the red flowers washing down The Cleft. (11)

The dream state is pre-spatial because there is no tension between relation and non-relation. This passage indicates that the arrival of non-identification among the Clefts is not just about a removal 'from themselves' but also a removal from nature. This is a very traditional expression of the collocation of males with artificiality and woman with the natural (Salvaggio 1988: 33). However, the role of females and males in the novel is not so straightforward. The change they bring about is not simply a removal, but a contradictory removal and not-removal from what came before. This contradictory position has been present in many of the texts looked at so far, and has in general fallen under the rubric of the Zug effect, meaning the presence of relatively dark objects within a novel. Another example from the first author looked at, Neil Gaiman, can be used to redefine the effect.

In Gaiman's *American Gods*, Shadow mirrors the economy of the Zug effect through his relationship with his dead wife, Laura. Shadow, who has just been released from a three-year stint in prison, comes home to a wife recently deceased. Laura has been killed in a car crash. The driver was Shadow's best friend, with whom his wife had been having an affair while he was locked up. Upon his release, Shadow meets Mr Wednesday, who seems to be more-than-human in some way. On the first night he spends outside jail, he is visited by Laura. She says she is there to watch over him. Laura is flesh-and-blood, although still dead, smelling of mothballs and tasting of bile when they kiss. In a moment of both touch and distance, it is actually the physical contact of the kiss that convinces Shadow that she is dead: 'Laura's tongue flickered into Shadow's mouth. It was cold, and dry, and it tasted of cigarettes and of bile. If Shadow had had any doubts as to whether his wife was dead or not, they ended then' (Gaiman 2004: 70). It is only when Shadow experiences Laura as both relation and non-relation that is able to start to begin a phase of mourning her death (72–3).

In *The Cleft*, the tension of time and space, indicating that a new phase of life has been entered, is seen when the Monsters venture back to the rocks where the females live. They describe what they see thus:

> They lay on the rocks, the waves splashing them, like seals, like sick seals, because they are pale and seals are mostly black. At first we thought they were seals. Singing seals? We had never heard seals sing, though some say they have heard them. Then we knew they were the Clefts. (Lessing 2008: 29)

The Clefts are first like seals, then not like seals but sick seals, because they are not black like seals but pale. This is an expression of the simultaneous relation and non-relation of space, except that there is no distance between the Monsters and the Clefts: they are in the same vicinity, but the paradox of space is still present. Then there is a tension between the sensual object of the sick seals and the sensual quality of singing: when these two are fused together there is a tension because it is an unusual combination. This tension leads to revelation: the real objects are the Clefts, not seals, nor sick seals, nor singing sick seals. This tension leads to a break in the life of the Monsters between pre-Cleft and Cleft. A new phase has begun.

Yet not all phase changes are accompanied by tension. In fact, some of them are notable for their lack of tension. In Octavia Butler's *Dawn* (1987), the first book of her *Xenogenesis Trilogy* (later renamed *Lilith's Brood*), the earth has been destroyed by nuclear war. Aliens, called the Oankali, have rescued a few remaining humans, brought them to their large spaceship orbiting Earth, and put them to sleep for over 200 years before beginning a programme to repopulate the planet. Lilith is a human who has been woken up in order to bond with the Oankalis and eventually train other humans to accept their new situation. Living with the Oankalis is hard because they are so alien. The main indicator of strangeness, which China Miéville indicated in the last chapter, is tentacles. As Lilith experiences them:

> The tentacles were elastic. At her shout, some of them lengthened, stretching toward her. She imagined big, slowly writhing, dying night crawlers stretched along the sidewalk after a rain. She imagined small, tentacle sea slugs – nudibranchs – grown impossibly to human size and shape, and, obscenely, sounding more like a human being than some humans. Yet she needed to hear him speak. Silent, he was utterly alien. (Butler 2007: 14)

Tentacles are one of the main features that remain alien to Lilith and the other humans who are woken up (33, 48, 191). It is only when Lilith is able to form a symbiosis with an Oankali first though sex (162) and then by saving one's life by stripping naked and holding a severed tentacle against the alien body so it can heal again (232) that tension disappears and a new phase of her life begins. In other words, what is key to change in *Dawn* is not tension, but, as with *American Gods* and *The Cleft*, symbiosis between one being and another. In the case of Gaiman's novel the symbiosis is between Shadow and Laura, in Lessing's between the Clefts and the Monsters.[1]

Sex and Authority

In Harman's *Immaterialism*, many of the phase changes of the Dutch East India Company are changes for the worse, including slavery and murder (Harman 2016: 57–60). In a similar way, it should not be assumed that all of the changes introduced by the males into the society of the Clefts are of a positive nature. In a very basic sense the males are terrible. For example, the first song they create as a group takes up the theme of the annihilation of the Clefts:

> Kill the Clefts,
> Kill them, kill them,
> They are our enemies
> Kill them all. (Lessing 2008: 28)

In addition, the males are responsible for actual crimes, such as rape and murder (46–7). In another example, the young males are full of disgust when they first see the Clefts after having been thrown out of their company. The males witness a birth:

> What we were seeing had to surprise, no matter what we had been told. More, we were disgusted. Those large pale *things* rolling in the waves, with their disgusting clefts, which we saw for the first time, and as we looked, from the cleft of one of those slow lolling creatures emerged a bloody small-sized thing. We saw it was a tiny Cleft. Only later did we reason that it might just as well have been a Squirt – one of us. We ran back, past the big Cleft in the cliffs, with its reddish stains and fuzzy growths. We ran and we vomited and we went back up the mountain and over down to our place. (29–30)

This passage is greatly different to the one quoted above, in which the Monsters first saw the Clefts and compared them to seals. In that passage, a tension was developed in the identification of the Clefts as Clefts. In the birthing passage quoted here, there is very little confusion, and no tension. Only in 'Only later did we reason that it might just as well have been a Squirt' is there the slightest hint of tension between an object and the way it is perceived, but this is short-lived and without any real consequences for the parties involved. Yet this is a lack of tension without symbiosis, so it is unlike what took place in Butler's *Dawn*. Instead, the birth scene in *The Cleft* is described from an attitude of disgust, which ends in them vomiting and leaving the scene to go back home, instead of being an experience of a life-changing event.

So what is the difference between the first passage and the second? Sex. The Clefts gave birth to males from the very beginning, but this did not cause an existential crisis until the males were caused by sex with males, rather than through impregnation by the moon or the waves. In the birthing passage, it is not the creation of one sex or another that is disturbing. This is, and has been, the basic fact of their existence, and is therefore too strong a tie between them to lead to transformation (Harman 2016: 89). On the other hand, symbiosis through sex is represented as a phase-making event. It causes a tension between objects and qualities that the birthing of difference is too fundamental to contain.

The central role of sex has grounded many strands of feminism in new forms of materialism. As Rosi Braidotti argues, there are two main types of feminist materialisms. A focus on embodiment develops the transversal of bodies and power. This led to a sensitivity to the entwining of body and mind, nature and culture (Dolphijn and van der Tuin 2012: 21). Another consequence is that 'oppositional consciousness combines critique with creativity' which 'does not stop at critical deconstruction but moves on to the active production of alternatives' (22).

Sex demands attention to the material in such discussions. Yet sex also has an additional function in *The Cleft*. It mediates. In the last chapter, the essence of objects was seen to be the part of an object that is withdrawn. Objects are always relatively dark, and the speculation of sf is one mode that can help make this idea understandable. However, because objects are always relatively dark, they can never come into direct contact with each other. Instead, they come into contact with their sensual qualities, and these qualities make contact with each other (Harman 2011a: 72–5). Yet it is the tension between sensual qualities and real objects which can be a sign of change. It is in the realm of sensual qualities that symbiosis takes place, and it is the sensual that sex represents in Lessing's novel.

In opposition to contrasting sex (male/female) and gender (masculine/feminine), two fundamental texts have rescheduled sex in order to highlight it as a force of tension: Camille Paglia's *Sexual Personae* sees sex as the mediator between nature and culture, and Judith Butler's *Bodies that Matter* aims to foreground the constraints imposed by sex on the performativity of gender. What both have in common is that sex is not in a positive or negative position, but rather occupies a locus of creating an opportunity for change through disruption.

For Paglia, 'Sexuality and eroticism are the intricate intersection of nature and culture' (Paglia 1991: 1). Nature is not good or bad; rather, it is excess:

> Everything is melting in nature. We think we see objects, but our eyes are slow and partial. Nature is blooming and withering in long puffy respirations, rising and falling in oceanic wave-motion. A mind that opened itself fully to nature without sentimental preconception would be glutted by nature's coarse materialism, its relentless superfluity. An apple tree laden with fruit: how peaceful, how picturesque. But remove the rosy filter of humanism from our gaze and look again. See nature spuming and frothing, its mad spermatic bubbles endlessly spilling out and smashing in that inhuman round of waste, rot and carnage. From the jammed glassy cells of sea roe to the feathery spores poured into the air from bursting green pods, nature is a festering hornet's nest of aggression and overkill [. . .] Nature is the seething excess of being. (28)

It is difficult to see exactly what is 'excessive' about nature as described in this passage. On the one hand it falls into one of the dangers of the Anthropocene, what Timothy Morton calls 'ecomimesis'. This means that the passage engages in a form of narration that acts as 'an authenticating device' (Morton 2007: 33), using an abundance of detail in order to try and convince the reader that the author has real access to nature, outside of the page. However, Paglia is using ecomimesis in order to foreground its shortcomings. Her use of verbs such as *melting, blooming, withering, rising, falling*, all of which are found in just the first sentence, are not meant to convince the reader that nature is real, but rather to show how nature is always in excess of language. This is the 'excess of being' that Paglia claims for nature at the end of the quotation.

However, this is not an argument for idealism, since Paglia locates sex as a mediator between nature and culture. The latter, as Paglia describes it, was born from males and their need to aim, through urination and ejaculation, and through their always projecting 'into the beyond' through erections (Paglia 1991: 20, 21). In *The Cleft* the males reflect this aspect of Paglia's thought first of all in their names: Squirts. However, as seen in the difference of two passages from the novel above, there are moments when a different kind of symbiosis takes place. For Paglia, sex is a name for this symbiosis. This is because sex takes on the 'as' structure which was brought forth by Harman from Heidegger's reading of the tool: 'Sex is the point of contact between man and nature, where morality and good intentions fall to primitive urges. I call it an intersection' (3). The males in *The Cleft* represent not only masculinity (culture, in Paglia's sense) but also a point of contact between nature and culture through the introduction of the sexual act to the once-all-Mothers females. The figure of Horsa, one of the first children born from sex between male and female, will both clarify and problematise the way in which this intersection functions.

But first, another reading of the role of sex comes from Butler's revision of the way in which performativity was extracted from her work. In her classic *Gender Trouble*, Butler does focus on the relation of sex to gender, as can be seen in her discussion of Simone de Beauvoir and Monique Wittig:

> Simone de Beauvoir wrote in *The Second Sex* that 'one is not born a woman, but rather *becomes* one.' The phrase is odd, even nonsensical, for how can one become a woman if one wasn't a woman all along? And who is this 'one' who does the becoming? Is there some human who becomes its gender at some point in time? Is it fair to assume that this human was not its gender before it became its gender? How does one 'become' a gender? And, perhaps most pertinently, when does this mechanism arrive on the cultural scene to transform the human subject into a gendered subject? (Butler 1990: 111)

Here the human before gender is raised as a problem but not given much space, as Butler soon closes it off by showing how

Wittig sees sex itself as a *'gendered* category' (112). In this sense Butler's thought is fairly close to Paglia's, but with an important difference. Both see sex as unnatural: Paglia sees it as a mediation tool with culturally dependent codes; Butler sees the body as already sexed before it comes to a gender (129). The difference is that Paglia posits nature as coming 'before' sex, while Butler assumes that there is nothing natural that can be inscribed into the body as such (129). This last point, however, indicates an important refocusing on materiality in Butler's thought, which can be found in *Bodies that Matter: On the Discursive Limits of 'Sex'*, which she opens with just this point: 'Is there a way to link the question of the materiality of the body to the performativity of gender? And how does the category of "sex" figure within such a relationship?' (Butler 1993: 1). In a reading similar to the gap found in castration, Butler argues that the body is to be found in its misrecognition within a symbolic structure:

> The linguistic categories that are understood to 'denote' the materiality of the body are themselves troubled by a referent that is never fully or permanently resolved or contained in any given signified. Indeed, that referent persists only as a kind of absence or loss, that which language does not capture, but, instead, that which impels language repeatedly to attempt that capture, that circumscription – and to fail. (67)

Yet rather than staying with the 'as' structure, Butler continually reinforces her argument that 'any recourse to the body before the symbolic can take place only within the symbolic, which seems to imply that there is no body prior to marking' (98; cf. 106–7).[2] Although seemingly pre-critical at first, the challenge that the thought of Quentin Meillassoux and others have brought to this position finds a literary counterpart in the figure of Horsa from Lessing's novel. Horsa represents the mediating aspect of sex's role in the change of an object from one phase to another.

Horsa is one of the new children, born from the coupling of man and woman. These new children are described as having a 'double heritage' (Lessing 2008: 103), bringing 'restlessness and curiosity' to the Clefts. With these New Ones came not only fire (103–4) but also danger, in that they were not content merely to loaf around The Cleft but instead got into trouble exploring their world (106). Thus the introduction of sex mediates the presence of movement, which Paglia connected to the overabundance of nature. In Lessing's novel the pre-sex infants are often characterised as sedentary – 'the infants of the old kind were passive, easy, seldom cried, staying where they were set down' (103) – while the new infants bring about difference, movement and change.

When two of these New Ones are introduced in the last third of the story, the female Maronna and the male Horsa, they are done so *in media res*, as the records that the narrator has of these times are incomplete (163). The first scene this couple occupies together is one of agitation and change: 'Something in the stuff and substance of life had been agitated – by what?' (50). Maronna is berating Horsa for putting the younger male children's lives in danger by making up stupid dangerous games of skill and daring. However, the 'double heritage' of the New Ones comes forth in Horsa's reaction: eventually he listens to Maronna, apologises, and changes his ways (164). And again, the next time the pair appear in the narrative, Horsa first acts as a force for peace by ending the infighting that is taking place among the splintering groups of males and females, and then acts as a force of difference by fighting with and then breaking from Maronna and moving his group of males somewhere that is difficult for her to find (172–3). What these two scenes set up when looked at together is an aporia of authority, seen above both in Paglia's eschewing of ecomimesis and Harman's paradox of relation and non-relation, which brings tension into the authority of knowledge.

Theodore Sturgeon's debut novel *The Dreaming Jewels* (1950) – published under the title *The Synthetic Man* in the Pyramid Press edition that I own – provides another telling example of relation and non-relation in sf. Horton Bluett, an adopted boy, runs away from an abusive father and winds up joining a carnival. The head of the carnival, Pierre Monetre, is shown in flashback to have discovered strange alien jewels. What is important about this novel for the discussion here is the manner in which Monetre found the jewels. He was walking in a forest near his home and spotted two trees that were exactly the same:

> The trees were the same size. Each had a knotted primary limb snaking off to the north. Each had a curling scar on the first shoot from it. The first cluster on the primary on each tree had five leaves on it.
> [...]
> What he saw was impossible. The law of averages permits of such

a thing as two absolutely identical trees, but at astronomical odds. Impossible was the working word for such a statistic.

Monetre reached and pulled down a leaf from one tree, and from the other took down its opposite number.

They were identical – veining, shape, size, texture. (Sturgeon 1967: 39–40)

However, there is even a greater similarity between the two trees than is indicated here. When Tree A is affected by something, having a branch snapped off or a figure carved into it, after a short period of time the same appears on Tree B (40–1). Therefore 'Tree A was the original. Tree B was some sort of . . . copy' (41). What makes these trees an important image of a spatial tension, however, is their incorporation of difference within similarity. After studying the trees for two years, Monetre learns that 'aside from the function of exact duplication, Tree B was different' (41). What is different about Tree B is that it contains 'a single giant molecule, akin to hydrocarbon enzymes, which could transmute elements' (41). The difference in Tree B indicates that the presence of the 'noise' of difference within similarity engenders change, or transmutation. Although these powers of transmutation are eventually tied to a crystal found underneath the tree (43), what is important here is that change is born out of the proximity of relation and non-relation.

The Dreaming Jewels and *The Cleft* have moments when both relation and non-relation coexist. Such moments are examples of the Zug effect. One of the strategies for representing this paradox is what was above called dismantling. In *The Cleft* dismantling takes the form of an absence of authority. Avital Ronell examines a number of thinkers on authority in her *Loser Sons: Politics and Authority*. The two core satellites around which she revolves are Alexandre Kojève and Hannah Arendt. Put briefly, she takes both respectfully to task for remaining 'historical': Kojève locates authority in Hegel's master/slave dialectic, then God, and then finds it absent in Marx, while Arendt takes an even earlier approach by locating it in Plato's taking up of the pen of philosophy in contradistinction to the orality of Socrates (Ronell 2012: 25). What is important for Ronell is to retain the violence of authority in her own thought, something she sees missing from Arendt (31). What Ronell finds common to both thinkers (and Levinas and Blanchot too) is the location of inequality within their constructions of authority (33),³ something that the figure of Horsa challenges in the manner of what will be seen as his weak authority, and that Ronell rallies against here because of her seeming paradox of seeing a number of simultaneous aspects of authority: one needs it and hates it at the same time (35) and it can be utilised for critique and disrupted by questioning (21). Thus Ronell constructs authority around the trope of the aporia, meaning, in Derrida's formulation, an impossible passage (Derrida 1993: 8).

What Ronell's programme seems to imply, on the other hand, is a critique of paternal authority in particular, for it is in the name of the Father that an 'honorable politics' becomes impossible (Ronell 2012: 46). This impossibility arises out of the economy of survival, in that it is through paternal authority that the past comes to haunt the present. Thus derives the title of her work, *Loser Sons*, in which she traces the effects of the paternal hand on figures such as George W. Bush, Osama bin Laden, Franz Kafka and others. In her readings of these figures, Ronell sees the position of childhood as determined by an adulthood which wishes to see itself in a position of non-identification, and thus places childhood under the coordinates of the pre-male Clefts:

> The complicity between figures of idiocy and childhood, in unexpected ways rich and telling, was created basically to prompt the adult capacity for reflective memory. Childhood was from the start a stand-in for live feed – for story anterior to memory that showed, together with the lockdown of idiocy, an uninhabitable space where memories could not be retrieved. The constitutive blur of childhood had to be separated from the expanding discursive empires of history and autobiography, for developmental theories of selfhood and its historical becoming. (Ronell 2012: 68)

On the one hand, *The Cleft* is a novel of separation, a new phase between pre-sex childhood and symbiotic adulthood. However, the figure of Horsa does not allow this to be the end of the story, instead calling for another construction of identity, one which is open to a childhood disruption.

Horsa becomes the leader of the boys, but his leadership is challenged by a splinter group that does not recognise his authority. Their 'problem' has to do with parental time, for they are children who are presumptively assuming the role of adults: 'The little boys thought of themselves as big boys, and emulated the hunters and food gatherers [. . .] They were very pleased with their accomplishments, would come swaggering back to the beach with the animals they had killed, just like the youths who had achieved their men's bodies' (Lessing 2008: 208–9). This misappropriation of adulthood attempts to reschedule non-identification with childhood. Horsa is an interesting figure here because he loses out in keeping this separation clean; he and an unnamed friend attempt to cross the sea in order to discover a new land for their people, but the journey is too rough – the friend dies and Horsa is seriously injured, and then thrown back upon his native shore (214–15). In his weakened state Horsa's position as leader has all but disappeared:

> The children were dancing and singing, wild with their independence and mocking their elders who were around their own fires. Horsa shouted at them to come over and join the main feast but the children ignored him. Horsa was being generally ignored, and he did not understand it, nor did he see that an air of hilarity and anarchy that prevailed was because he was not there, leader of them all, in command, always visible as central focus of authority. No, he was lying on the sand, or crawling, trying to sit up, and weak with pain. (218)

This contrast between Horsa and the young is not being foregrounded here in order to side with one or the other. As Ronell states, 'Is it at all serious to pronounce oneself "for" or particularly "against" authority?' (Ronell 2012: 50). Instead what is being developed is the dismantling of authority, which, as seen in the struggle with sex above, is that there is the potential that weakened figures of authority such as Horsa can bring forth Shaviro's universe of things. This universe takes the form of the 'as' structure entailed in authority rather than coming down on one side or the other.

This 'as' structure, as seen in *The Road*, is one in which the authority of language is confused by its own babbling. Or, as it is stated in Lessing's novel, 'If you have had authority all your life, because of your nature, something you never knew you had, and then you lose it, then it is hard even to ask the right questions' (Lessing 2008: 220). Going back to work done in the first chapter, in sf in particular foregrounding of a lack of knowledge might be said to be especially prevalent in the genre. The 'science' of the term 'science fiction' can refer to the genre's dependency on the experimental method, which is a way of thinking that participated in the birth of the genre but is also what 'separates' sf from fantasy (cf. Bailey 1972: 26, 80; Amis 1960: 14–17; Malmgren 1991: 5–6; Csicsery-Ronay 2008: 69–70). However, this is both a naive reading of science and of the genre of sf: both take the concept of ambiguity very seriously. An illustration of this can be seen in the classic sf novel *When Worlds Collide* (1933), by Philip Wylie and Edwin Balmer. Two new planets have been discovered. However, they are heading straight for Earth, captured by the gravity of our sun. They will make one pass by the planet, destroying the moon, and then orbit the sun and return to wipe out the Earth the second time through. A small group of scientists have decided to try and 'leap' off the Earth and land on the smaller and more Earth-like of the two planets, Bronson Beta. Because it is known that the planets will collide with the Earth, and that they will pass by twice (the first time causing environmental catastrophes that wipe out four-fifths of the population), the novel sets up an opportunity for its protagonists to appropriate an experience of their potential non-being. However, what they do instead is decry that such an appropriation is impossible. After the planets pass the Earth the first time, Tony rallies the survivors. The narrator states that

> No wonder, really, that these men responded and that he exhorted and urged them on. They, and he, could not realize that the world was doomed, any more than a man could realize that he himself must die. Death is what happens to others! So other worlds may perish; but not ours, on which we stand! (Wylie and Balmer 1970: 96)

In this scene the narrator is sharing a knowledge with the implied reader that Tony does not have: that a knowledge of one's own death is impossible. However, Tony later comes to the same conclusion himself, and this awareness of a lack of awareness has its rewards: Tony tells his love Eve, whose father has barred him from marrying her because she will be needed to repopulate their new home, that the survivors, who have all been explicitly told what will happen the next time the planets pass, still cannot have any inkling of facticity: 'But they don't *know it*,' Tony tells Eve. 'They can't *know* a thing like that just from being told – or even from what they've just been through' (98). This explication of a lack of knowledge, which is perhaps the most profound kind of knowledge available, prompts Tony to act as never before: 'Tony seized and held her with a fierceness and with a tenderness in his ferocity, neither of which he had ever known before' (100). The coordinates being developed in *When Worlds Collide* are not that of an experience of awareness of one's own death, but of an experience of its lack.

This lack is also seen in the place Horsa occupies in the history of *The Cleft*: his name remains – it 'was the name of a star before it acquired Egyptian names, Greek names, our Roman names' (Lessing 2008: 252); however, the meaning of this name is lost, and it is this lost meaning that indicates the 'as': 'If we knew what that star meant then, perhaps we might hear Horsa speaking at last. Or imagine we did' (252). The point of this passage is that neither is possible: neither hearing the real Horsa speak nor the totality of the imagined version of him. This is the function of castration, which is a figure of tension that leads to a new phase. Yet disturbingly, it is also one of the strongest figures of authority itself. For, as Ronell argues, a complete relation to authority is a sign of weakness; what is needed is both a relation and a non-relation to it:

> If I have to call security or start stomping around, raising my voice, I am lacking in authority. I should be able simply to cast a look, send out a glare, for the unwelcome intruder to slither away. Maybe flashing a glare signals too strong an action. In fact, the less said, the more authority. (Ronell 2012: 73)

The dismantling of authority is one way to increase spatial and temporal tensions. Like lifting off the top of a gaming console, when authority is disrupted the connections that objects can make, and the ways that objects can withdraw into themselves, become more varied than expected. Connecting and withdrawal are other words for fusion and fission, for relation and non-relation. Yet change does not only happen when dismantling takes place. *The Cleft* shows that symbiosis is another strategy for change. Symbiosis takes place during the heterosexual coupling of male and female, not in the birth of females or the birth of males. This does not mean that symbiosis is heterosexual, only that this is the example offered in *The Cleft*. In the first chapter, it was seen how Joanna Russ's *And Chaos Died* suffered from almost universal dismissal, mainly for its lack of coherence and the manner in which the main character, Jai Vedh, is a homosexual who is eventually converted to heterosexuality. Russ wrote each novel as a 'correction' to the one preceding it (except, of course, for the first). *The Female Man* immediately follows *And Chaos Died* and thus functions as a critique of it. *The Female Man*, with its complex structure interweaving four different characters in four different time periods, corrects the anti-homosexuality of the previous novel. However, *And Chaos Died* is not to be totally dismissed. The epigraph chosen to open this chapter indicates one of the strategies of *And Chaos Died* – it is a novel of the castrated self, which is another way to describe the tension between the real and sensual qualities of an object. This was seen as a strength in the first chapter, which used a description of a spaceship from the novel as an example of the Zug effect. Turning back to another previous example, that of the ability of the human eye to see ultraviolet light, castration would be the separation of the eye lens from the eye, which would remove the eye-bearer from the symbolic world of correct vision and traditionally locate them in a group of ill, handicapped or otherwise disabled persons. However, this disability is actually the ability to be connected with more qualities than is expected; thus castration is a function of the relatively dark object, in which the manner in which an object is connected to others is 'cut off' or fissioned, thus allowing that object to function with otherwise invisible objects (the eye can now see ultraviolet light). As the Laboria Cuboniks collective puts it in the manifesto for xenofeminism, 'It is through, and not despite, our alienated condition that we can free ourselves from the muck of immediacy' (Laboria Cuboniks 2015: 1). Various aspects of *The Cleft* have connected both the fission of castration and the fusion of symbiosis. The next chapter addresses a potential danger in this argument: the synthesis of disparate elements into a new entity sounds like a dialectical procedure. However, both speculative realism and the sf addressed in this book are non-dialectical. This difference is the focus of the following analysis.

Notes

1. In Alastair Reynolds's debut novel *Revelation Space* (2000), symbiosis not only takes place between a character and a clone of himself, but also between that character and a 'lo-res' version of its clone. A third of the way into the space opera it is revealed that Dan Sylveste is a clone of his father Calvin. Calvin created Dan in order to have a

suitable body to eventually transfer his consciousness into, once the technology became feasible. Dan is ignorant of both the fact that he is a clone and that he was created to be a potential host (Reynolds 2002: 182). However, the cross-section between Reynolds's novel and those discussed above lies in Calvin's back-up plan: in case the 'alpha' recording of Calvin's consciousness proved too complicated to transfer into Dan's brain, a 'beta' recording, which merely mimicked Calvin's personality rather than capturing it, was available for transfer. In fact, the alpha recording of Calvin is presumed lost: only the beta version remains (183). Dan is himself but distant from himself. In fact, he is not only distant from himself because his personality is actually his father's, but he is even removed from this, because his personality is only the beta version of his father's self. In this sense the 'revelation space' of the novel's title is not just its setting in outer space, but also the revelations in what J. G. Ballard called the more interesting 'inner space' (Ballard 1996: 197) of science fiction.
2. As Samuel Chambers and Terrell Carver argue, 'For Butler [...] the body can never serve as an ontological foundation [...] The body cannot ground a theory of feminist politics any more than it can ground a theory of gender. Nonetheless, to say this is not to dismiss the body; nor it is to ignore the critics' constant question: "what about the body?" [...] While Butler rejects any theory grounded in an ontology of the body, she still finds something fundamental about bodies: bodies, for Butler, are *vulnerable*. A body is both dependent upon others and subject to violation by another, by others. Through our bodies we always remain exposed to others, and our very vulnerability ties us to others' (Chambers and Carver 2008: 52). However, my point here is that Butler does not consistently remain with this 'as' structure.
3. For Arendt, this means that authority always comes from the outside (Arendt 2003: 468), for Kojève, that there is a certain pleasure in judging others (Kojève 2007: 101).

6

Animal Death: Paolo Bacigalupi

He did not look like a man. His name was Will Hartnett. He was an astronaut, a Democrat, a Methodist, a husband, a father, an amateur timpanist, a beautifully smooth ballroom dancer; but to the eye he was none of those things. To the eye he was a monster.

Frederik Pohl, *Man Plus* (1976)

History and the *Ngaw*

Paolo Bacigalupi's Nebula award-winning novel *The Windup Girl* (2009) sets up a dialectical situation which it then disrupts. This is important for two reasons. First, dialectic formations are often also assemblages or networks, meaning that their constituent parts are defined by how they interact with each other rather than by the essence which is withdrawn from such interactions. In the previous chapter, symbiosis was seen as a powerful tool for change. However, the way it was described often bordered on a dialectical structure, as did the doubling of double-vision and the contradiction of crisis energy. *The Windup Girl* offers a different strategy, the short circuit. In brief, this means that one of the terms of a symbiosis disrupts the symbiosis. This disruption takes the form of spatial and temporal tensions, as described above and developed below. In terms of the structure of sf, this strategy challenges a traditional reading of the novum. As Darko Suvin states, '*SF is distinguished by the narrative dominance or hegemony of a fictional "novum" (novelty, innovation) validated by cognitive logic*' (Suvin 2010: 67, italics in original). This chapter challenges this concept by using Samuel Delany's idea of inmixing. This in turn questions the cognitive logic involved in certain aspects of sf. The dismantling of both leads to indirect representations of the withdrawn nature of objects.

This challenge begins in Bacigalupi's novel with an example of temporal tension. The past, which is connected to a more natural time, is in tension with the artificiality of the present. The novel opens with Anderson Lake making his way through a food market in Bangkok. He has found a new kind of fruit, hopefully resistant to the 'blister rust' plague that contaminates almost all genetically engineered food (Bacigalupi 2009: 1). This is a time in the not-so-distant future in which all exertion, physical and mechanical, is measured out in the calories it costs to support. In this future there are almost no cars, and aeroplanes are reserved for only the richest. Anderson is interested in the fruit because he works for the 'calorie company' AgriGen and is in Thailand covertly searching for new genetic samples to broaden his company's offerings and to make their foodstuffs more plague-resistant. The new fruit he comes across is a *ngaw*. The first thing he notices is how much a part of the present the fruit is:

> [1] She hands back the fruit. Anderson sniffs tentatively. Inhales floral syrup. *Ngaw*. It shouldn't exist. [2] Yesterday, it didn't. Yesterday, not a single stall in Bangkok sold these fruits, [3] and yet now they sit in pyramids, piled all around this grimy woman where she squats on the ground under the partial shading of her tarp. From around her neck, a gold glinting amulet of the martyr Phra Seub winks at him, a talisman of protection against the agricultural plagues of the calorie companies. (Bacigalupi 2009: 2)

Sections 1, 2 and 3 designate the broad temporal segments of this passage. Regarding the order of these segments, 1 and 3 take place in the 'now' of the story time while 2 looks back to a time before (even of just before – yesterday) through analepsis. Although this simple back-and-forth between past and present merely reinforces the information that the fruit is new, the same structure is followed as the passage continues. On a larger scale, this zig-zag pattern of temporal shifts takes a prominent place in sf literature. One prominent example, Joe Haldeman's *The Forever War* (1974), features soldiers who make interstellar jumps which, because of the special theory of relativity, cause them to miss out on large chunks of the history of their home planet when they return. This interplay of past and present has a transformative effect, turning the soldiers into aliens as their home world becomes more and more strange (Haldeman 2006: 53). Haldeman's book was re-envisioned in John Scalzi's *Old Man's War* (2005), where the estrangement effects of movements in time are reflected by the strangeness of the creatures the soldiers are sent to fight:

> 'I'm not talking about who's ahead in the overall tally, Alan,' I said. 'I'm talking about the fact that our opponents are one fucking inch tall. Before this, we were fighting spiders. Before *that*, we were fighting goddamned pterodactyls. It's all messing with my sense of scale. It's messing with my sense of me. I don't feel human anymore, Alan.' (Scalzi 2007: 187)

This structure is important because, as *The Windup Girl* continues to bounce between past and present, an opposite movement of prolepsis is described. After the prolepsis, the return to the present becomes antagonistic.

> [1] A fist of flavor, ripe with sugar and fecundity. The sticky flower bomb coats his tongue. [2] It's as though he's back in the HiGro fields of Iowa, offered his first tiny block of hard candy by a Midwest Compact agronomist when he was nothing but a farmer's boy, barefoot amid the corn stalks. [3_1] The shell-shocked moment of flavor [3_2] – real flavor – [3_3] after a lifetime devoid of it. (Bacigalupi 2009: 2)

There are three broad temporal segments. Segment 1 takes place in the present, with Anderson tasting the new fruit in the middle of the Bangkok market. The strength of the flavour of the fruit triggers a memory, segment 2, which is that of tasting a kind of candy for the first time as a child. However, segment 3 seems less straightforward in its temporal designation, and therefore has been broken up into three sub-segments.

There is no transition, except for the sentence break, between segment 2 and subsegment 3_1. Therefore, 'The shell-shocked moment of flavor' can plausibly be connected with the item that was last mentioned being tasted, the 'hard candy' that Anderson had as a child in Iowa. While 'shell-shocked' and 'bomb' (the latter used in 'flower bomb' to describe the taste of the *ngaw* in the present) are two metaphors from the same domain – the military – perhaps this connection is not strong enough on an initial reading to overcome the presumed anachrony between segments 2 and 3. However, the next sub-segment, 3_2, fits less easily into the sequence, as 'real' is not the most common way in which to describe the flavour of 'hard candy', especially when there is actual fruit being tasted in the vicinity. Sub-segment 3_3 then seems to bring the story time back into the present, as a lifetime devoid of real flavour is more applicable to Anderson the man than to Anderson the boy. Thus, upon discovering that the whole segment takes place in the 'now' of the story time, the reader is retroactively back in the present.

However, segment 3 contains another ambiguity in the relationship between past and present. While the value of the *ngaw* in the present is tied to the manner in which it has been genetically engineered to avoid blister rust, segment 2 contains at least three signifiers pertaining to a 'more natural past': a farm, being barefoot and a field of corn (despite the ominous sounding HiGro also mentioned). Therefore in the first two segments a tension has been set up between the 'artificial' present and the more 'natural' past. However, segment 3 is a key feature of the passage: it does not provide a kind of synthesis of the past and present, but rather highlights the antagonism between the two. For if we, for the moment, disregard the apparent hyperbole and take sub-segment 3_3, 'a lifetime devoid of [real flavour]', literally, then the *ngaw* would actually be the first time Anderson is experiencing such 'real' flavour. He has never experienced it before, not even as a barefoot boy amid the cornfields of Iowa. But even if we allow for a less stringent reading of this statement, Anderson's past is still being connected to a nature that is only now being fulfilled.

In other words, for Anderson, nature is connected to his past life as the son of a farmer, walking amid the corn stalks barefoot, not even separated from the earth by a pair of shoes. This reminiscence shows how as a child he was supposedly not afraid of plague or disease; he was a part of nature rather than scared by it. However, segment 3 indicates that it is actually in his present state of fear and agitation (regarding food-borne illnesses) that nature can become fulfilled. In this sense Anderson's past is not contrasted with the present but rather fulfilled in it. The explosive taste of the *ngaw*, which had supposedly never existed before the present moment of the story time, actually fulfils a kind of flavour that began when he first tasted the hard candy as a child. On the one hand, what ties these two tastes together in symbiosis is simply their unexpectedness. However, on the other, the taste of the *ngaw* is something that Anderson had never experienced before, not even with the hard candy. For although as a child he was more a part of nature (not that a cornfield is particularly natural [Gould 1985]), the hard candy given to him by a worker from a genetic engineering company puts the status of nature in question. Here the idea of art fulfilling nature comes into play. The 'real' flavour of the *ngaw* both called to mind and obliterated the taste of the hard candy as a child. While the hard candy was collocated to the 'real' in Anderson's memory (childhood, farms, being barefoot), it is only now that this realness has been fulfilled in the taste of the (also genetically engineered) *ngaw*. Another way to say it is that the *ngaw*, in a strict sense, is sublime.[1]

Art Fulfilling Nature

But how is it that nature 'wants' to be fulfilled? How does nature have an image of itself, of where it wants to go? The relationship between art and natural beauty is a troubled and vast subject that has touched on a number of texts described here. In the Anthropocene, art and nature are inseparable; since nature is now a crisis created by humanity, it is 'a process that inextricably binds together human and nonhuman systems' (Trexler 2015: 17). The structure of this binding has found a key formulation in the work of an author not usually associated with speculative realism, Theodor Adorno. In the last chapter, a certain danger was mentioned. The structures of symbiosis and dismantling at first seem dialectic. In order to describe how they are not, Adorno will be key. He will be used both to define a certain kind of dialectics, and to show how the sf discussed here does not quite fit. The manner in which the fiction does not fit was mentioned above. Synthesis is denied. This is the important tension in the thought of Graham Harman, and in the role of a Type-2 world with Quentin Meillassoux. In short, change arises out of tension retained, rather than out of tension resolved. Developing this statement is the focus of this chapter.

In *Aesthetic Theory*, left unfinished but published in 1970, a year after the author's death, Adorno develops a dialectical reading of the two terms in which the antagonism between the two is actually read as the fulfilment of one in the other (Adorno 1997: 61–78). This paradox comes about through the dialectical process itself, in which nothing is only what it is, but rather carries the opposite within. This is an approach aligned much more closely to new materialisms rather than speculative realism because meaning is generated by the relation of things rather than the tension of withdrawn essences. However, Adorno's thought is much more complex than this simple formulation, and relates to both speculative realism and sf in how it contains a concept of time that Bacigalupi's novel mirrors and problematises.

At first sight it may be thought that the relationship between art and natural beauty would not allow for the kind of opposition Adorno indicates as existing, because art destroys nature through its artificiality. This line of thinking leads to assumptions about why people go for walks in nature – to have a reprieve from art.[2] But walks in nature are also artworks, for, as Timothy Morton argues, the traditional concept of nature as reprieve rather than threat is getting in the way of ecological thought (Morton 2007). One important dialectical aspect of the relationship between art and natural beauty is that nature actually calls out for humanity to put it into forms, to put it into art. For while pure nature is a myth, nature itself is amorphous. This is actually why people go for a walk in nature, to form nature into a reprieve. This is also why nature is futuristic, and why it plays a central role in sf (Murphy 2009; Hageman 2012); in other words, nature is futuristic because it calls out to humanity to form it, to complete it. Nature calls out to humanity to make nature what nature wants to be: 'The identity of the artwork with the subject is as complete as the identity of nature with itself should some day be' (Adorno 1997: 63).[3] This formation, or completion, is nature's future event. On the one hand, this future call is problematic, as it seems is the forming of nature that has taken place in the Anthropocene. However, on the other hand, this call takes the form of the unavoidable attention that the hyperobjects of the Anthropocene demand. As Morton argues, climate change, nuclear waste disposal and other long-term and widespread catastrophes are no longer invisible: hyperobjects have already 'ushered in' a new phase in human experience (Morton 2013a: 2). This ushering in is the future Adorno gives to his reading of the symbiosis of art and nature.[4]

The futurity of nature brings about another key element in Adorno's thinking on the construction of history. As Robert Hullot-Kentor, the translator of *Aesthetic Theory*, puts it in his essay 'Suggested Reading',

> Adorno conceived a dialectic at a standstill that would *potentiate in reflection the antagonistic content of history*. By pursuing the

mediation of the particular through the social totality, negative dialectics transforms the power of totality into the force of historical reflection by releasing the history stored in the particular as the power that vitiates it. (Hullot-Kentor 2006: 225, emphasis mine)

The key formula in this quotation is that reflection can bring about the potential of the antagonistic content of history. To understand this point, reflection, in this case, can be likened to theory. In the relationship between theory and practice, theory is often derided: practice is seen as doing something, while theory is constructed as doing nothing, as just thinking. However, as paradoxical as it might sound, there is something practical about theory itself (Adorno 2001: 4). The practicality of 'not doing' can be as simple as not doing 'something stupid' or as not doing something dangerous to one's self or others. However, in a more philosophical sense, not doing one thing leaves open the potentiality for doing something else; if I do not write these words down, then I could potentially write any words down, or even no words at all. Thus comes about the idea of the *tabula rasa* developed by Aristotle in *De Anima* (III.iv; Polansky 2007: 453–4) and expanded by Avicenna[5] – to have the ability to do something and yet not to do that thing; an act of 'not doing' brings forth the potentiality for change. Thus the 'potentiate' in Hullot-Kentor's quote.[6]

In the second half of this passage, Hullot-Kentor states that what becomes potentiated is 'the antagonistic content of history'. In tracing the idea that the events of history do not always fit into their telling, an important moment was Friedrich Schiller's inaugural lecture at the University of Jena in 1789. Schiller was hired as a professor of history and gave a talk on the subject, in which he called for the philosopher-historian to replace the academic-historian, meaning there was a need for someone who would step back from the recording of detail about the past and begin to think about it. Similar to Karen Barad's scientifically inspired concept of entanglement, discussed in the first chapter, one of the important consequences claimed for such thinking is that it opens the potentiality of the historical moment to 'being-with' other disciplines than just history in order to be understood:

As carefully as the bread-and-butter scholar keeps his discipline clear of everything extraneous, so the philosopher endeavors to expand his, and to restore its connections with the others [. . .] Where the bread-and-butter scholar puts asunder, the philosopher joins together. He has early reached the conviction that in the realm of understanding, as in the domain of sensation, everything is interconnected, and his active drive for coherence cannot remain satisfied with fragments. (Schiller 1972: 324)

While Schiller's discussion takes a sort of joyful multiplicity as its aim, much in line with the Weimar Classicism with which this period of his life is associated, when Nietzsche uses this lecture as an impetus for the writing of the second half of his *Untimely Meditations* (1874) he focuses on the connection between thinking and not-doing. As such, a kernel of his thought at this moment can be seen when he states that 'Forgetting is essential to action of any kind' (Nietzsche 1997: 62), indicating a practicality of theory. In a later example, Walter Benjamin also puts this idea into a forceful and well-known formulation in his 'Theses on the Philosophy of History', in which he contrasts the potentiality of the now with the smooth trajectories traced out in many historical accounts: 'History is the subject of a structure whose site is not homogenous, empty time, but time filled by the presence of the now [*Jetztzeit*]' (Benjamin 1969: 261). The fullness or potentiality of the moment is what needs to be developed by historians; in the present we do not know what actions will lead to what consequences in the future, and it is this plurality that makes up, in part, Benjamin's concept of the *Jetztzeit*. What both the relationship between art and nature and philosophy have in common is that they are 'dialectics at a standstill', meaning a confluence of stasis and change, which is a similar construction to the multiple paths open to the lack of movement that makes present the *tabula rasa*.

The stage is then almost set for the entrance of Adorno's thought on history, and the manner in which it both develops and disrupts the structure of the dialectic. But first it should be stated that it was Heidegger who made history a problem for thinking for much of the Frankfurt School (Jay 1996: 72). Heidegger sets out the differences between historicity [*Geschichtlichkeit*] and history [*Geschichte*], in which the former precedes the latter for *Dasein*:

> As a determination historicity is prior to what is called history (world-historical occurrences). Historicity means the constitution of being of the 'occurrence' of Dasein as such; it is the ground for the fact that

something like the discipline of 'world history' is at all possible and historically belongs to world history. (Heidegger 1996: 17)

Thus historicity is related to the being-in-the-world of *Dasein*, meaning that a contradiction is present in the way things become accessible in the world, meaning that the world is 'material for living . . . A totality of useful things is always already discovered *before* the individual useful thing' (64). Yet at the same time, *Dasein*'s relationship to world is what lets things that are invisible and part of a context become broken, unveiled and conspicuous (68). However, what happens with such a positive rendering of *Dasein*'s being-in-the-world is that it ignores the tension between objects that are invisible and fit into the world, and those that fail in their use and thus become unveiled. For, as Harman argues, if objects have the potentiality to break, then there must be something 'more' about them than just their functionality even when they are veiled in the world of everyday use (Harman 2013: 266–7). Or, in the words of Morton, *Dasein* is 'both potential and "impossible"', meaning that it represents a dialetheic quality in which objects are both themselves and not themselves (Morton 2013b: 203–4). Here lies Adorno's critique of historicity in Heidegger: *Dasein*, in its being-in-the-world, is closed off from the everyday strangeness of objects in the world. Instead, Adorno sees the proper place of being as an antagonistic relationship between the human and what are seen to be non-human attunements to the world. This is both Adorno's contribution to dialectics and a challenge to it. A tension of negativity. This can be seen in Adorno's *Negative Dialectics*:

> 'Dasein' is an abashed German variant of subject. It did not escape Heidegger that it is both direct and the very principle of indirectness, that as a *constituens* it presupposes the constitutum, factuality [thus historicity precedes history – BW]. The state of facts is dialectical; Heidegger proceeds at any cost to translate it into the logic of noncontradictoriness. The mutually contradictory moments of the subjects are turned into two attributes which he attaches to the subject as to a substance. But this is helpful to the ontological dignity: the undeveloped contradiction will assure a superiority as such, because it defies the conditions of discursive logic, the language into which it has been translated. By virtue of this projection, the substance called Being is to be something positive above both concept and fact. Such positivity would not withstand its dialectical reflection. (Adorno 1990: 107–8n)

The contradictory moments of dialectical reflection that Adorno is purporting are essential to the functioning of crisis energy, discussed above. Their structure is also similar to the call from Schiller and Benjamin for the removal of the multiplicity of the now from the imposition of historical thinking. However, Adorno argues that this multiplicity is located within rationality, and not outside it (Horkheimer and Adorno 2002: 31–2);[7] thus objects that are both functional in the world (rational) and dysfunctional (broken) exist together, or are the same. One is part of another, and the role of dialectics in Adorno is to make present this intrusive coexistence.

The mechanism of how one element can contain another is seen, for example, in how individuals show their power through the society they live in (wealth, prestige, influence), while society can only show its power through the individual (obedience, support, voting). The reason that an understanding of such a give-and-take can be profound is that it is not the reified, 'smooth' relationship of a completed understanding of a system, but rather an antagonistic relationship of dismantling. It is antagonistic because there is a remainder from this interaction, and the remainder takes the form of a lack of reconciliation between the elements of difference between the two poles (say, art/natural beauty) (Adorno 1990: 114), which in Harman's thinking can be connected, despite Adorno's materialism, to the withdrawn nature of objects (Harman 2013: 170). In other words, there is a refusal of one element to merge into another, although at the same time they are intimately bound (although in rationality, not contradiction).[8] This refusal is essence, or identity. Adorno argues that 'The concept of natural beauty rubs on a wound, and little is needed to prompt one to associate this wound with the violence of the artwork – a pure artifact – inflicts on nature' (Adorno 1997: 61–2). This is a more passive (or theoretical) and explicit engagement with being-with than is found in Heidegger.

The *Ngaw* is not Dialectical

The above analysis begins to highlight the antagonistic coordinates that the *ngaw* holds in Bacigalupi's novel. It could be used to state that the position of the *ngaw* is a dialectical one, but in truth it is not. In order to make sense of the strength of this difference, a criticism that Slavoj Žižek has laid against dialectical thinking can be taken into account. This criticism brings out the disruptive tension that challenges the dialectic. This disruptive tension is what was termed the Zug effect in the first chapter. Žižek's comments will also bring his take on the Lacanian real (Lacan 2001: 139; Žižek 2008: 63) into play, although it will be seen that Adorno has already made essential space for such a disruption in his own thinking; this disruption is vital because, as the work of Alenka Zupančič has foregrounded, the real, although not a part of reality, can reshape it, and thus the real engenders an ethical question: how the subject will incorporate this newness into its world (Zupančič 2000: 235).[9] In the thought of Alain Badiou, this question takes the form of fidelity to the (disruptive) event (Badiou 2004; Düttmann 2004).[10] In Bacigalupi, it takes the form of fulfilment, but with a twist.

In *The Sublime Object of Ideology*, Žižek claims that dialectical thought is oppressive because it encourages a reified understanding of a thing that, because it is constructed out of a defensive symbolic reaction to trauma, closes the door on the difficult 'kernel' of the real it proposes to understand.

> This dialectics of overtaking ourselves towards the future and simultaneous retroactive modification of the past – dialectics by which the error is internal to the truth, by which the misrecognition possesses a positive ontological dimension – has, however, its limits; it stumbles on to a rock upon which it becomes suspended. This rock is of course the Real, that which resists symbolization: the traumatic point which is always missed but nonetheless always returns, although we try – through a set of different strategies – to neutralize it, to integrate it into the symbolic order. (Žižek 1989: 69)

In one sense, Žižek's comment goes to the heart of the argument presented so far: a dialectical understanding of the antagonistic relationship between past and present excludes a place for the real because an understanding of misrecognition and revision is somehow positive, moving forward, and hence a part of a symbolic construction of reality. However, in order to call attention to the importance of facing this impasse, Žižek actually uses Adorno's concept of dialectics as a (Hegelian and Lacanian, in Žižek's reading) way of facing antagonism in a more truthful manner. In '"The Most Sublime of Hysterics": Hegel with Lacan', Žižek argues that when a problem leads to two seemingly insoluble options (such as whether society is a whole that transcends the individual or whether it is a multitude), the position of Adorno is that, rather than finding one or the other as the correct answer, '*it is the fundamental antagonism which constitutes the very thing that one wants to comprehend*' (Žižek 2005a: 39, italics in original; cf. Adorno 1990: 183).[11] Or, as Mauro Bozzetti words it in an essay on Hegel and Adorno, 'reconciliation must be opposed because reality itself is not reconciled' (Bozzetti 2002: 297).[12] This is another description of Ian Bogost's dismantling.

Yet Žižek differentiates himself from speculative realism at exactly this point. The 'radical imbalance' which disrupts the dialectic is what Žižek claims can be used to 'discern the limitation of speculative realism', a limitation that he sees reflected in the differences between the key figures of the movement who first met in 2007 (Žižek 2012: 640). Similar to the discussion here, Žižek sees speculative realists as mainly divided between those who believe that science is the key for challenging correlationism (Meillassoux, Brassier) and those who are considered to hold 'religious beliefs' (Harman and Grant), which is really just the argument that objects are withdrawn and that this withdrawn nature can be surprising. For Žižek, both positions miss something (and this is presumably why the split occurred). This something he finds in what Meillassoux calls 'weak correlationism'. This is based on the Kantian notion 'which maintained the conceivability of the in-itself' (Meillassoux 2009: 66), even though the world can only be known through rational cognition. Žižek's critique of speculative realism is based on his argument that Meillassoux does not take his reading of weak correlationism far enough, because for him, the fact that the world can only be known through rational cognition, and that there are things that exist outside of thought, are both found in reality itself. In other words,

> what Meillassoux calls 'sickened' or 'failed' correlationism, far from being a half-hearted break-out from the correlationist constraint, is the key component of any true escape: it is not enough to oppose to transcendental correlation a vision of reality-in-itself – transcendental correlation itself has to be grounded in reality-in-itself; i.e., its possibility has to be accounted for in the terms of this reality. (Žižek 2012: 643)

For Žižek, the coordinates of the real are always found in the symbolic. This is what he means by the possibility of escape being located in the terms of our reality. Thus escape, as he sees it, takes place in 'a short circuit between two spheres which are usually perceived as incompatible, as moving at ontologically different levels' (Žižek 2006: 13). This is what Harman calls temporal tension, meaning the 'tension between sensual objects and their sensual qualities' (Harman 2011a: 100). The prime example of this that we have looked at was Lin's way of seeing the world in *Perdido Street Station*. The fragmented nature of her insect vision allowed her to see the world in multiple ways at once, like a cubist painting. For Žižek, any statement about reality beyond this is religious, or spiritual. Yet Mr Motley offered an additional lesson, the relation of image and essence to temporal tension. This is not panpsychism but a statement about the withdrawn nature of objects. Like Meillassoux's weak correlationism, Harman also contends that real objects cannot be directly known: 'object-oriented realism holds that reality exists outside the mind and we *cannot* know it'; yet he also argues that there is access to reality, but that it is indirect (Harman 2016: 17), rather than mathematical as with Badiou and Meillassoux.

At first, it might seem that the *ngaw* fits too easily into the dialectical coordinates that Žižek initially questions above. One effect of the fruit, as argued above, is the foregrounding of a misrecognition between the present and the past.[13] This potentially sets up the coordinates for a 'smooth' dialectical relationship. This seems to be confirmed by what happens next in the novel, which is the enactment of a defensive mechanism on the part of Anderson, just the kind of response that Žižek warns against. Anderson is attracted to the fruit and he fights for the self-control to resist it, perhaps through a kind of displacement. Anderson's self-control takes the shape of lighting a cigarette. This defensive act happens in a cycle rickshaw weaving its way through Bangkok, which is carrying Anderson from the market back to his factory. However, rather than cancelling out the disturbing past through a synthesis of its opposition to the present, Anderson's tactic of resistance actually causes a space to open up for the antagonism of the past to become present in the form of a flashback regarding the previous head of Anderson's factory (Bacigalupi 2009: 5–6). Anderson's attention is only brought back to the present when the cigarette startles him by burning down to its tip (7). In this scene, the cigarette was meant to smooth over the disruption that the *ngaw* had caused. This disruption was seen in how the real flavour of the fruit did not represent choosing the present over the past, but rather presencing the antagonism between the two in the ambiguity of the temporality of the flavour. However, in attempting to 'move on' from the scene in the market, both in the form of the rickshaw ride and by smoking a cigarette to relax into the present, what is actually engaged is the past: the story of Anderson's predecessor reveals Anderson's own secret mission in Bangkok – to find new genetic strains for his company.

In Bacigalupi's novel, the tension between past and present that foregrounds the role of temporality is also contained within the *ngaw* itself, which is part of the reason that it functions as a disruptive object. When Anderson is first told what the fruit is called, his initial question relates to temporality: '"It's new?"' (Bacigalupi 2009: 1). The woman who is selling the fruit confirms this by restating the name of the fruit and then saying '"New. No blister rust."' However, the newness of the object, its lack of provenance,[14] perplexes Anderson further:

> [1] [he] turns the strange hairy fruit in his hand. [2] It carries no stink of cibiscosis. No scab of blister rust. No graffiti of genehack weevil engraves its skin. [3] The world's flowers and vegetables and trees and fruits make up the geography of Anderson Lake's mind, and yet nowhere does he find a helpful signpost that leads him to identification. (Bacigalupi 2009: 2)

Now, as this sequence progresses, the spatio-temporal aspect of the external focalisation widens. The near zero-focalisation of segment 1 incorporates comparison in segment 2. In segment 3 the panorama widens, taking in knowledge of the whole world (or at least Anderson's knowledge of the whole world). This widening scope mirrors Anderson's thought process: the fruit itself is confusing, and as Anderson scrambles together what he knows to try and make sense of it, he finds that the fruit does not fit into any area of knowledge that he possesses. In other words, the fruit is not a part of Anderson's world. It is signpost-less. It is 'a mystery'.

This is what differentiates Harman from Žižek. The *ngaw* is an object which agitates, yet it is also withdrawn, although not completely dark. It is both an object of relation and non-relation, as developed in the last chapter. One of the ways it does this is through a foregrounding of temporality, which takes place in opening up the present to history. The *ngaw* 'resembles nothing so much as the pickled onions served in martinis at research clubs in Des Moines' (Bacigalupi 2009: 2). However, the *ngaw* is not 'just' a node for negotiating the relationship between past and present. If that were true, it would fit too neatly into the dialectical pattern that Žižek initially criticises. Instead the critical potential that the *ngaw* represents is located in how it disrupts its own coordinates. As Adorno says, regarding philosophy, 'It must strive, by way of the concept, to transcend the concept' (Adorno 1990: 15). The figure of the *ngaw* is disruptive because it is new, it did not exist yesterday; and yet on the other hand, it did. 'Not a single one of these furry fruits should exist; he might as well be hefting a sack of trilobites. If his guess about the *ngaw*'s origin is correct, it represents a return from extinction as shocking as if a Tyrannosaurus were stalking down Thanon Sukhumvit' (Bacigalupi 2009: 4). Its provenance is in question. However, it is not that the *ngaw* is a regenerated part of the past that is now available, like the dinosaurs of *Jurassic Park*, but rather that it is a natural part of the past which is available through the artificiality of the story time of the novel.[15]

Žižek also laid a concrete criticism against speculative realism. Weak correlationism is actually much stronger than Meillassoux suggests. This is because correlationism is based in reality-in-itself (Žižek 2012: 643). The real, physical appearance of the *ngaw* seems to fit into the criticism nicely. It has a spiky rind but is incredibly smooth inside. As Anderson asks about the fruit in the market, the woman selling them opens one up for him to try: 'Her brown thumb easily tears away the hairy rind, revealing a pale core. Translucent and veinous' (Bacigalupi 2009: 2). Actually, as is discovered later in the novel, this is a description of the Southeast Asian rambutan, for which *ngaw* is simply the Thai word.

But the fruit does not function so smoothly in the novel. Its nature is actually withdrawn. This can be seen when Anderson returns to his SpringLife factory, which is ostensibly creating kink-springs, a kind of power source, although the process so far is wildly expensive and underproductive (10). However, for Anderson this activity is just a cover. He has been sent by the AgriGen corporation to see what kind of new foodstuffs the Thais are able to engineer from their secure seed bank, which is why the *ngaw* is potentially so valuable. Upon his return to the factory, Anderson shows the fruit to his not-so-devoted assistant, Hock Seng, who is a 'yellow card', meaning a Chinese immigrant in

Thailand. Hock Seng is one of the rare immigrants who has been given permission to hold a job legally, and is not simply interned in an Expansion tower, a type of immigrant housing complex, like most of his fellow immigrants. Upon seeing the fruit, Hock Seng is rendered speechless. The reaction it provokes is not one of interest, or denial, but rather of being left without words. There is no way to paraphrase the object he sees; its essence is inaccessible to direct contact. At first Hock Seng admits knowing what the Thais call this fruit, although when asked if they had them in Malaya, his previous home, he falters: '"I – " Hock Seng starts to speak, then stops. He visibly fights for self-control, his face working through a flicker-flash of emotions. "I – " Again, he breaks off' (13).

It is not that the fruit is immediately 'the thing' in the disruptive Žižekian sense. Eventually Hock Seng does name it; he knows what it is called. This quick-naming and yet being rendered speechless is similar to the relationship between past and present engendered by the fruit for Anderson, who does not know where the taste comes from; it is something new, and yet it completes a taste in the past, perhaps in a way he could only experience now in the present. As Žižek argues, this dialectical relationship is too neat. And yet, as he also argues, it needs to happen. It is only retroactively that the truth will out, which is a productive experience of what dialectics can do (Žižek 2010: 88, 195; Žižek 2005b: 26–9). Or, as Adorno stated above, it is the concept being transcended through the concept. There is nothing beyond representation, but there can be disruptions within the artificial itself. This is in fact the power of Harman's spatial and temporal tensions in which objects and qualities disrupt each other. This thought is captured in the way Harman describes the literary and philosophical style of H. P. Lovecraft, in which '(1) real objects are locked in impossible tension with the crippled descriptive powers of language, and (2) visible objects display unbearable seismic torsion with their own qualities' (Harman 2012: 27). Like the short circuit built into the crisis engine from *Perdido Street Station*, the fruit also disrupts its own coordinates, as can be seen in how Hock Seng, after naming the fruit, has trouble naming it again. It is as if the posing of the question can only be troubled after the question is posed. Here the question becomes the following: *how* is the *ngaw* able to transcend the easy dialectical understanding of a situation (say, history) and offer something more traumatically redistributive of reality? The answer is found in the way the thing itself is developed through

Animal Death: Paolo Bacigalupi

two other examples from *The Windup Girl* – the megodonts and Emiko, who is the windup girl of the title.

Another Thing: the Megodont, an Animal Dies

The *ngaw* is the first object in the novel that foregrounds the representation of the antagonism between two entities (natural beauty/art, past/present), and it sets the stage for the second thing (the megodont) and then the third (Emiko). At the end of the first chapter of the book, Anderson finds himself in the middle of a catastrophe at his SpringLife factory. A megodont has broken loose from its rusty chains and gone on a deadly rampage throughout the factory. This workhorse of a creature is like a modified woolly mammoth which, in its current state of agitation, is 'a mountain of genetically engineered muscle, fighting against the last of its bonds' (Bacigalupi 2009: 19). Anderson is able to kill it, using a spring pistol left by the previous head of the factory, Yates. However, as the animal dies, a kind of 'contact' is made between it and Anderson. The scare-quotes around *contact* indicate the modern history of philosophical readings of the relation between human and non-human animals, ranging at the very least from Heidegger (1995) to Thomas Nagel (1974), Levinas (1990), Derrida (2003) and Agamben (2004). However, what is meant by contact in the context of Bacigalupi's novel is not an experience of the animal world on the part of the human but rather a shared experience of both humans and animals of being relatively dark objects, joining together in a moment of symbiosis. As Sherryl Vint argues in a book on the function of animals in sf, *Animal Alterity*, both animal studies and sf are

> interested in foundational questions about the nature of human existence and sociality. Both are concerned with the construction of the alterity which disrupts dialectics, and what it means for subjects to be thus positioned as outsiders. Both take seriously the question of what it means to communicate with a being whose embodied, communicative, emotional and cultural life – perhaps even physical environment – is radically different from our own. (Vint 2010: 1)

In this sense a foregrounding of the antagonism of one entity being in symbiosis with another is being posited in this scene from Bacigalupi's novel:

> Slowly its forelegs sprawl before it and it sinks, groaning, into straw and dung. The megodont's eyes sink to Anderson's level. They stare into his own, nearly human, blinking confusion. Its trunk stretches out for him again, slapping clumsily, a python of muscle and instinct, all uncoordinated now. Its maw hangs open, panting. Sweet furnace heat gusts over him. The trunk prods at him. Rocks him. Can't get a grip. (Bacigalupi 2009: 20)

One key to understanding the direction of this passage is in the pronouns. In the first clause of the first sentence, the megodont is referred to as 'it' three times, as if to stress a non-human nature. Then 'it' becomes 'the megodont' in the second sentence, as if mirroring the human referent of 'Anderson'. Then the megodont sinks down to meet Anderson eye-to-eye. 'They stare' are the eyes removed from the 'It stares', which would be the megodont. The megodont is not human but 'nearly' so. This signals a coming apart of the animal, as it is not referred to as a 'megodont' again in the paragraph, but instead disintegrates into qualities: eyes, trunk and maw. However, this disintegration has a strange effect of bringing Anderson closer. In 'They stare into his own, nearly human, blinking confusion'; there is ample room for misunderstanding: 'his own' is left dangling. It is unclear whether this refers to the megodont (which has up to this point only been referred to as 'it') or to Anderson, the more logical referent of the pronoun. However, if 'he' refers to Anderson, then the line would read: 'They (Anderson's eyes) stare into his own (Anderson's), nearly human eyes, which are blinking confusion.' However, this is not the case: it is the megodont's eyes that are nearly human, that are blinking confusion. This loosening of the pronouns is key to understanding the symbiosis of this passage.

Anderson and the megodont are present together in a new object. For Harman, this is a kind of symbiosis, meaning an attachment to another 'that makes our life in some sense a different life' (Davis 2012). In *The Windup Girl*, symbiosis takes place when the objects of the megodont and Anderson weaken their ties to their animal and human qualities, respectively. Quentin Meillassoux argues that newness can arise from another kind of weakness, what he calls the 'divine inexistence' of God (Meillassoux 2011: 177). Two aspects of Meillassoux's work are highlighted for this task: the manner in which the divine can be considered to arise out of something lost, and how the narrative strategy of this co-presence can be developed under the rubric of the 'as if'. Both of these strategies are used to develop the disruptive tension of *The Windup Girl*.

The most extensive publication, in any language, of Meillassoux's 1997 doctoral thesis *L'Inexistence divine* are the excerpts to be found in the appendix to Graham Harman's *Quentin Meillassoux: Philosophy in the Making*. Meillassoux's thesis, as presented in Harman's excerpts, can be summed up as follows: to believe in a God which exists is offensive to such a God, because it assumes that this theist God would allow children to be killed by accidents and other tragedies (Meillassoux 2011: 227–8); not to believe in a God is the same, for, as Meillassoux argues in *After Finitude*, 'Once the absolute has become unthinkable, even atheism, which also targets God's inexistence in the manner of an absolute, is reduced to mere belief' (Meillassoux 2009: 46). There is, however, another option, which is to believe in a God who does not yet exist (Meillassoux 2011: 236); thus the title of his dissertation, the divine inexistence. The possibility of a future God comes about, in a problematic sense, through a different train of thought, one which brings out an ethical dimension. First, Meillassoux asks what the most fundamental form of justice is; his answer is that since the worst form of injustice is death (because there is no chance in life of mitigating injustice), the most fundamental form of justice is the removal of death for everyone who has ever died. Thus the immediate resurrection of every person who has ever lived is posited. This resurrection is put forth as taking place on the earth '*as an ethics of life with no elsewhere*' (Meillassoux 2011: 188, italics in original). While such a resurrection seems unlikely, Meillassoux argues that it is possible. He says that we have experienced three fundamental phase changes to our world thus far: the emergence of something when there was nothing; the emergence of life when there was none; and the emergence of human thought from a world of animal life (189). He argues that another change could (but not necessarily) take place and that this change could (but not necessarily) take the form of the birth of a God or the resurrection of all who have ever lived (192). This leads Adam Kotsko to claim that Meillassoux 'is doing something like independently rediscovering Christianity' (Kotsko 2012). From this brief overview, two aspects will be looked into in more depth: the way in which the inexistence of God can itself be seen as divine, and the 'weak' gesture needed for an ethical waiting for a possible coming of God.[16]

On the one hand, the divine aspect of the inexistence of God is a straightforward consequence of immanentism, but on the other, it poses a radical problem for beings in the world. First, Meillassoux argues that 'if immanentism is maintained in fully radical form, it implies a world with nothing outside that could limit its power of novelty' (Meillassoux 2011: 175). Thus comes the possibility for God or resurrection, since 'If advent is immanent, then it is absurd; thus it is capable of anything' (176). This leads to why the inexistence of God is itself divine, for without the limits of a creator anything is really possible, and this 'anything' is itself wondrous: 'the inexistence of God is what unveils the staggering power of novelty of *our own* world' (177, italics in original). In *The Road*, this idea was put more simply: 'There is no God and we are his prophets' (McCarthy 2006: 181). It is here that Noah Horowitz takes issue, because Meillassoux claims both that this immanence leads to the possible destruction of the world, and at the same time claims that it is necessary for there to be something rather than nothing (thus imposing a limit on advent). Thus Horowitz argues that 'Not only does it ruin Meillassoux's explanation of irruption from nothing as being non-divine, but it also shows that he cannot argue that the divine is not. For if contingent being is necessary, then there must always be something' (Horowitz 2012: 278). However, for Meillassoux, such advents can either take place or not (Meillassoux 2011: 177). In one sense, in Meillassoux's world, it does not matter how we act, for such random events as the emergence of life, thought or God will either happen or not happen. This is a basic tenet of speculative realism: emergence is not dependent on an attitude or viewpoint. But at the same time, the most ethical way to live one's life is in preparation for such an event. For while Martin Hägglund argues that it is a desire for survival which forms both the atheist's and believer's attitude to the world (Hägglund 2011: 127), Meillassoux argues that such comportment is not necessary but only best (Meillassoux 2011: 224). What makes the death of the megodont a key and challenging image here is that Meillassoux posits weakness as the proper attitude (223); thus the loosening of ties between the qualities of the megodont and the essence of its being is the reason that a new symbiosis can occur with Anderson.

The megodont undergoes the fission of properties from its essence and the fusion of Anderson's properties to it. Its trunk is actually a python, another animal, removed from the dying elephant-like creature. The megodont's actions are becoming 'uncoordinated', meaning that they lack a central organising node – this would be the megodont's mind, which is slowly fading away in the last moments of its life. Such a dissembling into parts is central to what Thomas Disch calls a 'defining moment in the history of SF', David Bowman's transformation at the end of Arthur C. Clarke's *2001: A Space Odyssey* (1968) (Disch 2000: 68). In Bacigalupi's novel, these are moments of 'muscle and instinct' – of the visceral body which functions on its own rather than being controlled by the master-system of the mind. The creature's mouth hangs open, without the will to close. Yet this is not the image of an assembly, for the uncoordinated qualities create a tension, out of which comes a new object formed by the megodont and Anderson together. Then Anderson comes back into the picture: furnace heat blowing over him, now being prodded by the trunk which is only running on nerves. But then the megodont also comes back in full force. The last two fragments of the paragraph – 'Rocks him. Can't get a grip' – introduce another level of collusion. The trunk rocks Anderson, perhaps out of anger. However, maybe this is not the rocked of being bowled over, but rather that of soothing a baby to sleep. In the fragment 'Rocks him', 'him' still indicates Anderson's humanity, although this too is removed from the last moment: 'Can't get a grip' supposedly refers to the trunk being unable to grab on to Anderson, and thus being in the process of trying to kill him. But it might also refer to the mental state of the megodont, unable to coordinate its parts. The megodont is 'losing it'. In this sense the phrase can also refer to Anderson, who is being lost in the grammatically ambiguous moments of this passage. Perhaps it is best said that this phrase refers to them both, at once, in this moment of symbiosis at the death of an animal.

Science Friction

Temporality becomes foregrounded though the introduction of an incongruent element, like the *ngaw* or the megodont. In the domain of sf studies, the disruptive role of the incongruent element has been thought along with two terms, both developed by Darko Suvin: cognitive estrangement and the novum. This section aims to develop the role of these two terms in the discussion of the emergence of the new in sf, while also being aware of the work that has been done on both.

The past has been waiting for the future to complete it; in fact it has called out to the future for fulfilment. In this sense the *ngaw* occupies a rather traditional place in sf, that of an unknown object that provokes a 'conceptual breakthrough'. Traditionally, objects that provided such a change in thinking were large, and they have fallen under the half-serious moniker of a 'big dumb object' (Kaveney 1981), or BDO, which itself is related to Suvin's cognitive estrangement and the novum. While all three terms are quite common in sf criticism, the coordinates of the manner in which the *ngaw* functions are not. The *ngaw* is not a location of juxtaposition (Suvin 1979: 64) or even of inmixing (Delany 2009: 144), but rather of incorporation and desisting, both of which are essential if the reified dialecticism that Žižek challenged is to be obviated.

The history of the BDO is long and varied. However, it is of note that the term's canonisation – although done at first only as a joke (Nicholls 2000: 13) by Peter Nicholls and John Clute in *The Encyclopedia of Science Fiction* – lays much more focus on the size of the BDO than on its transformative properties (Nicholls and Clute 1999: 119). For example, Arthur Clarke's spaceship *Rama* (from the book of the same name) is only barely large enough to be included by Nicholls and Clute, although Roz Kaveney himself, who is credited with coining the term in the early 1980s, sees *Rama* as a prime example, and includes it in his updated definition in *From 'Alien' to 'The Matrix': Reading Science Fiction Film*:

> I created the term 'Big Dumb Object' to describe plots, common in the 1970s, in which the protagonists found a location so vast and complex that the entire book was taken up with their traversing it. Typical examples of this are Arthur C. Clarke's *Rama* and Larry Niven's *Ringworld*, both of which demanded whole series devoted to their exploration – more recent examples like Ian Macdonald's *Chaga* have actually been referred to textually as Big Dumb Objects, which is flattering. Nick Lowe has usefully suggested that genres like SF and fantasy are themselves Big Dumb Narrative Objects, that part of the pleasure of them is learning to move around them with more than a tourist's sense of location. (Kaveney 2005: 3–4)[17]

However, Peter Nicholls keys in on the aspect of the BDO that allows the fruit-sized *ngaw* to be included: 'Big Dumb Objects, like space, make us feel vulnerable and threatened and lost' (Nicholls 2000: 16). This 'making vulnerable' connects the BDO to two other key concepts in sf criticism: cognitive estrangement (or defamiliarisation – *ostranenie* as developed by Viktor Shklovsky) and the novum. Both terms were introduced by Suvin, first in his *Metamorphoses of Science Fiction: On the Poetics and History of a Literary Genre* (1979), and were then elaborated upon throughout his career. At the beginning of *Metamorphoses*, Suvin states that 'SF is, then, a literary genre whose necessary and sufficient conditions are the presence and interaction of estrangement and cognition, and whose main formal device is an imaginative framework alternative to the author's empirical environment' (Suvin 1979: 7–8). The element of cognition is related to Meillassoux's reading of more standard sf, in which certain events, even if found strange at the time, are posited as being eventually understandable. As Suvin puts it: 'SF sees the norms of any age, including emphatically its own, as unique, changeable and therefore subject to a *cognitive* view' (7).[18] Suvin takes the concept of estrangement from the formalists, focusing on how, in order for something familiar to become unfamiliar, a certain shared world-view must be supposed; a certain 'zero world' is proposed that the author and the implied reader share (11), which can then function as a springboard for the strange: 'the essential tension of SF is one between the readers, representing a certain number of types of Man of our times, and the encompassing and at least equipollent Unknown or Other introduced by the novum. This tension in turn estranges the empirical norm of the implied reader' (64).[19]

The impetus for this estrangement is the novum, a concept that Suvin adapts from Ernst Bloch, who said that 'A novum of cognitive innovation is a totalizing phenomenon or relationship deviating from the author's and implied reader's norm of reality' (cited in Suvin 1979: 64).[20] For Suvin, the novum is a 'mediating category whose explicative potency springs from its rare bridging of literary and extraliterary, fictional and empirical, formal and ideological domains, in brief from its unalienable historicity' (64). As such, the 'mediating' aspect of Suvin's construction of the novum functions as a lodestone, in that if there are two seemingly distinct elements (past/present, art/nature, literary/extraliterary), in what way can their being-with each other be described? When can it be said that one ends and the other begins? For dialectical materialism, this question takes the form of the role of the Communist Party in mediating both proletarians and intellectual anarchists (Jameson 2009: 28); for an ontological approach, it takes the form of the role of the 'with' or the 'in' in the relation of two items to a third (Sloterdijk 2011). However, for speculative realism, it is important to understand Suvin's structuring of the way in which the novum engages with and disrupts preconceived relationships between objects and qualities.

The traditional example for understanding Suvin's bridging, which can also be used as a catalyst to move beyond it, consists of three words from the opening scene of Robert Heinlein's *Beyond the Horizon* (1942): 'the door dilated' (Heinlein 2002: 2).[21] As Samuel Delany explains,

> The occurrence of unusual, if not downright opaque, signifiers in the syntagm focuses our attention on the structures implied (since the 'objects' that define the structures are themselves so frequently mysterious in one way or another), whether internal, external, implicit or explicit to any given signifier (or set of signifiers) in a given SF text. (Delany 2009: 139)

A door does not usually dilate. Thus, when confronted with this situation in a piece of fiction, the reader is taken out of their empirical experience and into another. Being taken out of one's world is what Suvin terms 'estrangement', which is caused by contact with an unfamiliar element (the novum).[22] A reader understands the novum through cognition, or the use of reason – which is especially important for Fredric Jameson's reading of Suvin (Jameson 2007: 63)[23] – which thus forms the 'bridge' to the alternative world of the novel. While this pattern is a part of all fiction and non-fiction, it is especially prevalent in and central to sf.[24]

As was briefly mentioned in the first chapter, Delany's reading of some of the standard tropes of sf foregrounds the difference between the assemblage and speculative realism. For Suvin, one important element of the novum is that it allows for the setting of '*one thing by the side of another*' (Suvin 1988: 142, italics in original). Peter Paik summarises this position:

> A text portraying a society in which the political institutions, social norms, economic system, and ways of life are superior – i.e., more harmonious, reasonable, virtuous, enlightened, and pleasurable – than those of the author's own society serves to estrange the reader by underscoring for her or him the bitter gulf that exists between the injustices and oppressions plaguing the society she or he inhabits and

the more humane and enlightened political order on display in the fiction. (Paik 2010: 3)[25]

Delany takes issue with this kind of juxtaposition, instead offering a notion of 'inmixing', which he does based on a reading of the classic example of Heinlein's 'the door dilated'. For Delany, it is not that one world is set against another, but rather that something new is created out of the mixing of the two:

> In terms of difference, however, the mental image of the door has undergone (because of the new predicate) a catastrophic change of form. The imagined door has gone from rectilinear to round; it is now composed of interleaved plates; quite likely its material composition has changed as well [...] We are dealing here neither with a familiar door suddenly estranged, a familiar process suddenly distanced, nor even a familiar sentence removed from its ordinary environment [...] What is significant about the signifier 'The door dilated,' is not how the mental image is *like* either a conventional door or a conventional camera aperture, but rather how it *differs* from both. (Delany 2009: 141)[26]

Delany offers his own version of such a difference in his novel *Stars in My Pocket like Grains of Sand* (1984) in which he states, in one scene, that 'The door deliquesced' (Delany 1985: 244). What is interesting about Delany's version is that it does not negate Heinlein's door but rather foregrounds one of the difficulties of the novum: for although *to deliquesce* simply means to melt away or dissolve, the relative infrequency of the term points to the fact that it is not important *what* the door does (dilate or deliquesce) but rather that it is simply fused with qualities that are different from everyday experience. However, this is not all that Delany's example does, for he challenges Suvin's 'alongside one another' with the 'in' of inmixing; this can be seen in what happens with the door of *Stars in My Pocket* after it deliquesces: it forms a puddle on the floor which at first it is thought requires to be stepped over, but then is decided requires to be stepped in. Delany's novel indicates a kind of immersion that functions differently than Suvin's medium of the novum: instead of forming a bridge, the novum forms a puddle; in other words, what is being approached is not just the setting beside one another of different qualities, but also the weird unknown of a dark object.

One of the limits of Suvin's view can be seen in how the phrase 'the door dilated' becomes normalised in Heinlein's novel, while Delany keeps it strange (by having the puddle stepped into, although we are not given the reason why this needs to be done). For example, in *Beyond this Horizon*: 'She ushered him as far as the door to the Moderator's private office, dilated it, and left him [...]'; '"Do you know, Phillis," he said as he dilated the door for her, "I have a feeling [...]"' (Heinlein 2002: 28, 82). Through repetition, the strange becomes familiar; in this sense what is strange to the 'world', in the Heideggerian sense, is being incorporated back into it (Thacker 2011: 4–5). Bacigalupi himself seems to enter this discussion through the use of the door motif in his short story 'Pocketful of Dharma', which is an example of inmixing in that there is no single-word novum attached to the door, which simply 'swings', and yet when it is touched it behaves in an unfamiliar manner:

> They came to a level nearly complete. Her feet echoed in a hallway, and she came to a door. Her hand leaned gently on the surface of the door and its skin moved slightly under pressure so that Wang Jun was unsure if the door molded to her hand or reached out to caress it. The door swung open and Wang Jun saw the luxury of the heights of which he had always dreamed. (Bacigalupi 2010: 19)

However, at the beginning of Bacigalupi's short story 'The People of Sand and Slag', a hatch does simply dilate (Bacigalupi 2010: 49).

Another instructive counter-example to Suvin's concept of the novum may be found in the use of the word 'soul' in Brian Aldiss's 1961 novel *Hothouse*. Although the story takes place in the distant future, near the end of Earth's lifespan, it is a prescient representation of the Anthropocene. Both the Earth and the moon have stopped spinning, and the overbearing sun on one half of the planet has created a hothouse atmosphere that encourages a plethora of voracious plant-life that puts the few remaining humans under constant threat. After one of the humans, Clat, is killed, the rest go back to her residence. It is then that the first instantiation of the term 'soul' is found, and it seems pretty much to fit into Suvin's standard definition of the novum: 'On the cot lay Clat's soul. Lily-yo took it and thrust it into her belt' (Aldiss 2008: 6). The oddity of a soul having the physicality to be thrust into a belt puts the soul in the traditional position of a novum.

Animal Death: Paolo Bacigalupi

In *Hothouse*, the soul does not maintain these coordinates, but goes through two alterations. First it is desacralised: two pages later it is revealed that the soul is a wooden totem carved at a child's birth, which is buried in place of their body, since bones rarely survive the body's demise in the violent forest (Aldiss 2008: 8). But then the soul is estranged again. At the end of part one of the novel, the Adam and Eve-esque pair Gren and Poyly have both been 'infected' by a fungus, which is the most intelligent being on the planet at the moment, and which enters into a kind of symbiosis with the humans, restoring their lost critical abilities, for better and for worse. As the two become infected, they make love. When they get up afterwards Gren sees that they have forgotten something:

> Gren glanced down at their feet. 'We've dropped our souls,' he said.
> She made a careless gesture. 'Leave them, Gren. They're only a nuisance. We don't need them any more.' (90)

The location of the term 'soul' with explicit reference to Adam and Eve, along with the loaded phrasing of 'dropping' souls which are a nuisance and no longer needed, act as triggers that the reader is now meant to relocate the wooden soul back into its transcendental function, which was removed in the initial encounter with the term 'soul' as a novum. Although disruptive objects have a more complicated economy in *The Windup Girl*, this movement from novum to not-novum and back again sets up a disruptive reading of an object. This movement can be seen in the figure of Emiko, as developed in the next section.

In short, the crux of Delany's inmixing is that it is 'more' resistant to being reincorporated in narration (at least when compared to the novum) than in a dialectic. It thus performs a short circuit. In this sense, inmixing lies on the side of 'theory', in that its potentiality is enacted through a removal, or desisting from incorporation. In the scene of the death of the megodont, both animal and human become more than they were before by being removed, both mentally and grammatically, from their current forms. Yet this removal is not something new, but rather something extrapolated from the dark, withdrawn potentiality of objects. This is one of the strengths of sf as a genre. As Steven Shaviro says in *No Speed Limit*,

> Science fiction takes up certain implicit conditions of our personal and social lives, and makes these conditions fully explicit in narrative.

It picks out 'futuristic' trends that are already embedded within our actual social, technological situation. These trends are not literal matters of fact, but they really exist *as* tendencies or potentialities. (Shaviro 2015b: 2)

The really existing tendencies are the antagonistic remainder that objects are not completely known, and this unknown is what can create an unusual symbiosis.

Emiko and Agitation

A novum such as Heinlein's 'the door dilated' was seen as being too 'one-sided', at least in comparison to the inmixing developed by Delany. Suvin's later development of the 'not only but also' in his *Positions and Presuppositions to Science Fiction* is closer to the 'unstable equilibrium' (Suvin 1988: 55) developed throughout this book. However, the focus of Bacigalupi's novel is not on equilibrium (no matter how unstable) but rather the antagonism that disrupts the dialectic he initially sets up.

The windup girl Emiko does not figure as a representation of two entities in an antagonistic relationship (past/present in the *ngaw*, animal/human in Anderson); rather, she performs a short circuit in that she both posits and disrupts the coordinates of her own fulfilment. Thus the windup girl questions the representation of the bipolarity of the dialectic and instead posits a singularity which carries the seeds of its own tension.

When Emiko is introduced she is sitting at a bar, drinking whiskey, trying to dull the pain of an unspecified act of humiliation she is about to be a part of: 'Emiko sips whiskey, wishing she were drunk, and waits for the signal from Kannika that it is time for her humiliation' (Bacigalupi 2009: 34). Here Emiko 'sips' her whiskey. This is an indication of enjoyment, of having time, of not being in a rush, which is in direct conflict with the next phrase, 'wishing she were drunk'. If Emiko wants to be drunk, and she has whiskey in front of her, why does she not 'down it' and, if there is more where that came from, have another? Thus Emiko is introduced through agitation: she has a will, she has a desire, but she is either controlled or controlling; she sips but she wants to gulp. This mystery is both advanced and further complicated by the end of the sentence: 'and waits for the signal from Kannika that it is time for her humiliation'. The humiliation can now be connected to the wishing to get drunk, and the sipping instead of gulping to being under the thumb of Kannika. Whatever the actual reasons for Emiko's conflict, the conflict is here, and it is a human conflict rather than any sort of specifically windup one, since at this point there is no clue offered in the text regarding Emiko's non-human status.

The rest of the paragraph brings this struggle to the fore: 'A part of her still struggles against it but the rest of her – the part that sits with her midriff-baring mini-jacket and tight *pha sin* skirt and a glass of whiskey in her hand – doesn't have the energy to fight' (34). The 'it' that is being struggled against is presumably either the humiliation or being under the control of someone who can humiliate her. The part that resists this is set up against the part that is putting on a show, dressed up, exposed, playing a role. So the first part of her, the resistance, is set up as the 'real', while the subservient part is the 'artificial'. An 'easy' dialectical relationship between these would be that she would experience her artificial self to such an extreme that she would find out that that is who she really is. But things are messier here. The next paragraph begins: 'And then she wonders if she has it backwards [. . .]' (34). She posits a reversal of the self-understanding that is proffered in the first paragraph: 'if the part that struggles to maintain her illusions of self-respect is the part intent upon her destruction. If her body, this collection of cells and manipulated DNA – with its own stronger, more practical needs – is actually the survivor: the one with will' (34). It is not important here which argument is correct, but rather that Emiko forms the site of her own questioning. In this sense she short-circuits the way that two different entities 'inmixed' with each other in the previous two sections of this chapter.

However, the narrational strategy of inmixing emerges when this interpretation is coupled with the 'whiskey' paragraph. Emiko sips instead of swills; she wonders if it is her DNA that stops her from breaking with her training, that ensures her survival. In this paragraph she wonders if she lacks the will to die or if she is too stubborn. Thus, in looking at the two paragraphs together, the following matrix is developed:

sip	swill
DNA	will
lack	stubborn

If we read each column from top to bottom, what the matrix makes clear is that Emiko sips the whiskey because her DNA lacks the capacity to will death. This in fact keeps her alive. She does not get drunk not because she does not have the will to do so, but because she is not stubborn enough to kill herself. What is foregrounded by this matrix, however, is not such an interpretation per se but rather the being-with or symbiosis of a number of contradictions within the same entity. In fact, Emiko is the 'thinking' of such contradictions together. This is why Adorno's thought is essential, for Emiko seems to be a representation of what Adorno means by 'negative dialectics':

> Nor is dialectics a simple reality, for contradictoriness is a category of reflection, the cogitative confrontation of concept and thing. To proceed dialectically means to think in contradictions, for the sake of the contradiction one experiences in the thing, and against the contradiction. A contradiction in reality, it is a contradiction against reality. (Adorno 1990: 144–5)

For Adorno, it is important that the thinking of such a contradiction is both 'in' and 'against' reality. Fredric Jameson shows the centrality of such 'negativity' to Adorno's view:

> Now perhaps we can grasp the nature of the dialectical effect – indeed the dialectical shock – more clearly as we follow the process whereby we are led to a critical and negative position, then brutally canceled in a second moment to which we are less likely to lend our absolute credence, having how learned the experience of the linguistic and conceptual untrustworthiness of such positions in general. To be sure, this ought to have been a lesson taught by the doctrine of ideology, but the latter still seems to promise a truth ('science'), a final correction [what Suvin calls equilibrium], a moment of resolution, or knowledge, for which there is little place in Adorno's implacably negative dialectic. (Jameson 2009: 56–7)

Delany's use of 'the door deliquesced' functions, at least in part, on the level of negative dialectics in that it is a concept (and is thus 'in' reality) that disrupts itself (and is thus against reality). This double movement takes place on a larger scale in relation to the windup girl Emiko, although both sides are contained in a singularity. It is in this sense that representation 'must strive, by way of the concept, to transcend the concept' (Adorno 1990: 15).

However, the revelation that Emiko is a machine is also disrupted. Following this new information, a stand-alone paragraph, in italics, seemingly represents the thoughts or comments of the crowd in general who see Emiko put through these acts and who realise that she is not human, although the comment is unattributed: '*Look! She is almost human!*' (Bacigalupi 2009: 35). Emiko is brought down to the level of 'just below' humanity, but it is done through the gaze, indicated by the imperative *Look!* and Emiko's role as a performer in the club. At the same time, it should be remembered that the economy of the gaze indicates that there is no mirror or other which is returning the gaze, but rather it is an action of misrecognition. Thus Emiko would seem to function in a similar way to the clones of *Never Let Me Go*, highlighting a lack of humanity in humanity itself through its own mistaken identification. What makes the coordinates of the figure of Emiko different, though, is that just as this smoothly dialectical comment is offered, it is contradicted. The narrative tells us that someone else thought differently, at some point, about her. Someone thought that her differences from humanity indicated not lack but surplus:

> Gendo-sama used to say that she was more than human. He used to stroke her black hair after they had made love and say that he thought it a pity New People were not more respected, and really it was too bad her movements would never be smooth. But still, did she not have perfect eyesight and perfect skin and disease- and cancer-resistant genes, and who was she to complain? At least her hair would never turn gray, and she would never age as quickly as he, even with his surgeries and pills and ointments and herbs that kept him young. (Bacigalupi 2009: 34–5)

Here on a pedestrian level it is made clear what is more- and what is less-human about Emiko: she has heightened senses and is resistant to disease; however, there is a tell. The clinamen of difference is located in Emiko's body: her movements will betray her. Gendo-sama says that her movements will never be 'smooth', that the jerky movements of her body will always be a sign of her 'almostness'. Thus Emiko occupies the coordinates of agitation. It is the remainder of difference within the more-than-human of the artificiality of Emiko that puts her in the position of the dialectical pluralism described above.

Short Circuit

In Emiko, both relation and non-relation coexist within a single object: herself. The importance of this doubled-self is that it short-circuits the easy dialectic of materialism that can take place between two objects. However, this short circuit does not negate the dialectic, for difference still exists; in fact it is maintained (between windup and human, past and present, individual and universal). It is from a 'position' of dialectical pluralism that Emiko functions in the novel.

Emiko's positioning in the novel is that she is both the thing and that which is disrupted by the thing. Emiko is a kind of double-character, or doppelgänger, as defined by John Herdman. Herdman argues that there are true doubles in literature, such as those found in Dostoyevsky and Hoffmann, or, as discussed above, Fat Charlie and Spider in Neil Gaiman's *Anansi Boys*. However, some characters are 'internally' double, or, looking at the work of Joseph Frank, 'quasi-double' (Herdman 1990: 14). The reason that the literary device of internal doubling can be profound is that 'the psychological power of the device lies in its ambiguity, in the projection of the subject's subjectivity upon a being whose reality the structure of the novel or story obliges the reader to accept' (Herdman 1990: 14). As such, self-division is about potentiality within ambiguity, at least in the sense that William Empson describes as his third type of ambiguity, which can

> describe two situations and leave the reader to infer various things which can be said about both of them; thus I should call it an ambiguity of this type when an ornamental comparison is not merely using one thing to illustrate another, but is interested in two things at once, and making them illustrate one another mutually. (Empson 1966: 112)

The short circuit that Emiko performs is that the 'two things' that Empson mentions are one, as Herdman indicates in his 'internal' form of doppelgänger. This is why Emiko is a powerful character: at times there is nothing outside her that reflects her struggle; she is struggle herself. 'Emiko puts her head in her hands. She wonders if she will find a date, or if she will be left alone at the end of the night, and then wonders if she knows which she prefers' (Bacigalupi 2009: 35).

What is being described is Harman's spatial tension of relation and non-relation, which is reflected in Emiko's origin in Japan, which makes her life in Thailand difficult. She is designed for upper-class service, and the work she does in Bangkok literally overheats her body. As she sits waiting for her turn to be displayed, she plays with the bar rings left by sweaty glasses, including, presumably, her own glass of whiskey. These rings turn into the wet, smooth skin that traps her into a life of servitude, for she must be continuously cooled in a culture in which all forms of energy are scarce, including that needed for keeping ice on hand for an illegal windup:

> Emiko traces her fingers through the wetness of bar rings. Warm beers sit and sweat wet slick rings, as slick as girls and men, as slick as her skin when she oils it to shine, to be soft like butter when a man touches her. As soft as skin can be, and perhaps more so, because if her physical movements are all stutter-stop flash-bulb strange, her skin is more than perfect. Even with her augmented vision she barely spies the pores of her flesh. So small. So delicate. *So optimal*. But made for Nippon and a rich man's climate control, not for here. Here, she is too hot and sweats too little. (Bacigalupi 2009: 35)

At first the description Emiko seems to offer of herself here mirrors that of the *ngaw*: the fruit was spiky and impenetrable on the outside, but had almost unbearably smooth flesh inside. Emiko is similar: her jerky movements and artificial, New People status are only the rough coating to her smooth, almost too smooth interior. But the structure of this passage is more complex. The passage from the sweating beer to the windup that cannot sweat enough both engages in the structure of the dialectic and provides a short circuit within it. This progression can be mapped out as follows:

Beer sits and sweats
Beer is slick as Emiko's skin for others
   → Her skin softer than skin
   → Movements stutter-stop
      → Skin is more than perfect
      → Augmented vision
      → She is optimal
         → Too hot, cannot sweat

The dialectical aspect of this schema is that something artificial – a glass of beer – has some qualities that Emiko possesses – a wet outer surface – a comparison which then shows that even though both artificial things are slick, Emiko's skin is even better than a non-augmented human's because of its extra-smoothness. However, this understanding is, in the end, short-circuited by the fact that Emiko cannot sweat herself, as a beer and a human can, and thus her perfection is only due to the traumatic kernel of a lack that is always ready to disrupt itself.

The issue that the figure Emiko raises here and throughout the novel is that of freedom, both from the known and the unknown:

> She wonders if she were a different kind of animal, some mindless furry Cheshire, say, if she would feel cooler. Not because her pores would be larger and more efficient and her skin not so painfully impermeable, but simply because she wouldn't have to think. She wouldn't have to know that she had been trapped in this suffocating perfect skin by some irritating scientist with his test tubes and DNA confetti mixes who made her flesh so so smooth, and her insides too too hot. (Bacigalupi 2009: 35–6)

Freedom from her present condition is not seen as a positive condition but rather a tautological one: if she were an animal, trapped in its world, she would not have to know she was an animal, trapped in its world. This is not freedom but annihilation. However, in another sense this is a description of the short circuit: freedom is not to be found in the interaction between objects but rather within the 'unfreedom' of the object itself. In part this is what Adorno means in his section on freedom in *Negative Dialectics* when he states that 'freedom itself and unfreedom are so entangled that unfreedom is not just an impediment to freedom but a premise of its concept' (Adorno 1990: 265). Such a 'doubling', however, is due in part to the structure of thought itself. As Jean-Luc Nancy argues in *The Experience of Freedom*, there is a doubling that happens on the level of thinking, in that freedom is not only the ground but the subject of thought:

> Above all, freedom is what expends: freedom is primarily prodigal liberality that endlessly expends and dispenses thinking. And it dispenses thinking primarily as prodigality. In this way, freedom gives without counting [...]; it gives thinking, it gives something to be thought about, yet it also simultaneously gives itself to be thought about in every thinking. (Nancy 1993: 53)

Symbiosis of One

Harman discusses change in relation to a symbiosis of two objects: 'We find that the key moments in a human life rarely result from introspective brooding in one's private chambers. Instead, they happen most often through symbiosis with a person, a profession, an institution, a city, a favorite author, a religion or in some other life-changing bond' (Harman 2016: 46). Yet with Emiko, symbiosis takes place within a single object. And it is not because she is thinking about some problem in a particularly philosophical manner. Instead, it is due to her structure, meaning the fact that the essence of her being is based on a contradictory tension. In this sense she performs a symbiosis of one.

Inspired by her new-found, if momentary, freedom as seen in the surplus of her gesture in the bath, Emiko tries to make a run for it, to go 'north' to where Anderson said the free windups live. It is dangerous for her to be on the streets of Bangkok; she is easily recognisable as an illegal windup, betraying herself by every step she takes with her jerky movements. Her main issue is with 'passing' for a non-windup: 'if Emiko is very careful, and fights her nature and her training – if she wears *pha sin*, and does not swing her arms – she almost passes' (Bacigalupi 2009: 103). Emiko's goal is to blend in. However, it is her movements that betray her. Much of the scholarly work done on 'passing' is in relation to transgender studies. For example, Jack Halberstam indicates the disruptive effect that performing gender can have in a film on those who are not transgender:

> The transgender film confronts powerfully the way that transgenderism is constituted as a paradox made up in equal parts of visibility and temporality: whenever the transgender character is seen to be transgendered, then he/she is both failing to pass and threatening to expose a rupture between the distinct temporal registers of past, present, and future. [...] Visibility, under these circumstances, may be equated with jeopardy, danger, and exposure, and it often becomes

necessary for the transgender character to disappear in order to remain viable. The transgender gaze becomes difficult to track because it depends on complex relations in time and space between seeing and not seeing, appearing and disappearing, knowing and not knowing. (Halberstam 2005: 77–8)[27]

Emiko struggles with passing. She eventually abandons this struggle and foregrounds the tension between art and nature that makes up her identity. She has escaped her relatively safe if wretched housing in order to find freedom in the windup village. The only way to get there is to move, to get on a river boat or board a train. This movement, however, is what betrays her. Although 'she blends in if she does not move' (Bacigalupi 2009: 104), because she needs to move she is eventually outed. It is here that Emiko illustrates the difference between the stasis of the withdrawn nature of objects and the movement of their sensual qualities on the surface. In stasis, Emiko's essence is unknown. But in movement, identity is assigned, but her identity also moves, since Emiko is never considered either totally natural or totally fake.[28]

Eventually Emiko is confronted by a man who was a soldier who fought military versions of the windups. He puts a knife to her throat and Emiko knows that she has to do something. But she does not simply react. She thinks, and even prays before taking him down: 'Emiko closes her eyes and prays to Mizuko Jizo Bodhisattva, and then the *bakeneko* Cheshire spirit for good measure. She takes a breath, and then with all her strength she slams her hand against the knife. The blade slices past her neck, a searing line' (107). Emiko is responding to the world rather than merely reacting to it, a difference developed above in relation to the animal and its world. However, such knowledge has a price. She runs, but she knows she will burn. She can go beyond herself in her actions, but what she has left behind will not be far. She knows she will die in both cases, under the knife of the soldier or burning up in the street, but she also knows that one is better than the other: 'She will burn, but she will not die passive like some pig led to slaughter' (107).

Emiko embraces her augmentation. This is where the symbiosis of one occurs. She is not in a relation to another idea or person, but rather to a part of herself that she tries to ignore. In this way Emiko is the monster she was sent to kill, as was developed in the first chapter with regard to Damon Knight's *Beyond the Barrier*. Emiko fails to pass, and in this failure the tension between art and nature that makes up her self becomes apparent. However, this is not the end of Emiko 'embracing' her augmentations. Another example is seen in the representation of spatial tension. This whole scene moves very slowly for Emiko, who for the first time is experiencing her sped-up state of being more than herself:

> Her attacker, shouting and waving his knife as he clambers through bamboo scaffolding. She's amazed that he's so slow, so much slower than she would have expected. She watches, puzzled. Perhaps he is also crippled from his time in the war? But no, his gait is correct, it's just that everything around her is slow: the people, the traffic. Odd. Surreal and slow. (108)

However, upon being rescued by Anderson, Emiko 'forgets herself' and her efforts at passing for a human being; thus her machine-like aspects become foregrounded. She calls Anderson a fool for helping her. Then 'she pushes damp hair away from her face. A surreal stutter-stop motion, the genetic bits of her unthinking. Her smooth skin shines between the edges of her slashed blouse, the gentle promise of her breasts. What would she feel like? Her skin gleams, smooth and inviting' (108). The symbiosis Emiko represents in this scene arises from a tension of time. For Harman, time is defined. The new phase enacted by this symbiosis is actually an evolutionary leap for both human and machine.

Emiko's next appearance in the novel comes filtered through Anderson's thoughts. He thinks about their developing relationship during a business meeting. He is now paying for her company every night. His thoughts about her allow a different interpretation to emerge of Emiko's thoughts on the relationship between her body and its training. Previously she had stated that because of the genetic manipulations her body had undergone she was filled with animal hungers; these hungers could only be countered through training provided by the same generippers who were responsible for these hungers in the first place. In Anderson's musings, Emiko seemingly makes the same point again, although she contradicts herself: '"My body is not mine [. . .] The men who designed me, they make me do things I cannot control. As if their hands are inside me. Like a puppet, yes? [. . .] They made me obedient, in all ways"' (184). Previously the urges that came about because of her design had to be counterbalanced by training in obedience; now, these urges are in fact obedience itself. On the one hand, this change of perspective could be put down to sloppy writing: Bacigalupi might have forgotten what Emiko said before, and not much should be read into this. However, if we follow the caveat that everything in a work of art is intentional, whether the author is aware of it or not (and of course, the unthought of an author is often the most productive for interpretation, meaning, for releasing the unthought of the critic), this reversal needs to be taken seriously.

Emiko says that her urges are like an animal's. This is in contradistinction to a sense of freedom from one's bodily urges that corresponds to the positive sense of being-in-the-world that Adorno criticises. Thus, for Emiko at this moment, the animal is that which is poor in relation to its world. This is, in the words of Leonard Lawlor, a Heideggerian attitude in that 'For Heidegger, animalistic signs, quite simply, do not grant access to the "as such"' (Lawlor 2007: 50). Anderson thinks something similar, although he fits it into the new context of her servitude being the urge: 'She is an animal. Servile as a dog' (Bacigalupi 2009: 184). The first argument that Emiko makes, that her animal urges, created by the generippers, can only be granted the status of being-in-the-world (in Heidegger's sense) through training provided by the same generippers, is actually the opposite of the argument that no training is needed because the animal urges that arise from her body, which are often sexual in nature, are themselves products of a coded servitude. In this sense, Emiko once again figures the short circuit in that here it is the control of servitude that is actually seen as the perpetrator of the elements of Emiko's body that she cannot control. Emiko's argument follows the logic that Jean Baudrillard lays out in his chapter 'The Animals: Territory and Metamorphosis' from *Simulacra and Simulation*. Baudrillard asks what kind of confession scientists are trying to extract from animals that are manipulated and abused by science. His answer is that animals are meant to show that the animal does not exist, that animal urges can be explained and controlled by science itself:

> [Scientists mean to extort p]recisely the admission of a principle of objectivity of which science is never certain, of which it secretly despairs. Animals must be made to say that they are not animals, that

bestiality, savagery – with what these terms imply of unintelligibility, radical strangeness to reason – do not exist, but on the contrary the most bestial behaviors, the most singular, the most *abnormal* are resolved in science, in physiological mechanism, in cerebral connections, etc. Bestiality, and its principle of uncertainty, must be killed in animals. (Baudrillard 2006: 129)

Thus there is no contradiction in the fact that both Emiko's urges and her ability to suppress urges are engineered by the generippers: both serve to control and thus annihilate the animal inside in a symbiosis of one.

At the same time, Emiko provides the ground for posing a challenge to her reified urges. This can be seen in how Anderson, following his comment that Emiko is 'servile like a dog', thinks: 'And yet if he is careful to make no demands, to leave the air between them open, another version of the windup girl emerges' (Bacigalupi 2009: 184). The person that emerges, however, is not a return to the natural or non-coded; rather, following the logic of Adorno outlined at the beginning of this chapter, a change in thought (i.e. philosophy) 'must strive, by way of the concept, to transcend the concept' (Adorno 1990: 15). Emiko does not transcend her programming by somehow avoiding it, but rather by fulfilling it in the sense of experiencing its withdrawn nature. This can be seen when later Emiko is at Anderson's penthouse apartment, alone. Again she thinks about the windup free-town. However, her contemplation is interrupted because her sense of hearing, which has also been genetically enhanced, picks up the sound of the building being swept by government troops. It is the white shirts. If she, an illegal windup, is caught, it will be the end of her. She needs to escape out into the street, which is only another risk of exposure. Her body is working against her: 'She's already boiling from running back and forth like a frantic rat' (Bacigalupi 2009: 198). However, Emiko once again expresses herself in all of her enhanced ways. She is stronger and faster than the natural humans around her. Usually she needs to hide this fact, but now she begins to relish it, to become who she is (which is the artificial enhancements given to her by the generippers – the surplus above and beyond humanity). She naturally moves and thinks at such an enhanced rapid pace that when she lets herself go the rest of the world inexplicably seems to slow down: 'The white shirts are running for her – running full bore – and yet somehow, strangely, they suddenly seem slow. Slow as honey on a cold day' (199). Emiko is realising her potential, her difference, by here foregrounding a temporal tension.

Emiko likes what she is becoming. Later in the story it is said that: 'At speed, she marvels at the movements of her body, how startlingly fluid she becomes, as if she is finally being true to her nature. As if all the training and lashes from Mizumi-sensei were designed to keep this knowledge buried' (254). Both urges and the ability to suppress those urges are expressed, and it is now an experience of this tension that Emiko has. However, this experience is not just something Emiko 'has', but is something that she inhabits. After suffering more humiliation at the hands of Kannika, Emiko finally surpasses her training and kills one of the VIPs who have been a part of the evening (259). Emiko is then on the run, hiding out with Anderson in his apartment. Eventually the police learn of her location and they bang on the apartment door. Anderson tells Emiko to hide in a closet. When she dresses she is also faster than normal. However, in the description of her speed, a new element is seen: 'Already she is dressing. Her stutter motion is fast, almost a blur. Her skin gleams as she pulls on a blouse and a pair of loose trousers. Suddenly she's shockingly fast. Fluid in her movements, strangely and suddenly graceful' (269). It is not that the speed of Emiko's movements hides her jerky nature, but rather that this jerkiness is a part of the fluidity itself. In fact, it seems necessary for it. Her movement is both fluid and strange; there is the dialectical movement of one to the other but within that movement there is trauma, there is a thread of tension. Instead of hiding, as Anderson suggests, Emiko jumps off the balcony, which is now an easier feat since she has done it before.

Eventually Emiko makes her way through a city raging in civil violence back to Anderson's apartment, where she tends him at his death (347). The epilogue of the novel shows a city in which Emiko excels. She is free, but still in Bangkok.

> She lives by scavenge and the hunt. She eats cheshires and catches fish with her bare hands. She is very quick. Her fingers flash down to spear a carp whenever she desires it. She eats well and sleeps easily, and with water all around (because of broken dams), she does not so greatly fear the heat that burns within her. If it is not he place for New People that she once imagined, it is still a niche. (356)

But this is not the end of the windup girl. She runs into Gibbons, the generipper. He toys with her in his cruel manner, barking at her to stand up, which she does before she can think about it (357). He says that her training was not the best, that her servile genes were probably taken from a Labrador, but that she is basically better than a human (357–8). Emiko fights against this, pointing out her jerky movements and her sterility, although Gibbons says that neither is permanent. The novel ends with a promise of excess, that he will give her these things, and 'much, much more' (359). But Emiko has shown that the way in which to work through the scientific removal of the animal from her body is not to turn back towards nature (as seen in her refusal to 'die like an animal'), but rather through the fulfilment of who she is through the artificially coded enhancements that the scientists have provided her. In this sense, embracing the poverty of the animal is what sets her free, for, as Adorno says, 'The more our consciousness is extricated from animality and comes to strike us as solid and lasting in its forms, the more stubbornly will it resist anything that would cause it to doubt its own eternity' (Adorno 1990: 369). This is not a turn away from the constrictions of her being, but rather a rapturous saying yes to them.

The image of Emiko embracing both her human and automated aspects brings together a number of different topics covered in this chapter. The main aim has been to show how speculative realism is not a dialectical form of thinking. The issue with dialectics, in this basic sense, is that it precludes the essence of objects, meaning the withdrawn real aspect of objects that can never be fully captured by sensual experience. The *ngaw* was initially used both to set up a dialectics and to dismantle it. The figure of the fruit denied a synthesis of past and present, instead foregrounding an antagonism or tension between the two. This tension was then connected to Samuel Delany's theory of inmixing, which is a figure of tension, rather than being a figure of eventual resolution like Suvin's reading of the novum. The megodont and Emiko are also seen as objects, as Harman describes them, 'locked in impossible tension with the crippled powers of language' (Harman 2012: 27). However, Emiko is singled out in the novel because she shows how objects that 'display seismic torsion with their own qualities' (27) can form a symbiosis of one, meaning that she is a figure that disrupts her own coordinates. This short circuit is seen as one of the key strategies for developing non-dialectical figures in fiction.

Notes

1. In *The Postmodern Condition*, Jean-François Lyotard describes the Kantian dynamic sublime as 'a strong and equivocal emotion: it carries both pleasure and pain . . . in it pleasure derives from pain' (Lyotard 2004: 77). Something is sublime 'when the imagination fails to present an object which might, if only in principle, come to match a concept' (78). In the case of the *ngaw*, the taste of the hard candy was taken to be exquisite in the past, but now the taste of the *ngaw* is so wonderful that the taste of the hard candy pales in comparison. The concept of the sublime is important, for it leads to potentiality; as Johannes Bertens argues, the sublime 'does not lead towards a resolution; the confrontation with the unpresentable leads to radical openness' (Bertens 1996: 113).
2. Cf. §247 of Hegel's *Philosophy of Nature*, which begins with the statement that 'Nature has presented itself as the Idea in the form of *otherness*' (Hegel 1970: 13).
3. Richard Rorty seems to allow for such a position, although he denies any qualitative claims for it: 'Nature may, for all we know, necessarily grow knowers which represent her, but we do not know what it would mean for Nature to feel that our conventions of representations are becoming more like her own' (Rorty 2009: 299).
4. Mauro Bozzetti foregrounds the a priori nature of the ratio in Adorno's thought: 'ratio is not a category but a presupposition of thought: if the unity of ratio is questioned, if no distinction is drawn between the irrationality of historical phenomena and the contradictoriness of thought, we no longer have any categories at all, no philosophical language, no philosophy. This is indeed Adorno's greatest provocation and hard to accept' (Bozzetti 2002: 307).
5. Avicenna developed Aristotle's reading of potentiality by dividing it into three categories: absolute ability, a child who may one day learn to write but does not yet know how to; possible potency, the human who has obtained the basic knowledge of writing though it is not fully developed; perfect potency, a human in full capacity of an ability but not exercising it (Acar 2003: 79). It is the last category, perfect potency (or potentiality), which will be a focus of this chapter.
6. In *Potentialities*, Giorgio Agamben states that 'For Aristotle, all potential to be or to do something is always also potential not to be or not to do' (Agamben 1999: 215).
7. Cf. another member of the Frankfurt School, Siegfried Kracauer, and

his call for more, not less, rationality in combating the dehumanising aspects of the ornament (Kracauer 1995: 86; cf. Foster 2003: 75–6).
8. This has also been given a recent formulation by Manuel DeLanda in his *Philosophy and Simulation* under an investigation of the co-presencing of irreducible and decomposable wholes (DeLanda 2011: 185).
9. In Heideggerian terms, this question is taken up under *Gelassenheit*, or 'letting-be': 'man, *as* in-dwelling in releasement to that-which-regions, would abide in the origin of his nature, which in consequence we may paraphrase: man is he who is made use of for the nature of truth. And so, abiding in his origin, man would be drawn to what is noble in his nature. He would have a presentiment of the noble mind' (Heidegger 1966: 84–5). However, it is important to note that in the section '*Gelassenheit?* No, Thanks!' from *The Parallax View*, Žižek refers to 'letting-be' as sustaining 'the utmost violence of ontic engagements' because such a subordination to truth is a smoothing over of relations instead of an opening towards antagonism: 'everything is not just the interplay of appearances, there is a Real – this Real, however, is not the inaccessible Thing, but the *gap* which prevents our access to it, the "rock" of the antagonism which distorts our view of the perceived object through a partial perspective. And, again, the "truth" is not the "real" state of things, that is, the "direct" view of the object without perspectival distortion, but the very Real of the antagonism which causes perspectival distortion. The site of truth is not the way "things really are in themselves", beyond their perspectival distortions, but the very gap, passage, which separates one perspective from another, the gap (in this case: social antagonism) which makes the two perspectives radically *incommensurable*. The "Real as impossible" is the cause of the impossibility of ever attaining the "neutral" non-perspectival view of the object. There is a truth, everything is not relative – but this truth is the truth of the perspectival distortion as such, not the truth distorted by the partial view from a one-sided perspective' (Žižek 2006: 281).
10. For Badiou, disruption comes about through art, love, politics or science. Fidelity to a disruptive event (May 1968, Cubism, set theory, love) is to multiply the event without identity (Badiou 2004).
11. Much work has been done on foregrounding the antagonism within this dichotomy, including Nancy's *The Inoperative Community* (1991), Agamben's *The Coming Community* (2003), Anderson's *Imagined Communities* (2006) and Hardt and Negri's *Multitude* (2004).

12. However, it should be kept in mind that Adorno's 'path' to the unreconciled is not through a lack of rationality but rather through 'more' of it (cf. Jay 1996: 259–60).
13. I do not mean misrecognition in the valuable sense assigned to it by Pierre Bourdieu (Bourdieu 1996: 30–2) but rather that of Lacan's *méconnaissance* (Lacan 2001: 41).
14. The lack of provenance is one of the key disruptive aspects of the cyborg in Donna Haraway's well-known essay (Haraway 1991). The family is taken as a temporal and spatial issue by Jack (formerly Judith) Halberstam, the question of which can set up a 'queer' time and space: 'The time of reproduction is ruled by a biological clock for women and by strict bourgeois rules of respectability and scheduling for married couples. Obviously, not all people who have children keep or are even able to keep reproductive time, but many and possibly most people believe that the scheduling of repro-time is natural and desirable. Family time refers to the normative scheduling of daily life (early to bed, early to rise) that accompanies the practice of child rearing. This timetable is governed by an imagined set of children's needs, and it relates to beliefs about children's health and healthful environments for child rearing. The time of inheritance refers to an overview of generational time within which values, wealth, goods and morals are passed through family ties from one generation to the next. It also connects the family to the historical past of the nation, and glances ahead to connect the family to the future of both familial and national stability. In this category we can include kinds of hypothetical temporality – the time of "what if" – that demands protection in the way of insurance policies, health care, and wills' (Halberstam 2005: 5). A non-sf example of how a lack of provenance can set up an alternative 'lifestyle' appears at the beginning of Sarah Waters's *Fingersmith* (2002): 'My name, in those days, was Susan Trinder. People called me Sue. I know the year I was born in, but for many years I did not know the date, and took my birthday at Christmas. I believe I am an orphan. My mother I know is dead. But I never saw her, she was nothing to me. I was Mrs Sucksby's child, if I was anyone's; and for father I had Mr Ibbs, who kept the locksmith's shop, at Lant Street, in the Borough, near to the Thames' (Waters 2002: 3). Of course, one of the sources for alternative relationships based on alternative families is the Book of Ruth, from the Old Testament, in which Naomi and her husband move from Bethlehem to Moab because of drought. Their two sons marry in Moab, but then all three males die. Naomi is to return

to Bethlehem and she begs her daughters-in-law to stay in Moab and find new husbands. One does, but the other, Ruth, makes a pledge of friendship to Naomi that is seen as an early example of a representation of a strong female–female friendship: '1:16 And Ruth said, Intreat me not to leave thee, or to return from following after thee: for whither thou goest, I will go; and where thou lodgest, I will lodge: thy people shall be my people, and thy God my God: 1:17 Where thou diest, will I die, and there will I be buried: the LORD do so to me, and more also, if ought but death part thee and me' (KJV). As an indication of the 'radicalness' of this passage, part of it has now become a standard text to represent the romantic bond in marriage ceremonies between heterosexual couples.

15. However, the *ngaw* is strangely removed not only from Anderson's past but also from his construction of history. This is seen in the way Bacigalupi informs the reader that the *ngaw* is not the only fruit that lies in this nether-region of the past, for so do the more 'familiar' nightshades, potatoes, tomatoes and chilies (Bacigalupi 2009: 4). Therefore the *ngaw* is given a sense of concreteness for readers that it does not have for Anderson. For him it remains new, without signposts: a mystery.

16. Noah Horowitz, in his book *Reality in the Name of God, or Divine Insistence*, differentiates Derrida's and Meillassoux's messianic futuricity by equating Derrida's *différance* with idealism (Horowitz 2012: 115).

17. In Clarke's *Rendezvous with Rama* (1972), the ship is described as being so large that is difficult to comprehend: 'Its body was a cylinder so geometrically perfect that it might have been turned on a lathe – one with centers fifty kilometers apart. The two ends were quite flat, apart from some small structures at the center of one face, and were twenty kilometers across; from a distance, when there was no sense of scale, Rama looked almost comically like an ordinary boiler' (Clarke 1974: 12).

18. Suvin expands on this by saying that cognition 'implies not only a reflecting *of* but also *on* reality. It implies a creative approach tending toward a dynamic transformation rather than toward a static mirroring of the author's environment' (Suvin 1979: 10).

19. In *Alien Encounters*, Mark Rose states that estrangement 'may be regarded as the simplest as well as one of the most common patterns that science fiction narratives follow [. . .] The extraordinary intruder may be an alien creature, a novel and devastating disease, a climatic or ecological change, a technological innovation, or any of

a larger number of other possibilities. Sometimes the familiar world is either partially or wholly restored at the story's end, sometimes it is not. The narrative's emphasis may fall upon the threat of change, the process of change, or the effects of change' (Rose 1981: 26–7). In *Victorian Science Fiction in the UK: The Discourses of Knowledge and Power*, Suvin foregrounds the importance of the contexts of production and reception in relation to the novum (Suvin 1983: 299–300).

20. For an important historical contextualisation of the novum, see Patrick Parrinder's introduction to *Learning from Other Worlds: Estrangement, Cognition and the Politics of Science Fiction and Utopia* (Parrinder 2001: 6–8). In *Structural Fabulation*, Robert Scholes bemoans the fact that the novum is a 'thing' in a text rather than a stylistic element, as found in poetry (Scholes 1975: 47).

21. The tradition of interpreting these three words began with Harlan Ellison's essay 'A Voice from the Styx' (Ellison 1978).

22. The novum emerges in all of the presuppositions that this phrase (and all others) entails: 'The famous S-F sentence "The door dilated" presupposes – among many other things – that in this narration's universe of discourse there are intelligent beings (psycho-zoa) who use sight, locomotion, and constructed edifices, that these edifices incorporate building techniques not used in human history up to the writer's period, that the narration's "otherness" locus is normal for the implied narrator, and that the categories of visual observation, locomotion, constructed edifices, building techniques, and historical normality are relevant for understanding this universe of discourse' (Suvin 1983: 301).

23. The importance of the rational is also stressed by Stephen Burt, who argues that for Suvin, literature without the rational is just fantasy: 'for him, SF properly so-called presents a world set apart from our own by some new thing in science, technology, or nonhuman nature – the invention of teleportation, for example, or contact with space-faring species. That new thing – the "novum" – must be integral to the world or the plot of the fiction, and it must be imagined as subject to rational inquiry (so as to let us imagine that real life might change, too); otherwise we are reading fantasy, for Suvin almost by definition a conservative, regressive, bad thing' (Burt 2009: 600).

24. In *The Seven Beauties of Science Fiction*, Csicsery-Ronay stresses that both the novum and cognitive estrangement are *effects* and not things in themselves (Csicsery-Ronay 2008: 75).

25. Perry Nodelman, in an early review of *Metamorphoses*, claims that

'Suvin emphasizes estrangement for two reasons. The first is political. As a Marxist, he sees science fiction as a literature of revolt, "a genre showing how 'things could be different.'" The second is only a little less political. As a Marxist scholar, Suvin wants to reinvent literary history in Marxist terms – to show how science fiction has actually existed for centuries, but that little is known about it because it has always expressed the aspirations of the masses' (Nodelman 1981: 24). Suvin stresses the political aspect of estrangement in his afterword to a collection on the topic (Suvin 2001).

26. Delany limited the 'amount of new' generated from such inmixing in an interview from 1998 (Freedman 2009: 42–3).
27. Sadie Wearing takes a more critical approach to the initial motivations for wanting to pass in the first place in 'Subjects of Rejuvenation' (Wearing 2007: 285–7).
28. A classic example of the difficulty of identifying an android among humans is Philip K. Dick's *Do Androids Dream of Electric Sheep?* (1968). In hunting down a number of escaped androids in order to terminate them, Deckard comes up against a number of issues in applying the 'Voight-Kampff' test, which is meant to separate the human from the non-human. However, what usually gets in the way is either desire or the feminine. For example, when giving the female opera singer Luft the Voight-Kampff test, Deckard finds that he is unable to get a meaningful response. This is not because she refuses to answer his questions, but rather that she uses language to disrupt language itself, a language through which Deckard is attempting to substantiate her androidness. The first question is about killing a wasp. Deckard sets up the situation: '"You're sitting watching TV and suddenly you discover a wasp crawling on your wrist."' Luft interrupts because she does not know what a wasp is (Dick 1996: 102). Deckard explains, but Luft still does not understand. '"Tell me the German word"' (103) she demands. Deckard thinks about it, remembers *Wespe*, and by this time the original question has been forgotten. 'Impossible now to get a meaningful response' (103) the actual reader is told in free indirect speech. So they try again, this time skipping the details to get to the essentials, and he describes a meal of '"boiled dog, stuffed with rice"' (103). The response that the Voight-Kampff test is supposed to measure is blushing, or shame, which is the uncontrollable response of 'capillary dilation in the facial area' (46). However, Deckard is unable to get a measurable response because Luft meets his questions with counter-questions, misunderstandings, and requests for clarification. In response to

Deckard's question about boiled dog, Luft sidetracks him by talking about movies from the Philippines. The same happens when Luft needs the word 'verdant' explained, and when she mistakes the painter's name 'Currier' for the word 'curry' (103–4). Finally, Luft has had enough and pulls out her laser tube when Deckard seemingly gets fresh by asking a question about visiting a man's apartment.

7

Transcription: Kim Stanley Robinson

> Rather like my father a few years before, I'd be given another chance; and it would be the chance at a second life, with very little connection to the old one. I would have nothing to mourn.
>
> Michel Houellebecq, *Submission* (2015)

The Bardo

The reading of tension in sf continues in this chapter, which looks at a number of books by Kim Stanley Robinson, along with two early works by J. G. Ballard. The focus is on the transformations that take place when tension is foregrounded. This tension is seen as something that lies on the surface of things, rather than at any kind of depth. By focusing on the surface, the causal connection between objects and qualities is developed, along with the way that it can lead towards change. The concept of transcription is borrowed from musicology in order to develop a model for such transformation. In the Anthropocene, transcription is seen as essential in order to begin living in the new scales of time and space that are being thrust upon us.

Robinson's *The Years of Rice and Salt* is an alternative history about many reincarnations of the Buddha from the seventh century AD until the present day. Although it is never stated directly that the various reincarnations described in the novel are of the Buddha, the opening lines of the book indicate this: 'Monkey never dies. He keeps coming back to us in times of trouble, just as he helped Tripitaka through the dangers of the first journey to the west, to bring Buddhism back from India to China' (Robinson 2003: 3). The monkey is a key instantiation in the many reincarnations of Buddha, as can be seen in some of the *Jakata* stories (Sarma 2006). This alternate history, however, is not so much about Buddhism, but rather proposes that most of the population of Europe is wiped out by the Black Death, and Islam becomes the dominant, unmarked force on the planet. Robinson has 'attempted to consider seriously the nature of Islamic fundamentalism within an Islamic context rather than merely as oppositional to the West' (Mendelsohn 2003: 268). Foregrounding both Buddhism and Islam was one of the main goals of the novel, as Robinson himself stated in an interview in 2004: 'One of the effects of this structure is that you are able to offer readers extended encounters with religious beliefs and social practices with which many North Americans are likely to be unfamiliar, from the social character of Buddhism to the culture of the Islamic madressa' (Robinson, Szemen and Whiteman 2004: 179).[1]

Ten cycles of reincarnation are described. In each cycle the two main characters' names have the same first letters: 'b' and 'k'. In the first chapter they are Bold and Kyu, in the last Bao and Kung. As the novel opens, Bold is a Mongolian horseman who finds his encampment devastated by the Black Death. He is sent wandering by this event and, 'after he had long gotten used to living alone in the world' (Robinson 2003: 14), he eventually comes into contact with a village, and then cities, as he moves eastwards. Eventually he is captured and sold as a slave.

On a Chinese vessel heading to Bold's homeland he meets another slave, the boy Kyu, who is made a eunuch during the journey (33–4). Upon their arrival, Kyu's fortunes rapidly change, as he is skilful at court politics, while Bold remains where he began, minding the horses in the stable. Eventually Kyu has less and less to do with Bold, until they are both brought together again after their deaths. They meet again in the bardo (Tibetan for 'in-between state', or the place that lies between death and rebirth), and it is here that an analysis of certain aspects of speculative realism in the novel takes place.

Kyu's problem in the bardo has to do with his inability to form a symbiosis with what is around him. However, at first Kyu is ready to do so, and is thus ready for reincarnation; he is one with the void he encounters at death, just as this void is one with itself: 'At the moment of death Kyu saw the clear white light. It was everywhere, it bathed the void in itself, and he was a part of it, and sang it out into the void' (80). However, Kyu cannot remain focused; he is too distracted by the whirring of his own mind; he sinks into himself rather than being open to the otherness that is the wheel of rebirth. Kyu complains that what is distracting him is not his own mind, but rather a bloody scene before him. A Buddha, 'radiating calm', sits on a dais, surrounded by a number of 'peaceful deities' (81). Yet below them is bloodshed:

> The righteous dead were climbing long flying roads up to these gods. On the deck surrounding the dais, less fortunate dead were being hacked to pieces by demons, demons as black as the Lord of Death, but smaller and more agile. Below the deck more demons were torturing yet more souls. It was busy and Kyu was annoyed. This is my judgment, and it's like a morning abattoir! How am I supposed to concentrate? (81)

In this scene Kyu is having difficulty with his reincarnation because he cannot lose himself in the scene. Instead he exists in a state of tension with it. Tension arises from Kyu both being in relation to the bardo, since he is in it, and being in non-relation to it, because he cannot help questioning the bloodshed below him.

It was argued above that tension does not exist everywhere. As Graham Harman says, tension is 'a term that implies simultaneous closeness and separation' (Harman 2011a: 108). Therefore being in the bardo is supposed to be tension-free, with Kyu being one with everything around him. However, this scene represents the tension of space, which is foregrounded in the bardo in Robinson's novel.

The *Tibetan Book of the Dead*, or the *Bardo Thodol*, is an early fourteenth-century text aimed at offering guidance for the soul experiencing reincarnation, or passing through the bardo. The bardo is a place of transition, the space in which one phase changes into another. It is not a space of metamorphosis, which implies the complete change of one figure into another, but rather of modulation, in which some aspect of a figure remains the same throughout (Robinson 2003: 187; Shaviro 2010: 13–14), meaning its essence (Harman 2013: 27). Passage through the bardo lasts 49 days, and when Kyu sees bloodshed below him, it means he is in the central, violent part of this period. According to the *Bardo Thodol*, this period of the bardo is made up of 'the fifty-eight flame-enhaloed, wrathful, blood-drinking deities come to dawn, who are only the former Peaceful deities in changed aspect' (Evans-Wentz 2000: 131). The bardo is about transformation, and the different aspects of deities a person is confronted with are meant to cause a change in the subject, thus affecting the form they will take in the next life. However, Kyu's tension in the bardo indicates that it has another function in *The Years of Rice and Salt*. For although Kyu was distracted before he saw the bodies, it was his distracted state that allowed him to experience the bardo for what it is (at least in part): a torture chamber.

Kyu is in the beyond, meaning that which lies beyond both life and death, and yet he brings the bardo to the surface, seeing it as torture and bloodshed rather than just an unreal transition in which psychological change can take place. In this sense, Kyu brings the bardo out in front, rather than letting it reside behind or beyond. In *Realist Magic*, Timothy Morton makes a similar claim for a speculative realist reading of the bardo. The abyss of the bardo is '*out in front of objects*' (Morton 2013b: 178), meaning that it is located in the tension of space and time rather than at any kind of depth. For Morton, the bardo is a powerful figure for this tension because the spaces of the bardo are causal: 'In other words, what you do in them affects what happens next. And what you have done affects what happens in them, now' (178). Although Morton is more focused here on the interaction of things in a kind of assemblage rather than a tension between qualities and essence, his foregrounding of the reality of symbiosis is of great importance. 'OOO [Object-Oriented Ontology] and Buddhism share something very interesting,' he says. 'They both hold that the interstitial space between things is not a blank void. In fact, it's charged with meaning, even with causality' (197).

In *The Years of Rice and Salt*, the causality of the bardo is foregrounded through Kyu's tension with it. Kyu does not pass through the changes of the bardo without a fight. Instead, he is unable to focus, be calm and progress through the rings of reincarnation in the appropriate fashion. Kyu is tense in the bardo. 'How am I supposed to concentrate,' he wonders, amid all these horrors. And when the black god holds a mirror up to his face to reflect his mood, Kyu cannot look into it: 'he had to concentrate on it [the mirror], as Bold kept reminding him. And yet all the while the whole antic festival shouted and shrieked and clanged around him, every possible punishment or reward given out at once, and he couldn't help it, he was annoyed' (83). Kyu's annoyance is a kind of tension because it is a separation, a fission, of Kyu from reincarnation. He does not go through it smoothly, but rather is in conflict with his surroundings. This tension then leads Kyu to think about what is happening.

> 'Why is black evil and white good?' he demanded of the Lord of Death. 'I never saw it that way. If this is all my own thinking, then why is that so? Why is my Lord of Death not a big Arab slave trader, as it would be in my own village? Why are your agents not lions and leopards?' (83)

For Kyu, the bardo is when the connections between objects and qualities are not taken for granted. Why is black evil and white good? Why is the Lord of Death not a slave trader, why are the agents not beasts of prey? The reason that his questions capture tension is because they indicate figures of both relation and non-relation. The Lord of Death is not a slave trader in the novel, but acts like one. The agents are not bloodthirsty animals, but just as well could be. As Harman says of tension,

> on the one hand, two poles might be kept so entirely separate as to have no relation at all, and on the other hand they might be so fused together that a state of utterly banal attachment would be the result. We need to identify the conditions under which both extremes are able to pass into tension, whether through a fission of banality (as in the case with sensual objects) or through fusion of what was previously separate (as is the case with real ones). (Harman 2011a: 108–9)

In Robinson's work, the bardo is the name for a time in which these conditions arise, and it does not only appear in *The Years of Rice and Salt*.

The bardo makes a brief appearance in *Blue Mars* (1996), the final book of Robinson's Mars Trilogy. A brief inter-chapter takes the form of a fable. Gyatso Rinpoche, the eighteenth reincarnation of the Dalai Lama, is in the bardo looking for a body into which to transmigrate. Reincarnation on Earth is rejected for political reasons: China rules Tibet. However, Mars is not a clear option because everyone is simply too busy to be bothered being the next Dalai Lama. Time is running out, the bardo is getting cold. Then a new form of reincarnation is suggested, one which matches the new kind of life being forged on the red planet. 'We'd be honored' to be your next reincarnation, some of the Martians say, 'Only it will have to be all of us at once. We do everything like that together' (Robinson 1997: 112). It is thus, as McKenzie Wark says, that the trilogy 'is making the near-utopian aspect of the most advanced forms of collaborative labor a general condition' (Wark 2015: 186), even in reincarnation.

Another example of the bardo in Robinson's work is found in *2312*, which was discussed in the first chapter. The main character, Swan, travels on a large, hollowed-out asteroid called a darkliner. Everyone in a darkliner is submerged in complete darkness, and this allows new combinations of objects and qualities to arise. However, one point that was not made above is that Robinson calls the darkliner a bardo. 'She was floating in the bardo, trying to think like someone unborn would think. Full of dubitation, child of a poverty. Would be reborn some other Swan' (Robinson 2012: 92). Like Kyu, Swan is full of doubt. This feeling arises from being in the complete dark, while for Kyu is arises from being surrounded by torture. Yet the result of doubt is the same: Swan, like Kyu, imagines both fission and fusion. Fission appears in her rebirth as another Swan, while fusion is seen in the way she is trying to taking on the qualities of the thought of a child. The reason the bardo functions in this way is because it is a relatively dark object, meaning that it foregrounds both new, unexpected, yet still possible connections between objects along with the fact that objects remain withdrawn from any kind of complete knowing.

Yet the bardo is not a place, but rather a time. It is the intermediate time between life and death. The removal of the bardo from both the time of life and the time of death is one reason for the doubt that Kyu and Swan feel. It is also the reason that it can function as a figure of both the fusion and fission of qualities. The bardo is an important image in Robinson's work because it represents a time of possibility and change, of new phases. As Fredric Jameson, Robinson's PhD mentor, says of the Mars Trilogy, it does not present utopia, but rather it 'opens the space into which it is to be imagined' (Jameson 2007: 409). Yet the mechanism of this opening has not been mapped out. Another scene in *2312* will provide a clue for this task: the work of *transcription*.

Transcription

On Mercury, Swan is convinced by Wahram (a politician from Titan who will eventually become her husband) to attend a

Beethoven concert. Afterwards, Mercury's capital is attacked, starting one of the main plot threads of the novel. However, it is during the Beethoven concert that the idea of transcription is developed.

The evening features

> a triple bill of rarely played transcriptions: first a wind ensemble playing a transcription of the *Appassionata* piano sonata; then Beethoven's opus 134, which was his own transcription for two pianos of his *Grosse Fugue* for string quartet, opus 133. Lastly a string quartet was to play a transcription of their own for the *Hammerklavier* sonata. (Robinson 2012: 142)

Musical transcription began as a learning tool for students before the advent of recording devices. The importance of transcription here is how the withdrawn essence of an object, a piano sonata for example, becomes tangible not through its direct representation, but rather through a multitude of indirect representations (or in the case of music, presentations) across different media. Music philosopher Stephen Davies argues that the essence, or '*musical content*', of a piece is 'preserved in the different medium of the transcription' (Davies 2005: 50). A change of medium, from piano to string quartet, is essential to the definition of transcription. Thus when the same words are copies from one piece to another, this is not transcription, for the same content appears in both media (51). Yet Davies does not draw out the consequence of both the preservation of an essence and the change involved when two different media are used. Although a historian and not a philosopher, Cecil Gray does a better job of capturing this contradiction when he says that in transcription, 'what one medium has in common with the other greatly exceeds, both in quantity and importance, that which belongs to it alone' (Gray 2009: 100). However, even Gray's formulation will need to be expanded in order to understand what is going on in Robinson's novel.

There are more musicians than audience members for the Beethoven concert on Mercury. However, those who are there enjoy it immensely, at least for the most part. The first piece is the piano sonata transcribed for wind instruments. The change from one medium to another causes the creation of something new: 'The transcription to winds made it a new thing in the same way that Ravel had made Mussorgsky's *Pictures at an Exhibition* a new thing' (Robinson 2012: 142). The third piece is similar. However, the description of the second piece develops what is meant by 'a new thing'. It is not a new entity, so to speak, but rather, unexpected qualities are fused to the old piece, while familiar qualities are fissioned off it. Regarding the transcription that Beethoven made for the *Grosse Fugue*, the musicians 'had to pound away' on the piano 'like percussionists, simply hammering the keys'. Treating the piano like a string instrument does not create a new piece, but instead makes Wahram aware of aspects of the work that he missed while hearing it played on the strings: 'More clearly than ever Wahram heard the intricate wave of the big fugue, the crazy energy of the thing ... The sharp attack of struck piano keys gave the piece a clarity and violence that strings with the best will and technique in the world could not achieve' (142). In this example, nothing new is created, but unexpected properties of the piece are discovered. At the same time, this does not mean that all the properties of the piece have been discovered. The piano does not exhaust the possibilities of the strings; many other transcriptions could be made, but not an infinite amount. The piece could not be transcribed to be played on a rock, or transcribed into cotton candy. This is what Davies means by a transcription needing to contain the '*musical* content' of the original piece. In the language developed above, a transcription, just like what happens in the bardo, must contain relation along with non-relation.

Harman defines spatial tension in terms of relation and non-relation. This tension plays a large part in a technique that he describes called *ruination*, which has much in common with Robinson's transcription. Harman's example is a joke which is ruined by being described literally (Harman 2012: 38–9). Yet ruining a joke can say something about the joke, about the kernel of its humour. And the more ways a joke (or anything else) can be ruined, the more can be known about it, although in an indirect fashion. Ruination thus indicates something about the power of a joke, statement or piece of music, but indirectly. 'I would ... say not only that a statement is effective only when it can be ruined, but that the statement is of higher quality the more ways it can be ruined' (41). In relation to transcription, the more transcriptions possible, the more powerful the piece.

Ruination is connected to the spatial tension of relation and non-relation in the following way. If the original and the transcription, for example, are too close to each other, then one has no chance of ruining the other. They are too related, so to speak (Harman 2016: 73). However, if the transcription has the chance of ruining the original, then something can be learned about the original itself (what was ruined). In the example from 2312, ruination takes place at the end of the performance but in the opposite manner. It is not that the transcription is too thickly related to the original, but too thinly. The two fugues of the concert are reprised, although both are played together. 'The two pieces overlapped with the wrong instruments applied to each, increasing the cognitive confusion' (Robinson 2012: 144). Wahram enjoys the piece, although for Swan it was '"Too crazy at the end"' (144). For Swan, the finale is too much a piece of non-relation. It says nothing about what came before. It is an example of Meillassoux's Type-3 world object, something that is so random that there is nothing to learn from it whatsoever.

The Transcriptionocene

Yet the type of transcription found in the second piece, when the strings of the *Grosse Fugue* were recalibrated for the piano, mirrors an important strategy that is developed throughout Robinson's work: transformation by design, which is also open to unexpected outcomes. This is the mode of transcription which is a planned remediation that can expose unexpected qualities of the original piece. This type of transcription is also an important strategy for living in the Anthropocene, as Robinson shows in his novel *Aurora* (2015). A group of humans are travelling on a multi-generation starship to colonise the nearest Earth-like planet, Aurora. The journey takes 170 years travelling at 1/10 of light speed. Upon reaching Aurora, the colonists find a deadly protein that kills all the people who descend on to the planet. About half of the remaining people decide to try again on a nearby planet, while the other half thinks that 'life is a planetary expression' (Robinson 2015: 428), meaning that all beings evolve along with smaller life forms, and this makes it impossible for a life form from one solar system to ever live on a planet outside that system (178–9).

Upon returning home, Freya, the main character, engages in an act of transcription by reconstructing beaches that were washed away when the sea levels rose due to climate change, an activity hinted at in 2312 (Robinson 2012: 449). When Freya returns to earth, all the beaches are gone. This is because of the irrevocable damage caused during the Anthropocene: 'Sea level rose twenty-four meters in the twenty-second and twenty-third centuries of the common era, because of processes they began in the twenty-first century that they couldn't later reverse; and in that rise, all of the Earth's beaches drowned' (Robinson 2015: 436). Some of those on Earth engage in a semi-illegal activity called 'beach return' (437). This is not an example of the quick-fix de-extinction offered by regenesis (Dawson 2016: 78–9). A couple of decades are needed for the work of beach return. Starting with heavy industry such as 'mines, rock grinders, barges, pumps, tubing, scoops, bulldozers, earthmovers' (Robinson 2015: 437), beach return aims to 'make beaches that are as similar to those that went away as can be arranged' (438). However, this work is not so much based on nostalgia as transcription. It is not a return to nature but uses technology to create nature anew. While on the one hand this falls into an anthropocentric reading of the Anthropocene, in which, as The Invisible Committee warn, the only way beyond it is through human invention and ingenuity (The Invisible Committee 2015: 32), the end of the novel posits a different reading. After agreeing to work with the beach returners, Freya goes for a swim in a natural ocean for the first time in her life (she was raised on a starship). Then there is a five-page description of her getting tossed about by the waves. The under-turn tugs, waves crack, break and pitch, crests swell, bubbles infuse, bodies are tossed and ripped off the sandy bottom (Robinson 2015: 462–3). This struggle of Freya with the sea is the last real image of the novel, and it is an image of transcription.

The strategy of transcription is important for speculative realism because it is an indirect strategy for representing the withdrawn nature of objects. As Steven Shaviro says in *Discognition*,

> I may still be affected by a light that I cannot see. I may sense it unawares, as happens in the case of blind-sight. Or the functioning of my body may be altered by it in some way, as happens when I am exposed to radioactivity, or to electromagnetic radiation at frequencies outside the visible spectrum. (Shaviro 2015a: 38)

This kind of perception happens alongside direct perception, but is 'no less real for happening indirectly or *vicariously*' (38). Indirect representation is essential for hyperobjects because, due to their non-human scale, they cannot be experienced directly. One privileged location for indirect representation of non-human scales is sf. As Shaviro says,

> Science fiction can *allude* to, or recount and approach to, states and conditions that exceed any possibility of direct depiction or explicit conceptualization . . . naturalist or mimetic fiction often follows the banal rule that one must show, rather than tell; but speculative fiction makes a point of telling – allusively and indirectly – that which, quite literally, cannot be shown. (38)

Some of the terms that Shaviro is using, such as *vicarious* and *allure*, come from the work of Harman. No matter how detailed a description is provided of an object, that description will never actually become that object: there is always a gap between experience and the real object (Harman 2012: 237). Yet this does not mean that there is no contact whatsoever with objects, that all experiences are just in the mind (or in language); there is contact, it is just indirect contact. This is what Shaviro means when he says that vicarious experience is 'no less real' than direct experience. As Harman says, such forms of allusion are 'pointing towards a thing without making it present' (238). Fictional visibility is another name for this kind of allusion.

As discussed numerous times above, Harman develops two strategies of indirect experience out of the processes of nuclear energy: fusion and fission. When qualities are connected with an object that they are not usually associated with, this is a case of fusion (240), while when qualities are separated from the objects that they are usually associated with, as in a cubist painting, this is a case of fission (241). Both can be strategies for representing non-human scales of time and space: qualities of the human scale can be fused with that of the supra-human scale of the Anthropocene, while the qualities of a human scale can be split from humanity, as normal experiences of time and progress are abandoned in *The Road*. What both strategies have in common is that they provide an experience of a scale which is beyond the human; they just do it indirectly.

As a precursor to Robinson's work, J. G. Ballard's *The Drought* (1964) connects time to progress in order to dismantle the two in a representation of the Anthropocene. In the novel, the only way to face the long-term scale of the destruction caused by the spread of nuclear waste is to abandon progress altogether. The whole world is undergoing a drought, although its causes are not known at first. The characters who believe that the drought is short-term perish, and those like the main character Ransom, who realise that there will never be anything else but drought in the imaginable future, have a better chance of survival. For example, in one scene Ransom tries to convince a rich man's personal driver that the little remaining water is about to run out, while the driver is convinced, 'with a wild misanthropic hope' (Ballard 1968: 47), that the rain will return in a few weeks. The driver is running away from the devastating scale of the drought, and will suffer for it, while Ransom shows that the only thing to do is try and face it.

Facing the drought means not fighting against it, but living with it. In order to accept the permanence of the drought, notions of time and progress must be forgotten. An early sign that Ransom abandons any hope of change is seen at the end of the first chapter, when he is thinking about the drying river on which he lives in his houseboat:

> With the death of the river, so would vanish any contact between those stranded on the drained floor. For the present the need to find some other measure of their relationships would be concealed by the problems of their own physical survival. None the less, Ransom was certain that the absence of this great moderator, which cast its bridges between all animate and inanimate objects alike, would prove of crucial importance. Each of them would soon literally be an island in an archipelago drained of time. (11–12)

Before the drought, the scale of Ransom's connections to the animate and inanimate world around him was defined by the river. With its disappearance, 'some other measure of their relationships' will need to be found. But at the moment there are no connections, and everyday survival takes precedence. The scale of everyday survival is to be 'an island in an archipelago drained of time'.[2]

This feeling of 'isolation in time' (96) indicates a shift from viewing the world through the scale of humanity to viewing humanity through the scale of the world. For 'When substance is replaced by scale, domains become just a matter of perspective' (Roderick 2016: 36). The cause of this fission of qualities is nuclear waste, meaning a significant decrease in precipitation due to 'a thin but resilient mono-molecular film formed from a complex of saturated long-chain polymers, generated with the sea from the vast quantities of industrial wastes discharged into the ocean basins during the previous fifty years' (Ballard 1968: 31). The 'millions of tons of highly reactive industrial wastes' which formed this film include 'unwanted petroleum fractions, contaminated catalysts and solvents' which 'mingled with the wastes of atomic power stations and sewage schemes' (31). This film covers enough of the world's oceans to disrupt the cycle of precipitation. The film creeps back after all attempts to remove it.

The film is a product of nuclear waste, and it is *viscous*, one of the traits Timothy Morton identifies in hyperobjects. Viscosity means that 'the more you know about a hyperobject, the more entangled with it you realize you already are' (Morton 2010). In *The Drought*, feeling isolated in time means facing the drought because the non-human timescale of the drought is being experienced. Morton says that 'Viscosity is a feature of the way in which time emanates from objects, rather than being a continuum in which they float' (Morton 2013a: 33). In Ballard's novel, once the scale of destruction caused by the toxic ocean film is felt, it is seen elsewhere, in crowds and on beaches, as if the viscosity of this new timeframe has seeped into the whole earth. This is what is meant by the drought making the scale of nuclear waste more visible.

In Ballard's next novel after *The Drought*, *The Crystal World* (1966), another world-wide catastrophe influences humanity to undergo a different experience of time: due to what is called the 'Hubble Effect', large portions of the earth's forests in the Gabonese Republic are being crystallised. In an earlier version of the novel, published as *The Terminal Man* in 1964, the same crystallisation hits the Florida Everglades. Although the crystallisation is a change in form, the manner in which it is described is through a change in time. A biologist describes the Hubble Effect thus: '"It's almost as if a sequence of displaced but identical images were being produced by refraction through a prism, but with the element of time replacing the role of light"' (Ballard 1965: 29). The transformation of the forests is temporal: 'We know now that it is time . . . which is responsible for the transformation' (39). The way in which this takes place is not exactly clear, but like antimatter, anti-time exists, and the relation of both time and anti-time 'eliminate each other, subtracting from the universe another quantum from its total store of time. It is random charges of this type, set off by the creation of anti-galaxies in space, which have led to the depletion of the time-store available to the materials of our own solar system' (39). Just as in *The Drought*, to understand change is to understand a different scale of time. The crystals are not an absence but rather 'a compression of time' (47). Although the Hubble Effect is not due to nuclear radiation, it is an earlier example of a collision between two scales of temporal experience.

In *The Drought*, Ransom and a few others leave town to go to the sea. When they arrive they find the shore fenced off by police and masses of people waiting for the scant daily rations of water given out by the occupying forces. Ransom decides to leave the crowded main gate and find a free place to park, but the scale of the crowd is enormous:

> They set off along the coast road below the cliffs. The motor camps stretched ahead of them to the right, the backs of trailers jutting out over the empty pavement. On the left, where the cliffs had been cut back at intervals to provide small lay-bys, single families squatted under make-shift awnings, out of sight of sea and sky, gazing at the camps separating them from the beach. (Ballard 1968: 91)

The scale of the crowd extends into the unseen: the coast lies behind other rows of trailers, awnings block the view of both the sea and the sky. The crowd is a small example of non-locality, meaning that the effects of a hyperobject seem dispersed in space, like isolated islands, because the connection between effects remains unseen; 'action at a distance is involved' (Morton 2013a: 39). Even when Ransom drives to the top of a small hill, he cannot see the end of the crowd: 'Half a mile ahead they climbed a small rise, and could see the endless extent of the camps, reaching far into the haze beyond the cape ten miles away' (Ballard 1968: 92). Both the abandonment of the time of progress and the inability to see the edges of the crowd on the beach are representations of larger-than-human scales of time and space. Because the drought is a product of nuclear waste, the characters in the novel are grappling with a scale in which they were always living, but of which they were not necessarily aware. The scale of the half-life of nuclear waste is huge. It is a scale that humans have been living in at least since the controlled reactions of Chicago Pile 1, the first nuclear reactor. This scale is one of the 'concentric temporalities' in which humanity exists, which also includes the life cycle of stars, bacteria and thoughts. The representation of such temporalities allows us 'to see history as a nested series of catastrophes that are still playing out rather than as a sequence of events based on a conception of time as a succession of atomic instants' (Morton 2016: 69). Representations of the scale of the catastrophe of nuclear waste make the viscosity of the world we live in more transparent.

In Ballard's work, viscosity creates difference, meaning a new phase in the life of humanity. Roy Scranton describes this new phase of life in the Anthropocene as a kind of dying, meaning a leaving behind of the enemy that we are. For 'The enemy isn't *out there* somewhere – the enemy is ourselves. Not as individuals, but as a collective. A system. A hive' (Scranton 2015: 85). The manner this leaving-behind takes in Ballard's work is through adapting new scales of time and space. In Robinson's work, it takes place through transcription.

Yet transcription is not about doing anything whatsoever. This would lead to a Type-3 world of non-relation. Instead transcription is about the tension between laws and freedoms, limits and agency. When the tension between the two is foregrounded, a new phase of being is possible. This is true for Freya, who survives the tumult under the sea to start a new life on Earth (Robinson 2015: 466). Transcription is an engagement with the material properties of real objects, but with a sense of play or fun (Bogost 2016: 55). The Anthropocene is forcing an age of transcription upon us, since we are being required to think about the kinds of change possible within the material constraints of climate change. In 2312 Robinson calls the Anthropocene the Dithering, meaning an in-between state like the bardo. Such states are full of potential because the tension between objects and qualities becomes more visible. These states are also full of danger because the bardo is growing cold, and the time for the next phase of reincarnation is upon us.

Notes

1. This is a seemingly different approach from most 'What If?' novels dealing with alternate histories which, according to Žižek, is a genre 'homogenized by conservative historians' (Žižek 2010: 85). However, the analysis of the ending of the novel will show novel not to be so far from the mark after all.
2. A removal of the connectedness of things can also be seen in the revisions that the opening of the novel underwent before publication. *The Drought* and its earlier version, *The Burning World*, have identical

opening paragraphs in which Ransom is introduced on his houseboat. The main event of this paragraph is Ransom seeing Quilter, the son of another barge dweller. In contrast, the original opening paragraph of the manuscript framed the whole narrative within the context of the drought; it reads: 'The abandonment of the city after many false starts and alarms, finally began in earnest on the morning of July 14, and was, however, to the majority of its inhabitants, distracted by the endless heat and dust of the rainless summer, this great evacuation revealed itself only in cold signs and omens' (National British Library ADD MS 88938/3/5/2). Framing the whole story through the evacuation, and including the exact date it happened, features a more controlled sense of time than the more now-oriented final opening.

Conclusion

> A bottomless abyss exists in every inch.
> Cixin Liu, *Death's End* (2010)

Speculative realism and sf have one main feature in common. Both challenge an anthropocentric view of the world by considering non-human objects worthy of serious thought. This book has developed this connection through a reading of various works that fit into the continuum between sf and fantasy. More specifically, it is an investigation into the role that ambiguity plays in divesting the world of human domination.

In the first chapter, the overarching strategy for representing tension was called the Zug effect. Quentin Meillassoux drew a line between sf, which anticipates a scientific future to make sense of the currently unknown, and extro-science fiction, which represents the unknown without such anticipation. However, it was seen that both science and sf incorporate ambiguity to a much greater extent than Meillassoux allows. Damon Knight's *Beyond the Barrier* was used as a key text because it incorporates unexplained ambiguity within its narrative. These moments of ambiguity, called relatively dark objects following Levi Bryant, deform the sensual world, indirectly indicating that something beyond the barrier of human thought exists. The ecological crisis of the Anthropocene is seen not only to force relatively dark objects into our awareness, but demands new strategies to ensure their continued visibility.

Cormac McCarthy's *The Road* was seen to develop the Zug effect with a key insight. Dismantling the dominance of language makes the world visible. 'The ponderous counterspectacle of things ceasing to be' (McCarthy 2006: 293) takes place when the language of the old world falls away in post-apocalyptic destitution. Dystopia is not read as an escape from the world, but rather the manner in which, as Timothy Morton says, humanity is becoming fixed 'more firmly to the spot, which is no longer an embeddedness in a world' (Morton 2013a: 144). Along with Meillassoux, the removal from world is seen as divine because the connections between objects and their qualities become tenuous, and new connections begin to take place.

The divine separation of objects and qualities is made visible through a specific strategy in the work of Neil Gaiman. Double-vision is the name for when the dominance of vision, rather than language, becomes fuzzy. In moments of double-vision, objects modulate, meaning that connections between objects that were previously dark now become visible. These connections take on the form of metaphor, which is about the tension between the relation and non-relation of one object with another. China Miéville's *Perdido Street Station* was then seen as reinserting the importance of essence within the change of double-vision. Rather than forming an assemblage or network, the characters of Mr Motley and the Weavers, along with Isaac's invention of the crisis engine, are figures that insist on the power of the withdrawn nature of objects, which can also be called their essence.

Up to this point, one of the key aspects of the connection between speculative realism and sf has been underdeveloped: tension. Doris Lessing's *The Cleft* was read as a novel that not only develops strategies for representing both temporal and spatial tension, but also foregrounds the way that objects change when such tension takes place. Mirroring aspects of Harman's reading of symbiosis in *Immaterialism*, Lessing's novel inserts the role of sex in the middle of the tension between real objects and sensual qualities.

The Cleft was used to develop tension, but it nearly overdevelops this idea into a dialectic. Paolo Bacigalupi's *The Windup Girl* was offered as a corrective to this danger. By refusing a synthesis between oppositions, the novel both presents a dialectical assemblage and disrupts its coordinates. This disruption was read along with Theodor Adorno's thought on art and nature, and Samuel Delany's concept of inmixing, which is meant to retain a notion of difference within Darko Suvin's idea of the novum. In addition, the figure of Emiko from the novel performs a short circuit in the way that she represents a symbiosis of one, meaning that she is a single object which, like all objects, carries the seeds of her own tension.

Conclusion   199

The final chapter of the book considered a number of Kim Stanley Robinson's novels. Both tension and change were combined in a reading of the bardo, the time in which the transformation of one being into another takes place in reincarnation. The bardo foregrounds the causality of objects, meaning the way that tension is connected to change. This connection is termed transcription, a term taken from musicology. Taking a musical piece for one set of instruments and transcribing it for another highlights both the way that connections between objects and qualities are taken for granted, and the way that such connections remain relatively dark. The work of J. G. Ballard was also used to show the way that transcription can become one way to see the large hyperobjects of the Anthropocene which are making themselves felt in ever-increasing fashion.

Ballard's work is located in a long tradition of sf which uses radiation and other non-visible forces to explore their strange effects on humanity and other creatures. Yet Ballard's work is less about the physical effects of mutation and more about the new forms of knowledge and experience necessary to begin to see the non-human scales of time and space of the Anthropocene. Thus this book will close with a short reading of the different ways in which some sf texts have confronted such large scales, thus foregrounding both the weakness of an anthropocentric position and the flimsy givenness of connections between objects and qualities.

H. P. Lovecraft's 'The Color out of Space' (1927) represents a radiation-like poisonous gas emanating from a crashed meteorite which deforms animals and plants while turning everyone in its vicinity insane. 'The Thing' from John Campbell's 'Who Goes There?' (1938) acts like radiation, spreading uncontrollably and eating its human hosts from the inside out. The creature is even connected to atomic energy, as it is seen creating an atomic generator to power a ship to escape and infect all the living beings on Earth (Campbell 1948: 73). And in Stanley Kubrick's *Dr Strangelove: Or How I Learned to Stop Worrying and Love the Bomb* (1964), nuclear weapons are supplied with 'Cobalt Thorium G' in order to increase the effects of their nuclear fallout. Yet while all these examples raise awareness of a number of important issues which can be related to nuclear weapons, the massive timescale of their effects is missed out. This work thus has more in common than might at first be expected with films such as *Them!* (Gordon Douglass) and *Godzilla* (Ishirō Honda) (both

1954), because when the effects of nuclear radiation are limited to a single creature, it appears to be an issue that can eventually be eradicated.[1] The result of nuclear waste being a hyperobject is different. It means that there is no simple solution to the problems it causes, there is no local enemy that can be defeated once and for all. However, such limitations should not be unexpected, for 'Many characteristics of the Anthropocene are largely outside the range of past experience from an environmental governance perspective' (Steffen, Crutzen and McNeill 2007: 854), as well as being outside an artistic one.

The death of Concepcion Picciotto on 15 January 2016 marked the end of a 35-year protest against nuclear arms. She spent these decades of her life in a peace camp on Pennsylvania Avenue, participating in 'the longest-running act of political protest in U.S. history' (Gibson 2016). Speaking during the latter Bush administration, Picciotto said her goal was 'to remove the president before engaging into a nuclear war' (Austermuhle 2005).

Nadav Kander's photographs of the Semipalatinsk nuclear test site in Kazakhstan focus on the rusting remains of the location of the test of the Russian atomic bomb that the Americans dubbed Joe-1 (referring to Stalin). The large seismograph recorders that resemble the tail section of a jumbo jet, inhabitable bomb crater lakes and radioactive weeds show the long legacy of the plutonium left behind by the 456 nuclear tests made between 1949 and 1989 in this inhabited area.

The experience of foreign scales is at the heart of Raymond Briggs's 1982 graphic novel *When the Wind Blows*. It tells the story of a nuclear attack by the Soviet Union on Britain. A nuclear strike is imminent and the useless preparations of the elderly Jim and Hilda Bloggs are contrasted with full-page illustrations of missiles and submarines, thus highlighting the difference 'between rudimentary home preparations and the horrible spread of death following a nuclear bomb blast' (Lowe and Joel 2013: 53).

The Nuclear Guardianship movement seeks to store nuclear waste in above-ground central locations so that it is not swept under the rug. Even encasing the waste in gold has been suggested, 'which has the advantage of absorbing gamma rays'; hence 'plutonium could become an object of contemplation' or even 'a member of a democracy expanded beyond the human' (Morton 2013a: 121). The Nuclear Guardianship movement seeks to make the long-term effects of nuclear waste not only visible, but a central part of life.

All of these examples are real-world strategies for making the scale of nuclear waste visible. However, making nuclear weapons and their waste a part of everyday life is not enough, for visibility is not about presence but rather the conception of a supra-human timescale through fission and fusion. In fact, nuclear weapons were originally seen to be much more a part of everyday life, perversely in line with the Nuclear Guardianship movement. In 1957 'Project Plowshare' began in the United States. It was concerned with developing the peaceful application of nuclear weapons, which included plans for digging a second Panama Canal with 300 nuclear explosions, using 764 bombs to construct another canal across Columbia, and clearing land for a highway across the Mojave Desert in California with 22 explosions (Bonneuil and Fressoz 2015: 131–2). Project Plowshare was also about the visibility of nuclear weapons in everyday life, although if implemented it would have had tragic results (the only use of nuclear weapons in peacetime on US soil was in 1962 for the extraction of gas in Colorado, but the resulting product was too radioactive to sell [Bonneuil and Fressoz 2015: 132]).

Martin Amis's 'The Immortals' is the last short story from his *Einstein's Monsters* (1987). Each story in this collection is about nuclear war, and 'The Immortals' represents the scale of nuclear fallout through a man who was born before humans evolved and is now dying in a nuclear winter. The story begins with the narrator stating that those suffering around him will soon be gone, while he will remain, because he is immortal: 'The human beings around here are in very bad shape, what with the solar radiation, the immunity problem, the rat-and-roach diet, and so on . . . But let the poor bastards be. Now I feel free to bare my secret. I am the Immortal' (Amis 1987: 135). The way the narrator explains his difference from those around him is in terms of scale: 'when you've been around for as long as I have, the diurnal scale, this twenty-four-hour number, can really start to get you down. I tried for a grander scheme of things. And I had my successes' (136). Staying awake for seven years straight, picking his nose for 18 months and giving himself a handjob for a whole summer are just some examples.

The narrator 'came from another planet which ticked to a different clock' and had to wait through the cooling of the earth and the arrival of biology in order to eventually meet up with any human beings. Throughout his immortal life, bouts of depression caused him to attempt suicide many times, but it never worked (143). Nuclear weapons are a different story, because they are objects that exist on the same scale as him, and thus in them he has met his match: 'Nothing else had ever managed to kill me, and I reckoned that a direct hit from a nuke was my only chance. I'm cosmic – in time – but so are nukes' (139). Although he laments not being in the right place at the right time for the largest of nuclear tests, the bomb is the only chance he feels that he has for ending his sentence of immortality.

However, the end of the story reveals that the character of the Immortal is a fake, a form of sublimation used by the narrator to deal with the horror he finds himself in, although he reveals this in a kind of 'reverse' delusion:

> I have a delusion also, sometimes. Sometimes I have this weird idea that I am just a second-rate New Zealand schoolmaster who never did anything or went anywhere and is now painfully and noisily dying of solar radiation along with everybody else. It's strange how palpable it is, this fake past, and how human: I feel I can almost reach out and touch it. There was a woman, and a child. One woman. One child ... But I soon snap out of it. I soon pull myself together. I soon face up to the tragic fact that there will be no ending for me, even after the sun dies (which should at least be quite spectacular). I am the Immortal. (148)

The Immortal is able to represent the scale of nuclear waste through the 'cosmic' scale in which he lives, and on which he meets the bomb. However, although this representation is a fake, it still functions as a means for conveying the immensity of nuclear warfare, although not so much the initial explosion but rather the long fall out. The narrator falls asleep during the blast – 'The BMP you don't have to worry about. Take it from me, it's the least of your difficulties' (140), he says. The issue rather is the long slow seep of radiation poisoning, which has such a massive scale that the only way to comprehend it is to come up with the figure of the Immortal. As Amis said in an interview around the time of *Einstein's Monsters*, 'the fact that you think you can enslave this cosmic force. It's clear instantly that we have become enslaved by it' (McGrath 1987). This, once again, is a shift from viewing the world through the scale of humanity to viewing humanity through the scale of the world. Yet this view is not only a kind of fiction, but also a way to scientifically understand radiation. In order to see radiation, it has to be fictionalised. William Scheick says of *Einstein's Monsters* that Amis was convinced 'that a post-nuclear holocaust would be as fantastical a version of hell as ever conceived by humanity, that such a world would in its non-human nature be almost beyond imagining' (Scheick 1991: 77). Fictionalisation takes place through the Immortal deluding himself into having cosmic traits. This is Harman's concept of fusion, the joining of traits of one scale with the objects of another (Harman 2012: 240). Or, as Morton says,

> A unit of radiation is some kind of quantum, such as a gamma ray. It is very hard to see a gamma ray in itself. You have to cause it to be deflected in some way, or to mark some inscribable surface such as a photographic plate. So you can see gamma rays when they illuminate a body, like in an X-ray photo. Gamma rays tune to us, gamma ray-pomorphizing us into a gamma ray-centric parody of ourselves. Radioactive materials are wonderful for thinking about how causality is aesthetic. At the quantum level, to see something just is to hit it with a photon or an electron: hence to alter it in some way. Every seeing, every measurement, is also an adjustment, a parody, a translation, and interpretation. A tune and a tuning. (Morton 2013b: 33)

Nuclear radiation is influential in that it indirectly manipulates human scales in order to be seen. This is why fiction is a valid form for representing the long-term effects of nuclear waste: nuclear waste attunes fiction to its own needs, since the scale of its existence cannot be immediately experienced.[2] This is seen in how the narrator of 'The Immortals' invents a 'cosmic' scale for himself in order to make sense of the slow death that surrounds him. And Ransom in *The Drought* abandons time and progress in order to experience the drought on its own terms, the only way to survive it. Everything that these characters provide is influenced by scales beyond their understanding. However, this influence is not only an effect of nuclear radiation. There are many other large-scale problems attempting to influence us enough to be able to hear them, including climate change, the sixth great species extinction and the inequality of resource distribution. The fact that all of these problems are human-generated adds a special urgency to this influence.

Notes

1. Laurence Rickels makes a similar point in reference to *Star Wars: A New Hope* (1977), saying that 'when an entire planet is annihilated at one point in the first film, only a little over one million inhabitants dies. This minimization of catastrophic loss, which increases the outside chances for survival, was on one dotted line with the pomo diplomacy of Reaganomics: it proved possible to calculate nuclear risk in terms of survival, even following exchanges of strikes' (Rickels 2010: 71).
2. Radiation is fictionalised on an even larger scale in Cixin Liu's *The Three Body Problem* (2014), when aliens manipulate the background radiation of the entire universe in order to trick Earthlings into believing that nature is random and science is useless in comprehending it.

Bibliography

Acar, Rahim. 2003. 'Intellect versus Active Intellect: Plotinus and Avicenna.' In *Before and after Avicenna: Proceedings of the First Conference of the Avicenna Study Group*. Ed. D. C. Reisman et al. Danvers: Brill, 69–87.
Adorno, Theodor. 1983. *Prisms*. Trans. Samuel and Shierry Weber. Cambridge, MA: MIT Press.
Adorno, Theodor. 1990. *Negative Dialectics*. Trans. E. B. Ashton. London: Routledge.
Adorno, Theodor. 1997 [1970]. *Aesthetic Theory*. Trans. Robert Hullot-Kentor. Minneapolis: University of Minnesota Press.
Adorno, Theodor. 2001. *Problems of Moral Philosophy*. Ed. Thomas Schröder. Trans. Rodney Livingstone. Stanford: Stanford University Press.
Agamben, Giorgio. 1999. *Potentialities: Collected Essays in Philosophy*. Trans. Daniel Heller-Roazen. Stanford: Stanford University Press.
Agamben, Giorgio. 2004. *The Open: Man and Animal*. Trans. Kevin Attell. Stanford: Stanford University Press.
Agamben, Giorgio. 2007. *Infancy and History: The Destruction of Experience*. Trans. Liz Heron. London: Verso.
Agamben, Giorgio. 2011. *Nudities*. Trans. David Kishik and Stefan Pedatella. Stanford: Stanford University Press.
Aldiss, Brian. 2008 [1961]. *Hothouse*. Harmondsworth: Penguin.
Amis, Kingsley. 1960. *New Maps of Hell*. New York: Ballantine.
Amis, Martin. 1987. *Einstein's Monsters*. New York: Vintage.
Arendt, Hannah. 2003. *The Portable Hannah Arendt*. Ed. Peter Baehr. Harmondsworth: Penguin.
Austermuhle, Martin. 2005. 'DCist Interview: Conception Piciotto.' http://dcist.com/2005/08/dcist_interview.php
Ayache, Elie. 2010. *Blank Swan: The End of Probability*. Chichester: John Wiley.

Ayache, Elie. 2014. 'A Formal Reduction of the Market.' *Collapse* 8: 959–8.
Ayache, Elie. 2015. *The Medium of Contingency: An Inverse View of the Market*. London: Palgrave.
Bachelard, Gaston. 1994. *The Poetics of Space*. Trans. Maria Jolas. Boston: Beacon Press.
Bacigalupi, Paolo. 2009. *The Windup Girl*. San Francisco: Night Shade Books.
Bacigalupi, Paolo. 2010. *Pump Six and Other Stories*. San Francisco: Night Shade Books.
Badiou, Alain. 2004. 'Philosophy and Art.' In *Infinite Thought: Truth and the Return of Philosophy*. Trans. Oliver Feltham and Justin Clemens. London: Continuum, 91–108.
Badiou, Alain. 2005. *Being and Event*. Trans. Oliver Feltham. London: Continuum.
Bailey, J. O. 1972. *Pilgrims through Space and Time: Trends and Patterns in Scientific and Utopian Fiction*. Westport, CT: Greenwood Press.
Bakhtin, Mikhail. 1981. 'Forms of Time and Chronotope in the Novel.' In *The Dialogic Imagination: Four Essays*. Trans. Caryl Emerson and Michael Holquist. Austin: University of Texas Press, 84–258.
Ballard, J. G. 1963. *The Burning World* [*The Drought*]. National British Library ADD MS 88938/3/5/2.
Ballard, J. G. 1965. 'The Illuminated Man.' In *The Best from 'Fantasy and Science Fiction', Fourteenth Series*. Ed. Avram Davidson. New York: Doubleday.
Ballard, J. G. 1968. *The Drought*. Harmondsworth: Penguin.
Ballard, J. G. 1996. *A User's Guide to the Millennium*. London: HarperCollins.
Barad, Karen. 2007. *Meeting the Universe Halfway: Quantum Physics and the Entanglement of Matter and Meaning*. Durham, NC: Duke University Press.
Bartusiak, Marcia. 2000. *Einstein's Unfinished Symphony: Listening to the Sounds of Space-time*. Washington, DC: Joseph Henry Press.
Baudrillard, Jean. 2006. *Simulacra and Simulation*. Trans. Sheila Faria Glaser. Ann Arbor: University of Michigan Press.
Beckett, Tom. 2011. 'Interview with Graham Harman.' http://eeevee2.blogspot.hr/2011/10/interview-with-graham-harman.html.
Benjamin, Walter. 1969. *Illuminations: Essays and Reflections*. Trans. Harry Zohn. Ed. Hannah Arendt. New York: Schocken Books.
Bennett, Jane. 2010. *Vibrant Matter: A Political Ecology of Things*. Durham, NC: Duke University Press.

Bertens, Johannes. 1996. *The Idea of the Postmodern: A History*. London: Routledge.
Birns, Nicholas. 2009. 'From Cacotopias to Railroads: Rebellion and the Shaping of the Normal in the Bas-Lang Universe.' *Extrapolation* 50.2: 200–11.
Blanchot, Maurice. 2006. 'The Proper Use of Science Fiction'. In *Imagining the Future: Utopia and Dystopia*. Ed. Andrew Miller, Matthew Ryan and Robert Savage. North Carlton, Australia: Arena Publications Association, 375–83.
Bogost, Ian. 2012. *Alien Phenomenology: Or What It's Like to Be a Thing*. Minneapolis: University of Minnesota Press.
Bogost, Ian. 2016. *Play Anything: The Pleasure of Limits, the Uses of Boredom, and the Secret of Games*. New York: Basic Books.
Bonneuil, Christophe, and Jean-Baptiste Fressoz. 2015. *The Shock of the Anthropocene: The Earth, History and Us*. Trans. David Fernbach. London: Verso.
Bourdieu, Pierre. 1996. *The State Nobility: Elite Schools in the Field of Power*. Stanford: Polity Press.
Boyd, Brian. 2009. *On the Origin of Stories: Evolution, Cognition, and Fiction*. Cambridge, MA: The Belknap Press of Harvard University Press.
Bozzetti, Mauro. 2002. 'Hegel on Trial: Adorno's Critique of Philosophical Systems.' In *Adorno: A Critical Reader*. Ed. Nigel Gibson and Andrew Rubin. Malden, MA: Blackwell, 292–311.
Brassier, Ray. 2013. 'Unfree Improvisation/Compulsive Freedom.' http://www.mattin.org/essays/unfree_improvisation-compulsive_freedom.html.
Brooks, Cleanth. 1947. *The Well-Wrought Urn: Studies in the Structure of Poetry*. New York: Harcourt, Brace and World.
Bryant, Levi. 2012. *The Democracy of Objects*. Ann Arbor: Open Humanities Press.
Bryant, Levi. 2014. *Onto-Cartography: An Ontology of Machines and Media*. Edinburgh: Edinburgh University Press.
Burt, Stephen. 2009. 'Of Disembodied Mind Sparks and Speakers of Klingon: A New Model of Science Fiction.' *Contemporary Literature* 50.3: 599–609.
Butler, Judith. 1990. *Gender Trouble: Feminism and the Subversion of Identity*. London: Routledge.
Butler, Judith. 1993. *Bodies that Matter: On the Discursive Limits of 'Sex.'* London: Routledge.
Butler, Octavia. 2007. *Lilith's Brood*. New York: Grand Central Publishing.

Campbell, John. 1948. *Who Goes There? And Other Stories*. Cutchogue: Buccaneer Books.

Cartwright, Jon. 2013. 'Physicists Discover a Whopping 13 New Solutions to the Three-Body Problem.' *Science*. http://www.sciencemag.org/news/2013/03/physicists-discover-whopping-13-new-solutions-three-body-problem.

Chambers, Samuel, and Terrell Carver. 2008. *Judith Butler and Political Theory: Troubling Politics*. Abingdon: Routledge.

Clarke, Arthur C. 1974. *Rendezvous with Rama*. New York: Ballantine Books.

Clement, Hal. 1962 [1953]. *Mission of Gravity*. New York: Pyramid.

Collado-Rodríguez, Francisco. 2012. 'Trauma and Storytelling in Cormac McCarthy's *No Country for Old Men* and *The Road*.' *Papers in Language and Literature* 48.1: 45–69.

Critchley, Simon. 1997. *Very Little – Almost Nothing: Death, Philosophy, Literature*. London: Routledge.

Csicsery-Ronay, Istvan. 2008. *The Seven Beauties of Science Fiction*. Middletown, CT: Wesleyan University Press.

Davis, Brian. 2012. 'On Landscape Ontology: An Interview with Graham Harman.' *Landscape Archipelago*. https://landscapearchipelago.wordpress.com/2012/07/01/on-landscape-ontology-an-interview-with-graham-harman/.

Davies, Stephen. 2005. *Themes in the Philosophy of Music*. Oxford: Oxford University Press.

Dawson, Ashley. 2016. *Extinction: A Radical History*. New York: OR Books.

DeLanda, Manuel. 2006. *A New Philosophy of Society: Assemblage Theory and Social Complexity*. London: Continuum.

DeLanda, Manuel. 2011. *Philosophy and Simulation: The Emergence of Synthetic Reason*. London: Continuum.

DeLanda, Manuel. 2016. *Assemblage Theory*. Edinburgh: Edinburgh University Press.

Delany, Samuel. 1979. 'The Order of "Chaos" (Joanna Russ, *And Chaos Died*).' *Science Fiction Studies* 19.6. http://www.depauw.edu/sfs/reviews_pages/r19.htm#A19.

Delany, Samuel. 1985. *Stars in My Pocket like Grains of Sand*. New York: Bantam.

Delany, Samuel. 2009. *The Jewel-Hinged Jaw: Notes on the Language of Science Fiction*. Middletown, CT: Wesleyan University Press.

Deleuze, Gilles, and Felix Guattari. 2005. *A Thousand Plateaus:*

Capitalism and Schizophrenia. Trans. Brian Massumi. Minneapolis: University of Minnesota Press.

Derrida, Jacques. 1991. *Of Spirit: Heidegger and the Question*. Trans. Geoffrey Bennington and Rachel Bowlby. Chicago: University of Chicago Press.

Derrida, Jacques. 1993. *Aporias*. Trans. Thomas Dutoit. Stanford: Stanford University Press.

Derrida, Jacques. 2003. 'And Say the Animal Responded?' In *Zoontologies: The Question of the Animal*. Ed. Cary Wolfe. Minneapolis: University of Minnesota Press, 120–39.

Diacu, Forin. 1996. 'The Solution of the n-body Problem.' *The Mathematical Intelligencer* 18.3: 66–70.

Dick, Philip K. 1996 [1968]. *Do Androids Dream of Electric Sheep?* New York: Dell Ray.

Dickinson, Colby. 2011. *Agamben and Theology*. London: Continuum.

Disch, Thomas. 2000. *The Dreams Our Stuff is Made of: How Science Fiction Conquered the World*. New York: Touchstone.

Dolphijn, Rick, and Iris van der Tuin. 2012. *New Materialism: Interviews and Cartographies*. Ann Arbor: Open Humanities Press.

Dornemann, Rudi, and Kelly Everding. 2001. 'Dreaming American Gods: an Interview with Neil Gaiman.' *Rain Taxi*. http://www.raintaxi.com/online/2001summer/gaiman.shtml.

Düttmann, Alexander Garciá. 2004. 'What Remains of Fidelity after Serious Thought?' In *Think Again: Alain Badiou and the Future of Philosophy*. Ed. Peter Hallward. London: Continuum, 188–211.

Elden, Stuart. 2006. 'Heidegger's Animals.' *Continental Philosophy Review* 39: 273–91.

Ellison, Harlan. 1978. 'A Voice from the Styx.' In *The Book of Ellison*. Ed. Andrew Porter. New York: Algol Press.

Empson, William. 1966. *Seven Types of Ambiguity*. New York: New Directions.

Evans-Wentz, W. Y. 2000. *The Tibetan Book of the Dead*. London: Oxford University Press.

Foster, Hal. 2003. *Design and Crime (And Other Diatribes)*. London: Verso.

Fóti, Véronique. 1995. *Heidegger and the Poets: Poiēsis / Sophia / Technē*. Amherst, NY: Humanities Press.

Freedman, Carl. 2009. *Conversations with Samuel R. Delany*. Jackson: University Press of Mississippi.

Freedman, Carl. 2015. *Art and Idea in the Novels of China Miéville*. Canterbury: Gylphi.

Fynsk, Christopher. 2000. *Infant Figures: The Death of the 'Infans' and Other Scenes of Origin.* Stanford: Stanford University Press.
Gaiman, Neil. 2004. *American Gods: The Author's Preferred Text.* London: Headline.
Gaiman, Neil. 2005. *Anansi Boys.* New York: Harpertorch.
Gaiman, Neil. 2007. 'How to Talk to Girls at Parties.' In *Fragile Things: Short Fictions and Wonders.* New York: Harper, 239–54.
Garcia, Tristan. 2013. 'Crossing Ways of Thinking: On Graham Harman's System and My Own.' *Parrhesia* 16: 14–25.
Gibson, Caitlin. 2016. 'Concepcion Picciotto, who Held Vigil Outside the White House for Decades, Dies.' *Washington Post.* https://www.washingtonpost.com/local/concepcion-picciotto-who-held-vigil-outside-the-white-house-for-decades-dies/2016/01/25/e0f829e2-c3b0-11e5-a4aa-f25866ba0dc6_story.html
Giggs, Rebecca. 2011. 'The Green Afterword: Cormac McCarthy's *The Road* and the Ecological Uncanny.' In *Criticism, Crisis, and Contemporary Narrative: Textual Horizons in an Age of Global Risk.* Ed. Paul Crosthwaite. New York: Routledge, 201–18.
Gilding, Paul. 2008. 'The Great Disruption.' http://paulgilding.com/discussion-papers/scream-crash-boom-2/.
Gould, Stephen Jay. 1985. *The Flamingo's Smile: Reflections in Natural History.* New York: W.W. Norton.
Gray, Cecil. 2009. *History of Music.* Abingdon: Routledge.
Gunn, James. 2005. 'Toward a Definition of Science Fiction.' In *Speculations on Speculation: Theories of Science Fiction.* Ed. James Gunn and Matthew Candelana. Lanham, MD: Scarecrow Press, 5–12.
Hageman, Andrew. 2012. 'The Challenge of Imagining Ecological Futures: Paolo Bacigalupi's *The Windup Girl.*' *Science Fiction Studies* 39.3: 283–303.
Hägglund, Martin. 2011. 'Radical Atheist Materialism: A Critique of Meillassoux.' In *The Speculative Turn: Continental Materialism and Realism.* Ed. Levi Bryant, Nick Srnicek and Graham Harman. Melbourne: Re-Press, 114–29.
Halberstam, Judith. 2005. *In a Queer Time and Place: Transgender Bodies, Subcultural Lives.* New York: New York University Press.
Haldeman, Joe. 2006 [1974]. *Forever Peace: In Peace and War.* London: Gollancz.
Handwerk, Brian. 2005. 'Animals Eyes Provide High-Tech Optical Inspiration.' *National Geographic News.* http://news.nationalgeographic.com/news/2005/12/1205_051205_animal_eyes_2.html

Haraway, Donna. 1991. *Simians, Cyborgs and Women: The Reinvention of Nature*. New York: Routledge.
Haraway, Donna. 2015. 'Anthropocene, Capitalocene, Plantationocene, Chuhulucene: Making Kin.' *Environmental Humanities* 6: 159–65.
Haraway, Donna. 2016. 'Tentacular Thinking: Anthropocene, Capitalocene, Chthulucene.' *e-flux* 75. http://www.e-flux.com/journal/75/67125/tentacular-thinking-anthropocene-capitalocene-chthulucene/
Hardwig, Bill. 2013. 'Cormac McCarthy's *The Road* and "A World to Come."' *Studies in American Naturalism* 8.1: 38–51.
Harman, Graham. 2002. *Tool-Being: Heidegger and the Metaphysics of Objects*. Chicago: Open Court.
Harman, Graham. 2005. *Guerrilla Metaphysics*. Chicago: Open Court.
Harman, Graham. 2008. 'DeLanda's Ontology: Assemblage and Realism.' *Continental Philosophy Review* 41: 367–83.
Harman, Graham. 2010. *Circus Philosophicus*. Ropley, Hants: Zero Books.
Harman, Graham. 2011a. *The Quadruple Object*. Ropley, Hants: Zero Books.
Harman, Graham. 2011b. *Quentin Meillassoux: Philosophy in the Making*. Edinburgh: Edinburgh University Press.
Harman, Graham. 2012. *Weird Realism: Lovecraft and Philosophy*. Ropley, Hants: Zero Books.
Harman, Graham. 2013. *Bells and Whistles: More Speculative Realism*. Ropley, Hants: Zero Books.
Harman, Graham. 2014. 'Materialism is Not the Solution: On Matter, Form and Mimesis.' *The Nordic Journal of Aesthetics* 47: 94–110.
Harman, Graham. 2016. *Immaterialism: Objects and Social Theory*. Cambridge: Polity.
Harman, Graham, and Jon Cogburn. 2015. 'An Interview with Graham Harman.' https://euppublishingblog.com/2015/09/10/an-interview-with-graham-harman/.
Hegel, G. W. F. 1970 [1817]. *Philosophy of Nature*, Vol. 3. Trans. A. V. Miller. Oxford: Oxford University Press.
Heidegger, Martin. 1966. *Discourse on Thinking*. Trans. J. Anderson and E. H. Freund. New York: Harper Torchbooks.
Heidegger, Martin. 1995. *The Fundamental Concepts of Metaphysics: World, Finitude, Solitude*. Trans. William McNeill and Nicholas Walker. Bloomington: Indiana University Press.
Heidegger, Martin. 1996. *Being and Time*. Trans. Joan Stambaugh. Albany: State University of New York Press.

Heidegger, Martin. 2001. '... Poetically Man Dwells ...' In *Poetry, Language, Thought*. Trans. Albert Hofstadter. New York: HarperCollins, 209–27.

Heinlein, Robert. 2002 [1942]. *Beyond the Horizon*. Riverdale: Baen Books.

Herdman, John. 1990. *The Double in Nineteenth-Century Fiction*. Basingstoke: Macmillan.

Hogan, Craig. 2006. 'The Sounds of Spacetime.' *American Scientist*. http://www.americanscientist.org/issues/feature/the-sounds-of-spacetime/99999.

Horkheimer, Max, and Theodor Adorno. 2002. *Dialectic of Enlightenment: Philosophical Fragments*. Trans. Edmund Jephcott. Stanford: Stanford University Press.

Horowitz, Noah. 2012. *Reality in the Name of God, or Divine Insistence*. New York: Punctum Books.

Hullot-Kentor, Robert. 2006. *Things beyond Resemblance: Collected Essays on Theodor W. Adorno*. New York: Columbia University Press.

Invisible Committee, The. 2015. *To Our Friends*. Los Angeles: Semiotext(e).

Ishiguro, Kazuo. 2005. *Never Let Me Go*. London: Faber and Faber.

Jameson, Fredric. 2007. *Archaeologies of the Future: The Desire Called Utopia and Other Science Fictions*. London: Verso.

Jameson, Fredric. 2009. *Valencies of the Dialectic*. London: Verso.

Jay, Martin. 1994. *Downcast Eyes: The Denigration of Vision in Twentieth-Century French Thought*. Berkeley: University of California Press.

Jay, Martin. 1996. *The Dialectical Imagination: A History of the Frankfurt School and the Institute of Social Research, 1923–1950*. Berkeley: University of California Press.

Joshi, S. T., and David Schultz. 2001. *An H. P. Lovecraft Encyclopedia*. Westport, CT: Greenwood.

Kaveney, Roz. 1981. 'Science Fiction in the 1970s.' *Foundation* 22: 5–35.

Kaveney, Roz. 2005. *From 'Alien' to 'The Matrix': Reading Science Fiction Film*. New York: I.B. Tauris.

Kermode, Frank. 2002. *Romantic Image*. London: Routledge.

Knight, Damon. 1967. *In Search of Wonder: Essays on Modern Science Fiction*. Chicago: Advent Publishers.

Knight, Damon. 1970. *Beyond the Barrier*. New York: Macfadden-Bartell.

Koestler, Arthur. 1963. *The Sleepwalkers: A History of Man's Changing Vision of the Universe*. New York: The Universal Library.

Kojève, Alexandre. 2007. *Outline of a Phenomenology of Right*. Trans. Bryan-Paul Frost and Robert Howse. Ed. Bryan-Paul Frost. Lanham, MD: Rowman and Littlefield.
Kotsko, Adam. 2012. 'Quentin Meillassoux and the Crackpot Sublime.' *The New Inquiry*. http://thenewinquiry.com/essays/quentin-meillassoux-and-the-crackpot-sublime/
Kracauer, Siegfried. 1995. *The Mass Ornament: Weimar Essays*. Trans. T. Levin. Cambridge, MA: Harvard University Press.
Kramer, Miriam. 2014. 'Listen to This: Comet's Eerie "Song" Captured by Rosetta Spacecraft.' *Space.com*. http://www.space.com/27737-comet-song-rosetta-spacecraft.html.
Kunsa, Ashley. 2009. '"Maps of the World in Its Becoming": Post-Apocalyptic Naming in Cormac McCarthy's *The Road*.' *Journal of Modern Literature* 33.1: 57–74.
Laboria Cuboniks. 2015. 'Xenofeminism: A Politics for Alienation.' http://www.laboriacuboniks.net/20150612-xf_layout_web.pdf.
Lacan, Jacques. 2001. *Écrits: A Selection*. London: Routledge.
Latour, Bruno. 1987. *Science in Action: How to Follow Scientists and Engineers through Society*. Cambridge, MA: Harvard University Press.
Latour, Bruno. 2007. *Reassembling the Social: An Introduction to Actor-Network-Theory*. Oxford: Oxford University Press.
Lawlor, Leonard. 2007. *This is Not Sufficient: An Essay on Animality and Human Nature in Derrida*. New York: Columbia University Press.
Lecercle, Jean-Jacques. 2002. *Deleuze and Language*. Basingstoke: Palgrave MacMillan.
Leckie, Ann. 2013. *Ancillary Justice*. London: Orbit.
Lessing, Doris. 2008. *The Cleft*. London: Harper Perennial.
Lessing, Doris. 2009. 'Afterword.' In Olaf Stapledon, *Last and First Men*. London: Gollancz.
Levinas, Emmanuel. 1990. 'The Name of a Dog, or Natural Rights.' In *Difficult Freedom: Essays in Judaism*. Trans. Seán Hand. Baltimore: Johns Hopkins University Press, 47–9.
Ligotti, Thomas. 2015. *Songs of a Dead Dreamer and Grimscribe*. Harmondsworth: Penguin.
Liu, Cixin. 2014. *The Three-Body Problem*. Trans. Ken Liu. New York: TOR.
Lowe, David, and Tony Joel. 2013. *Remembering the Cold War: Global Contest and National Stories*. London: Routledge.
Lyotard, Jean-François. 2004. *The Postmodern Condition: A Report on Knowledge*. Trans. Geoffrey Bennington and Brian Massumi. Manchester: Manchester University Press.

McCarthy, Cormac. 1993 [1973]. *Child of God*. New York: Vintage Books.

McCarthy, Cormac. 2006. *The Road*. New York: Picador.

McGrath, Patrick. 1987. 'Martin Amis.' *Bomb* 18. http://bombmagazine.org/article/874/martin-amis.

Malabou, Catherine. 2012. *Ontology of the Accident: An Essay on Destructive Plasticity*. Trans. Carolyn Shread. Cambridge: Polity Press.

Malmgren, Carl. 1991. *Worlds Apart: Narratology of Science Fiction*. Bloomington: Indiana University Press.

Massumi, Brian. 2002. *Parables for the Virtual: Movement, Affect, Sensation*. Durham, NC: Duke University Press.

Meillassoux, Quentin. 2009. *After Finitude: An Essay on the Necessity of Contingency*. Trans. Ray Brassier. London: Continuum.

Meillassoux, Quentin. 2011. 'Excerpts from *L'Inexistence Divine*.' In Graham Harman, *Quentin Meillassoux: Philosophy in the Making*. Edinburgh: Edinburgh University Press, 175–238.

Meillassoux, Quentin. 2012a. 'Iteration, Reiteration, Repetition: A Speculative Analysis of the Meaningless Sign.' Trans. Robin Mackay. Talk given at the Freie Universität, Berlin. https://cdn.shopify.com/s/files/1/0069/6232/files/Meillassoux_Workshop_Berlin.pdf.

Meillassoux, Quentin. 2012b. *The Number and the Siren: A Decipherment of Mallarmé's 'Coup de dés'*. Trans. Robin MacKay. Falmouth/New York: Urbanomic/Sequence Press.

Meillassoux, Quentin. 2015. *Science Fiction and Extro-Science Fiction*. Trans. Aloyshe Edlbei. Minneapolis: Univocal.

Mendelsohn, Farah. 2003. 'Religion and Science Fiction.' In *The Cambridge Companion to Science Fiction*. Ed. Edward James and Farah Mendelsohn. Cambridge: Cambridge University Press, 264–75.

Merrell, Floyd. 2003. *Sensing Corporeally: Toward a Posthuman Understanding*. Toronto: University of Toronto Press.

Miéville, China. 2000. *Perdido Street Station*. London: Pan Books.

Miéville, China. 2008. 'M. R. James and the Quantum Vampire: Weird; Hauntological: Versus and/or and and/or or?' *Collapse* IV: 105–28.

Miéville, China. 2009. 'Cognition as Ideology: A Dialectic of SF Theory.' In *Red Planets: Marxist and Science Fiction*. Ed. Mark Bould and China Miéville. Middletown, CT: Wesleyan University Press, 231–48.

Miller, Tim. 2010. 'The Motley & The Motley: Conflicting and Conflicted Models of Generic Hybridity in Bas-Lang,' *Foundation* 108: 39–59.

Monk, Nicholas. 2016. *True and Living Prophet of Destruction: Cormac McCarthy and Modernity*. Albuquerque: University of New Mexico Press.

Moore, Jason. 2015. *Capitalism in the Web of Life: Ecology and the Accumulation of Capital*. London: Verso.

Moretti, Franco. 2007. *Graphs, Maps, Trees: Abstract Models for Literary History*. London: Verso.

Morton, Timothy. 2007. *Ecology without Nature: Rethinking Environmental Aesthetics*. Cambridge, MA: Harvard University Press.

Morton, Timothy. 2010. 'Viscosity.' *Arcade*. http://arcade.stanford.edu/blogs/viscosity.

Morton, Timothy. 2013a. *Hyperobjects: Philosophy and Ecology after the End of the World*. Minneapolis: University of Minnesota Press.

Morton, Timothy. 2013b. *Realist Magic: Objects, Ontology, Causality*. Ann Arbor: Open Humanities Press.

Morton, Timothy. 2016. *Dark Ecology: For a Logic of Future Coexistence*. New York: Columbia University Press.

Muntz, Kyle. 2014. *Green Lights*. Fairfax, VA: CCM.

Murphy, Patrick. 2009. 'Environmentalism.' In *The Routledge Companion to Science Fiction*. Ed. Mark Bould et al. New York: Routledge, 373–81.

Nagel, Thomas. 1974. 'What is it Like to be a Bat?' *The Philosophical Review* 83.4: 435–50.

Nancy, Jean-Luc. 1993. *The Experience of Freedom*. Trans. Bridget McDonald. Stanford: Stanford University Press.

Nicholls, Peter. 2000. 'Big Dumb Objects and Cosmic Enigmas: The Love Affair between Space Fiction and the Transcendental.' In *Space and Beyond: The Frontier Theme in Science Fiction*. Ed. Gary Westfahl. Westport, CT: Greenwood, 11–24.

Nicholls, Peter, and John Clute. 1999. *The Encyclopedia of Science Fiction*. London: Orbit.

Niemoczynski, Leon, and Iain Hamilton Grant. 2013. '"Physics of the Idea": An Interview with Iain Hamilton Grant.' *Cosmos and History: The Journal of Natural and Social Philosophy* 9.2: 32–43.

Nietzsche, Friedrich. 1997 [1874]. *Untimely Meditations*. Trans. R. J. Hollingdale. Ed. Daniel Breazeale. Cambridge: Cambridge University Press.

Nodelman, Perry. 1981. 'The Cognitive Estrangement of Darko Suvin.' *Children's Literature Association Quarterly* 5.4: 24–7.

Paglia, Camille. 1991. *Sexual Personae: Art and Decadence from Nefertiti to Emily Dickinson*. New York: Vintage Books.

Paik, Peter. 2010. *From Utopia to Apocalypse: Science Fiction and the Politics of Catastrophe*. Minneapolis: University of Minnesota Press.

Parrinder, Patrick. 2001. 'Introduction.' In *Learning from Other Worlds:*

Estrangement, Cognition and the Politics of Science Fiction and Utopia. Ed. Patrick Parrinder. Liverpool: Liverpool University Press, 1–16.

Peirce, Charles. 1991. *Peirce on Signs: Writings on Semiotic by Charles Sanders Peirce.* Chapel Hill, NC: University of North Carolina Press.

Polansky, Ron. 2007. *Aristotle's 'De anima'.* Cambridge: Cambridge University Press.

Reisman, Garrett. 2013. 'What Sounds Do Astronauts Hear during a Spacewalk?' *Quora.com.* http://www.quora.com/What-sounds-do-astronauts-hear-during-a-spacewalk.

Reynolds, Alastair. 2002. *Revelation Space.* New York: Ace Books.

Rickels, Laurence. 2010. *I Think I Am: Philip K. Dick.* Minneapolis: University of Minnesota Press.

Rieder, John. 2010. 'On Defining SF, or Not: Genre Theory, SF, and History.' *Science Fiction Studies* 37.2: 191–209.

Robinson, Kim Stanley. 1997. *Blue Mars.* New York: Bantam.

Robinson, Kim Stanley. 2003. *The Years of Rice and Salt.* New York: Bantam.

Robinson, Kim Stanley. 2012. *2312.* New York: Orbit.

Robinson, Kim Stanley. 2015. *Aurora.* New York: Orbit.

Robinson, Kim Stanley, Imre Szeman and Maria Whiteman. 2004. 'Future Politics: An Interview with Kim Stanley Robinson.' *Science Fiction Studies* 31.2: 177–88.

Roderick, Nick. 2016. *The Being of Analogy.* London: Open Humanities Press.

Ronell, Avital. 2002. *Stupidity.* Urbana: University of Illinois Press.

Ronell, Avital. 2012. *Loser Sons: Politics and Authority.* Urbana: University of Illinois Press.

Rorty, Richard. 2009. *Philosophy and the Mirror of Nature.* Oxford: Oxford University Press.

Rose, Mark. 1981. *Alien Encounters: Anatomy of Science Fiction.* Cambridge, MA: Harvard University Press.

Russ, Joanna. 1970. *And Chaos Died.* New York: Ace Books.

Russ, Joanna. 1995. *To Write Like a Woman: Essays in Feminism and Science Fiction.* Bloomington: Indiana University Press.

Salvaggio, Ruth. 1988. *Enlightened Absence: Neoclassical Configurations of the Feminine.* Urbana: University of Illinois Press.

Sarma, Visnu. 2006. *The Pancatantra.* Trans. Chandra Rajan. Harmondsworth: Penguin.

Scalzi, John. 2007. *Old Man's War.* New York: TOR.

Schaub, Thomas. 2009. 'Secular Scripture and Cormac McCarthy's *The Road*.' *Renascence* 63.1: 153–67.

Scheick, William. 1991. 'Post-Nuclear Holocaust Re-Minding.' In *The Nightmare Considered: Essays on Nuclear War Literature*. Ed. Nancy Anisfield. Bowling Green: Bowling Green State University Popular Press.

Schiller, Friedrich. 1972. 'The Nature and Value of Universal History: An Inaugural Lecture (1789).' *History and Theory* 11.3: 321–34.

Scholes, Robert. 1975. *Structural Fabulation: An Essay on the Fiction of the Future*. Notre Dame: University of Notre Dame Press.

Scranton, Roy. 2015. *Learning to Die in the Anthropocene: Reflections on the End of a Civilization*. San Francisco: City Lights Books.

Shaviro, Steven. 2010. *Post-Cinematic Affect*. Ropley, Hants: Zero Books.

Shaviro, Steven. 2014. *The Universe of Things: On Speculative Realism*. Minneapolis: University of Minnesota Press.

Shaviro, Steven. 2015a. *Discognition*. London: Repeater Books.

Shaviro, Steven. 2015b. *No Speed Limit: Three Essays on Accelerationism*. Minneapolis: University of Minnesota Press.

Skrimshire, Stefan. 2011. '"There is No God and We are His Prophets": Deconstructing Redemption in Cormac McCarthy's *The Road*.' *Journal for Cultural Research* 15.1: 1–14.

Sloterdijk, Peter. 2011. *Spheres, Volume 1: Bubbles, Microsphereology*. Trans. Wieland Hoban. Los Angeles: Semiotext(e).

Smithson, Robert. 1996. *The Collected Writings*. Ed. Jack Flam. Berkeley: University of California Press.

Srnicek, Nick, and Alex Williams. 2015. *Inventing the Future: Postcapitalism and a World without Work*. London: Verso.

Stableford, Brian. 2007. *Heterocosms: Science Fiction in Context and Practice*. Rockville, MD: The Borgo Press.

Steffen, W., P. J. Crutzen and J. R. McNeill. 2007. 'The Anthropocene: Are Humans Now Overwhelming the Great Forces of Nature?' *Ambio* 36.8: 614–21.

Sturgeon, Theodore. 1967 [1950]. *The Synthetic Man*. New York: Pyramid Books.

Suvin, Darko. 1979. *Metamorphoses of Science Fiction: On the Poetics and History of a Literary Genre*. New Haven, CT: Yale University Press.

Suvin, Darko. 1983. *Victorian Science Fiction in the UK: The Discourses of Knowledge and Power*. Boston: G. K. Hall.

Suvin, Darko. 1988. *Positions and Presuppositions in Science Fiction*. Kent, OH: Kent State University Press.

Suvin, Darko. 2001. 'Afterword: With Sober, Estranged Eyes.' In

Learning from Other Worlds: Estrangement, Cognition, and the Politics of Science Fiction and Utopia. Ed. Patrick Parrinder. Liverpool: Liverpool University Press, 272–90.

Suvin, Darko. 2010. 'Science Fiction and the Novum.' In *Defined by a Hollow: Essays on Utopia, Science Fiction and Political Epistemology.* Bern: Peter Lang, 67–92.

Taleb, Nassim Nicholas. 2007. *Black Swan: The Impact of the Highly Improbable.* Harmondsworth: Penguin.

Thacker, Eugene. 2011. *In the Dust of this Planet: Horror of Philosophy, Volume 1.* Ropley, Hants: Zero Books.

Todorov, Tzvetan. 1975. *The Fantastic: A Structural Approach to a Literary Genre.* Trans. Richard Howard. Ithaca, NY: Cornell University Press.

Trevor-Roper, Patrick. 1970. *The World through Blunted Sight: An Inquiry into the Influence of Defective Vision on Art and Character.* Indianapolis: Bobbs-Merrill.

Trexler, Adam. 2015. *Anthropocene Fictions: The Novel in a Time of Climate Change.* Charlottesville: University of Virginia Press.

van Vogt, A. E. 1948. *The World of Null-A.* New York: Simon and Schuster.

Vidler, Anthony. 2001. *Warped Space: Art, Architecture, and Anxiety in Modern Culture.* Cambridge, MA: MIT Press.

Vint, Sheryl. 2010. *Animal Alterity: Science Fiction and the Question of the Animal.* Liverpool: Liverpool University Press.

von Uexküll, Jakob. 1926. *Theoretical Biology.* New York: Kegan Paul, Trench, Trubner.

Wark, McKenzie. 2015. *Molecular Red: Theory for the Anthropocene.* London: Verso.

Waters, Sarah. 2002. *Fingersmith.* New York: Riverhead Books.

Watt, Ian. 1971. *The Rise of the Novel: Studies in Defoe, Richardson and Fielding.* Berkeley: University of California Press.

Wearing, Sadie. 2007. 'Subjects of Rejuvenation: Aging in Postfeminist Culture.' In *Interrogating Postfeminism: Gender and the Politics of Popular Culture.* Ed. Yvonne Tasker and Diane Negra. Durham, NC: Duke University Press, 277–310.

Westfahl, Gary. 1998. *The Mechanics of Wonder: The Creation of the Idea of Science Fiction.* Liverpool: Liverpool University Press.

Westfahl, Gary. 2005. 'Hard Science Fiction.' In *A Companion to Science Fiction.* Ed. David Seed. Malden, MA: Blackwell, 187–201.

Willems, Brian. 2009a. *Hopkins and Heidegger.* London: Continuum.

Willems, Brian. 2009b. 'Pet Fixations.' *artUS* 27: 92–9.

Willems, Brian. 2010. *Facticity, Poverty and Clones: On Kazuo Ishiguro's 'Never Let Me Go'*. Dresden: Atropos Press.

Willems, Brian. 2011. 'Sound, Image, Index.' In *Pierre Schaeffer: mediArt*. Ed. Jerica Ziherl. Rijeka: Muzej Suvremeni Umjetnost, 61–8.

Willems, Brian. 2015. *Shooting the Moon*. Ropley, Hants: Zero Books.

Woodard, Ben. 2013. *On an Underground Earth: Towards a New Geophilosophy*. New York: Punctum.

Wylie, Philip, and Edwin Balmer. 1970 [1933]. *When Worlds Collide*. New York: Paperback Library.

Žižek, Slavoj. 1989. *The Sublime Object of Ideology*. London: Verso.

Žižek, Slavoj. 1999. 'The Matrix, or, the Two Sides of Perversion.' *Lacanian Ink*. http://www.lacan.com/zizek-matrix.htm.

Žižek, Slavoj. 2005a. 'Lacan – at What Point is he Hegelian?' In *Interrogating the Real*. Ed. Rex Butler and Scott Stephens. London: Continuum, 26–37.

Žižek, Slavoj. 2005b. '"The Most Sublime of Hysterics": Hegel with Lacan.' In *Interrogating the Real*. Ed. Rex Butler and Scott Stephens. London: Continuum, 38–58.

Žižek, Slavoj. 2006. *The Parallax View*. Cambridge, MA: MIT Press.

Žižek, Slavoj. 2008. *Enjoy Your Symptom! Jacques Lacan in Hollywood and Out*. London: Routledge.

Žižek, Slavoj. 2010. *Living in the End Times*. London: Verso.

Žižek, Slavoj. 2012. *Less than Nothing: Hegel and the Shadow of Dialectical Materialism*. London: Verso.

Zupančič, Alenka. 2000. *The Ethics of the Real: Kant, Lacan*. London: Verso.

Index

2001: A Space Odyssey, 153

Adorno, Theodor, 7, 198
  Aesthetic Theory, 4, 137–44
  Negative Dialectics, 141–2, 162, 166, 171, 173
Agamben, Giorgio, 54, 65, 79, 149
Aldiss, Brian, 6
  Hothouse, 158–9
Alien, 11
Amis, Kinsley, 5, 129
Amis, Martin, 'The Immortals', 201–3
animal, 63–5
Anthropocene, 30–3, 44, 108, 122, 138, 190–1, 195, 199–200
Arendt, Hannah, 126
as if, 56, 128
Asimov, Isaac, 'The Billiard Ball', 46–7
assemblage, 88–90, 110
Ayache, Elie, 80–2, 84, 117

Bacigalupi, Paolo
  'People of Sand and Slag, The', 158
  'Pocketful of Dharma', 158
  Windup Girl, The, 133–80, 198
Badiou, Alain, 92–4, 100, 143
Bailey, J. O., 6, 129
Bakhtin, Mikhail, 68–9
Ballard, J. G., 5, 7, 181, 199
  Crystal World, The, 193
  Drought, The, 191–5, 203
  Terminal Man, The, 193–4
Balmer, Edwin, *When Worlds Collide*, 129–30
Barad, Karen, 8–9, 139

bardo, 4, 182–5, 195
Baudrillard, Jean, 7, 170–1
Beckett, Samuel, 62
Benjamin, Walter, 140
Bennett, Jane, 106
big dumb object, 154–5
bin Laden, Osama, 127
Blanchot, Maurice, 7
Bloch, Ernst, 155
Bogost, Ian, 50, 61, 71, 75, 77–8, 89, 144
Böhme, Jakob, 55
Bonneuil, Christophe, 201
Boyd, Brian, 76
Bozzetti, Mauro, 144
Braidotti, Rosi, 121
Brassier, Ray, 21, 144
Briggs, Raymond, 200
Brooks, Cleanth, 51–2
Bryant, Levi, 16, 34–5, 42, 65, 86, 197
Bush, George W., 127
Butler, Judith, 122–4
Butler, Octavia, *Dawn*, 119–21

Campbell, John, 18, 199
Cartwright, Jon, 46
Chicago Pile 1, 194
Clarke, Arthur, 154
Clement, Hal, *Mission of Gravity*, 18–20, 24–5
Clute, John, 154
Collado-Radríguez, Francisco, 41
Critchley, Simon, 65
Crutzen, Paul, 30–1, 200
Csicsery-Ronay, Isvtan, 129

Index

dark objects, 5, 16, 18, 22, 34–6, 42, 60, 62–3, 84, 86, 89–90, 98–9, 113, 121–2, 131, 157
Darwin, Charles, 116
Davies, Stephen, 187–8
Dawson, Ashley, 190
de Bouvoir, Simone, 123
de Saint-Just, Louis Antoine, 94
DeLanda, Manuel, 7, 89–90, 95, 106, 110–11n1
Delany, Samuel, 7, 8–9, 25–6, 154, 198
  inmixing, 20–1, 23, 133, 156–60, 162
  Stars in My Pocket Like Grains of Sand, 157
Deleuze, Gilles, 62, 76, 88–90, 97, 110–11n1
Derrida, Jacques, 92–3, 127, 149
Diacu, Forin, 46
Dick, Philip K., 83–4
  Do Androids Dream of Electric Sheep?, 179–80n28
Disch, Thomas, 19, 153
Dr Strangelove, 199
dormant objects, 63, 97
double-vision, 60–1, 63, 71, 73, 86, 90, 198
Dutch East India Company, 120
Düttmann, Alexander García, 143

Elden, Stuart, 64–5
Empson, William, 79, 164
Evans-Wentz, W. Y., 183
Evolved Laser Interferometer Space Antenna, 13

Fóti, Véronique, 84n4
Freedman, Carl, 102
Fressoz, Jean-Baptiste, 201
Fynsk, Christopher, 54

Gaiman, Neil, 59–84, 109, 112, 198
  American Gods, 2, 61, 66–74, 77, 118, 120
  Anansi Boys, 2–3, 60, 74–9, 164
  'How to Talk to Girls at Parties', 61, 78–83

Garcia, Tristan, 98
Gernsback, Hugo, 6, 7
Giggs, Rebecca, 48
Gilding, Paul, 37
Glaßmeier, Karl-Heinz, 12
Godzilla, 199–200
Gould, Stephen Jay, 136–7
Grant, Iain Hamilton, 21, 144
Gray, Cecil, 187
Guattari, Félix, 76, 110–11n1
Gunn, James, 29

Hageman, Andrew, 138
Hägglund, Martin, 152
Halberstam, Jack, 167–8, 176n14
Haldeman, Joe, *Forever War, The*, 134–5
Handwerk, Brian, 63
Haraway, Donna, 32–3, 108
Hardwig, Bill, 41, 43–4
Harman, Graham, 18, 21–4, 26–7, 29, 33, 35, 47, 53, 55, 63, 67–8, 82, 86, 90, 92, 97–9, 102–4, 106, 122, 123, 137, 141, 144–6, 148, 151, 164, 169, 173, 183–5, 191, 203
  fission and fusion, 47, 49, 59, 90–1, 203
  Immaterialism, 112, 114–15, 120, 198
  Quadruple Object, The, 23
  ruination, 188–9
  symbiosis, 114–15, 133, 150, 167
  tool-being, 48–9, 95–7
  Weird Realism, 22–3, 49, 52, 56
Heidegger, Martin, 42–4, 48–9, 65, 77–9, 92–3, 95–7, 108, 123, 140–1, 149, 158
Heinlein, Robert, 156–8
Herbert, Frank, 20
Herdman, John, 164
Hillcoat, John, 55, 57–8
Hogan, Craig, 12–13
Hölderlin, Friedrich, 78
Horkheimer, Max, 142
Horowitz, Noah, 152
House on the Rock, The, 61
Hullot-Kentor, Robert, 138–9

infans, 52–4, 57–9
Invisible Committee, The, 190
Ishiguro, Kazuo, *Never Let Me Go*, 101–2, 163

Jameson, Fredric, 7, 155–6, 162, 186
Jay, Martin, 72–3, 140
Jones, Gwyneth, 7, 9, 72
Joshi, S. T., 32
Joyce, James, 62
Jurassic Park, 147

Kafka, Franz, 127
Kander, Nadav, 200
Kaveney, Roz, 154
Kermode, Frank, 51
Knight, Damon, 26, 29–30, 108
   Beyond the Barrier, 14–16, 27–30, 33, 36–8, 42, 63, 97–8, 169, 197
Kojève, Alexandre, 126
Kornbluth, C. M., 6
Kotsko, Adam, 151
Kunsa, Ashley, 41

Laboria Cuboniks, 131
Laser Interferometer Gravitational Wave Observatory, 13
Latour, Bruno, 7–9, 96–7
Lawlor, Leonard, 170
Leckie, Ann, *Ancillary Justice*, 75
Lessing, Doris, 12
   The Cleft, 3–4, 112–32, 198
Levinas, Emmanuel, 149
Ligotti, Thomas, 44–5
Liu, Cixin, *Three-Body Problem, The*, 46–7
Lovecraft, H. P., 22–4, 26–7, 32–3, 148, 199

McCarthy, Cormac
   Child of God, 41
   Road, The, 2, 40–59, 75, 117, 128, 152, 191
Malabou, Catherine, 71
Malevich, Kasimir, 17
Mallarmé, Stéphane, 59, 95
Malmgren, Carl, 7, 129
Marx, Karl, 126

Meillassoux, Quentin, 13, 14, 49, 53, 59, 81–2, 92–3, 100–1, 124, 144–5, 147, 150–1, 155, 197
   After Finitude, 21–2, 80, 151
   L'Inexistence divine, 151–2
   Science Fiction and Extro-Science Fiction, 9–10, 46–7
   Type-1 world, 16, 35–6
   Type-2 world, 1, 16–17, 20, 24, 26, 35, 37, 60, 62, 72, 80–1, 137
   Type-3 world, 16, 26, 37, 46–7, 69, 72, 189, 195
Mendelsohn, Farah, 182
Merrell, Floyd, 65
metaphor, 67
Miéville, China, 83, 119
   'Cognition as Ideology', 9
   crisis energy, 99–105, 110, 133
   Perdido Street Station, 3, 86–111, 115, 145, 148, 198
Miller, Tim, 91
Mitford, Mary, 70
Modigliani, Amedeo, 72
modulation, 66–9, 80
Moore, Jason, 31–3
Moretti, Franco, 69–70
Morton, Timothy, 4, 43–4, 47–8, 52, 58–9, 122, 138, 141, 184, 193, 194–5, 198, 200–1, 203
Muntz, Kyle, *Green Lights*, 38–9n1
Murphy, Patrick, 138

Nagel, Thomas, 149
Nancy, Jean-Luc, 166
Nicholls, Peter, 154
Nietzsche, Friedrich, 140
Nuclear Guardianship, 200–1

Paglia, Camille, 122–5
Paik, Peter, 156–7
paraphrase, 51–2, 56
Picciotto, Concepcion, 200
Plato, 126
Pohl, Frederik, 6
Priest, Graham, 102
Project Plowshare, 201
Pythagoras, 12

Reisman, Garett, 10–11
Reynolds, Alastair, *Revelation Space*, 131–2n1
Rieder, John, 8–9
Robinson, Kim Stanley, 181–96, 199
  2312, 33–6, 186–9
  Aurora, 189–90
  Blue Mars, 185–6
  Years of Rice and Salt, The, 4–5, 181–5
Roderick, Nick, 192
Ronell, Avital, 62, 113, 126–8, 130
Rose, Mark, 7, 116
Rosetta probe, 11–13
Russ, Joanna, 108
  And Chaos Died, 24–6, 130–1
  Female Man, The, 131

Salvaggio, Ruth, 118
Scalzi, John, *Old Man's War*, 135
Schaub, Thomas, 58
Scheick, William, 203
Schiller, Friedrich, 139–40, 142
Schultz, David, 32
Scranton, Roy, 32, 35–6, 195
Shaviro, Steven, 24, 66–8, 71–2, 75, 89, 159–60, 190–1
Shipman, Barbara, 64
Shklovsky, Viktor, 155
Skrimshire, Stefan, 56, 59
Sloterdijk, Peter, 155–6
Smithson, Robert, 17
Socrates, 126
space sounds, 10–13
Srnicek, Nick, 35
Stableford, Brian, 18–19
Stapledon, Olaf, 12
Sturgeon, Theodore, *The Dreaming Jewels (The Synthetic Man)*, 125–6

Suvin, Darko, 7, 14–15, 17, 20, 26, 63, 133, 153–60, 198

Taleb, Nassim Nicholas, 81
Thacker, Eugene, 43–4, 52–3, 158
Thater, Diana, 64
Them!, 199–200
Tibetan Book of the Dead (Bardo Thodol), 183
transcription, 186–9, 199
transcriptionocene, 189–95
Trevor-Roper, Patrick, 35, 72–3
Trexler, Adam, 137
Tzvetan, Todorov, 7, 71

van Beethoven, Ludwig, 188
van Vogt, A. E., 30, 37
Vidler, Anthony, 18
Vint, Sherryl, 149
von Uexküll, Jakob, 64

Wark, McKenzie, 30–1, 186
Westfahl, Gary, 6, 18
Willems, Brian, 76
  Facticity, Poverty and Clones, 64–5, 102
  Shooting the Moon, 104–5
Williams, Alex, 35
Wittig, Monique, 123
Woodard, Ben, 117
world, 42–5, 51–4, 58–9
Wylie, Philip, *When Worlds Collide*, 129–30

xenofeminism, 131

Žižek, Slavoj, 7, 62, 142–8, 154
Zug effect, 2, 5, 6–39, 60, 86, 118, 126, 131, 143, 197
Zupančič, Alenka, 143

EU representative:
Easy Access System Europe
Mustamäe tee 50, 10621 Tallinn, Estonia
Gpsr.requests@easproject.com

www.ingramcontent.com/pod-product-compliance
Lightning Source LLC
Chambersburg PA
CBHW051115230426
43667CB00014B/2593